AMERICAN POLITICAL, ECONOMIC, AND SECURITY ISSUES

GOVERNMENT REPORTS ON GOVERNMENT OPERATIONS FOR MARCH 2019

AMERICAN POLITICAL, ECONOMIC, AND SECURITY ISSUES

Additional books and e-books in this series can be found on Nova's website under the Series tab.

American Political, Economic, and Security Issues

Government Reports on Government Operations for March 2019

Evie Boan
Editor

snova
New York

Library of Congress Cataloging-in-Publication Data

ISBN: 978-1-53615-928-8

Published by Nova Science Publishers, Inc. † New York

CONTENTS

PREFACE

This book is a comprehensive compilation of all reports, testimony, correspondence and other publications issued by the GAO (Government Accountability Office) during the month of March, grouped according to the topic: Government Operations.

Chapter 1 - The LDA, as amended, requires lobbyists to file quarterly disclosure reports and semiannual reports on certain political contributions. The law also includes a provision for GAO to annually audit lobbyists' compliance with the LDA. GAO's objectives were to (1) determine the extent to which lobbyists can demonstrate compliance with disclosure requirements; (2) identify any challenges or potential improvements to compliance that lobbyists report; and (3) describe the resources and authorities available to USAO in its role in enforcing LDA compliance. This is GAO's 12th annual report under the provision. GAO reviewed a stratified random sample of 99 quarterly disclosure LD-2 reports filed for the third and fourth quarters of calendar year 2017, and the first and second quarters of calendar year 2018. GAO also reviewed two random samples totaling 160 LD-203 reports from year-end 2017 and midyear 2018. This methodology allowed GAO to generalize to the population of 49,918 disclosure reports with $5,000 or more in lobbying activity, and 29,798 reports of federal political campaign contributions. GAO also interviewed USAO officials. GAO is not making any recommendations in this chapter.

GAO provided a draft of this chapter to the Department of Justice for review and comment. The agency stated that it did not have comments.

Chapter 2 - AOC is organized into 10 jurisdictions that operate and maintain the buildings and grounds of the U.S. Capitol complex. For projects such as renovations and repairs, the jurisdictions can use their own employees, a contractor, or AOC's Construction Division, which is staffed with trade workers such as electricians and plumbers. Most of the Division's staff are employed on a temporary basis and paid with funds the Division receives from the jurisdictions for projects it executes on their behalf. In March 2017, AOC laid off 30 of the Division's approximately 190 temporary employees, citing a lack of work from the jurisdictions. GAO was asked to review the Division's operations. This chapter examines the jurisdictions' use of the Division and the Division's management of its workforce, among other issues. GAO analyzed information on projects the Division completed during fiscal years 2014 through 2018, reviewed AOC policies, visited the sites of six projects that are illustrative of the work the Division performs for the jurisdictions, and interviewed AOC staff, including officials from AOC's 10 jurisdictions and five of the employees AOC laid off in 2017.

Chapter 3 - Federal agencies' ethics programs seek to prevent conflicts of interest and safeguard the integrity of governmental decision-making. GAO was asked to review compliance with ethics requirements for political appointees in the executive branch. This chapter examines the extent to which (1) existing data identify political appointees serving in the executive branch, and (2) selected agencies use internal controls to reasonably ensure that their ethics programs are designed and implemented to meet statutory and regulatory requirements. GAO reviewed available data on political appointees. GAO also reviewed three case study agencies selected to provide a range in agency size and number of political appointees. GAO reviewed ethics documentation for a nongeneralizable sample of political appointees at the three agencies at any point between January 2017 and 2018 and interviewed officials from the agencies and two non-governmental organizations.

Chapter 4 - Congress has authorized federal agencies to collect hundreds of billions of dollars annually in fees, fines, and penalties. These collections can fund a variety of programs, including programs related to national security, and the protection of natural resources. Data on collections are important for congressional oversight and to provide transparency in agencies' use of federal resources. GAO was asked to review the availability of government-wide data on fees, fines, and penalties. This chapter examines (1) the extent to which data on collections of fees, fines, and penalties are publically available and useful for the purpose of congressional oversight; and (2) the benefits and challenges to government-wide reporting of fees, fines, and penalties. GAO assessed government-wide fee, fine, and penalty data against criteria for availability and usefulness based on multiple sources, including prior GAO work and input from staff of selected congressional committees. GAO interviewed OMB staff, Treasury officials, and representatives of organizations with expertise in federal budget issues and reviewed prior GAO work to identify benefits and challenges of reporting these data.

Chapter 5 - Since 1989, an appropriations provision, colloquially known as the "Stevens Amendment," has reflected Congress's longstanding effort to ensure transparency and accountability in federal grant spending. GAO was asked to review agency guidance and grantee compliance related to the Stevens Amendment. This chapter (1) describes the guidance DOL, HHS, and Education provide to grantees regarding the Stevens Amendment; (2) examines the extent to which DOL, HHS, and Education are managing grantees' compliance with the Stevens Amendment; and (3) describes what is known about how grantees calculate the dollar amounts and percentages of their federal and nongovernmental funding disclosures. GAO asked for agency guidance documents, reviewed monitoring reports, interviewed officials on agencies' Stevens Amendment oversight efforts, and asked agencies how grantees calculate funding amounts.

Chapter 6 - USPS faces a challenging business environment that has led to reduced demand for its traditional services and significant financial losses. USPS aims to address this challenge by offering innovative products and services. The success of these efforts will depend, in part, on how effectively USPS tests each innovation's performance on a small scale to determine whether, how, and when to launch an innovation more broadly—a practice known as "piloting." GAO was asked to review USPS's efforts to develop postal innovations. This chapter (1) describes key innovations that USPS recently piloted and (2) examines the extent to which USPS's policies reflect leading practices for pilot design and evaluation. GAO analyzed information on USPS pilots from fiscal years 2013 through 2017; compared USPS policies for piloting innovations to leading practices for pilot design and evaluation in prior GAO work and relevant standards for internal control; and selected four key innovations based on various characteristics (e.g., innovation type) to serve as illustrative examples of USPS's piloting efforts.

In: Government Reports …
Editor: Evie Boan
ISBN: 978-1-53615-928-8

Chapter 1

2018 Lobbying Disclosure: Observations on Lobbyists' Compliance with Disclosure Requirements[*]

United States Government Accountability Office

Abbreviations

Clerk of the House	Clerk of the House of Representatives
FEC	Federal Election Commission
HLOGA	Honest Leadership and Open Government Act of 2007
LDA	Lobbying Disclosure Act of 1995

---

[*] This is an edited, reformatted and augmented version of United States Government Accountability Office, Report to Congressional Committees, Publication No. GAO-19-357, dated March 2019.

USAO	U.S. Attorney's Office for the District of Columbia
SAUSA	Special Assistant United States Attorneys

Why GAO Did This Study

The LDA, as amended, requires lobbyists to file quarterly disclosure reports and semiannual reports on certain political contributions. The law also includes a provision for GAO to annually audit lobbyists' compliance with the LDA. GAO's objectives were to (1) determine the extent to which lobbyists can demonstrate compliance with disclosure requirements; (2) identify any challenges or potential improvements to compliance that lobbyists report; and (3) describe the resources and authorities available to USAO in its role in enforcing LDA compliance. This is GAO's 12th annual report under the provision.

GAO reviewed a stratified random sample of 99 quarterly disclosure LD-2 reports filed for the third and fourth quarters of calendar year 2017, and the first and second quarters of calendar year 2018. GAO also reviewed two random samples totaling 160 LD-203 reports from year-end 2017 and midyear 2018. This methodology allowed GAO to generalize to the population of 49,918 disclosure reports with $5,000 or more in lobbying activity, and 29,798 reports of federal political campaign contributions. GAO also interviewed USAO officials.

GAO is not making any recommendations in this chapter. GAO provided a draft of this chapter to the Department of Justice for review and comment. The agency stated that it did not have comments.

What GAO Found

For the 2018 reporting period, most lobbyists provided documentation for key elements of their disclosure reports to demonstrate compliance with the Lobbying Disclosure Act of 1995, as amended (LDA). For lobbying disclosure (LD-2) reports and political contributions (LD-203) reports filed during the third and fourth quarter of 2017 and the first and second quarter of 2018, GAO estimates that

- 92 percent of lobbyists who filed new registrations also filed LD-2 reports as required for the quarter in which they first registered (the figure below describes the filing process and enforcement);
- 97 percent of all lobbyists who filed could provide documentation for lobbying income and expenses. However, an estimated 20 percent of these LD-2 reports were not properly rounded to the nearest $10,000;
- 19 percent of all LD-2 reports did not properly disclose one or more previously held covered positions as required; and
- 33 percent of LD-203 reports were missing reportable contributions, which was a statistically significant increase compared to prior years.

Except as noted above, these findings are generally consistent with prior reports GAO issued from 2010 through 2017.

GAO continues to find that most lobbyists in the sample reported some level of ease in complying with disclosure requirements and in understanding the definitions of terms used in the reporting. However, some disclosure reports demonstrate compliance difficulties, such as failure to disclose covered positions or misreporting of income or expenses.

The U.S. Attorney's Office for the District of Columbia (USAO) stated it has sufficient resources to enforce compliance. USAO continued its efforts to resolve noncompliance through filing reports or terminating registrations, as well as imposing civil and criminal penalties.

March 29, 2019
Congressional Committees

Questions regarding the influence of special interests in the formation of government policy have led to efforts to achieve more transparency and accountability from the lobbying community. The Honest Leadership and Open Government Act of 2007 (HLOGA) amended the Lobbying Disclosure Act of 1995 to require lobbyists to file quarterly lobbying disclosure reports and semiannual reports on certain political contributions.[1] HLGOA also increased civil penalties and added criminal penalties for failure to comply with lobbying disclosure requirements. In addition, HLOGA includes a provision for us to annually audit the extent of lobbyists' compliance with the Lobbying Disclosure Act of 1995, as amended (LDA) by reviewing publicly available lobbying registrations and other matters.[2] This is our 12th report under this provision.[3]

Consistent with our prior reports, our objectives were to (1) determine the extent to which lobbyists can demonstrate compliance with the requirements for registrations and reports filed under the LDA; (2) identify any challenges or potential improvements to compliance by lobbyists, lobbying firms, and registrants; and (3) describe the resources and authorities available to the U.S. Attorney's Office for the District of Columbia (USAO) in its role in enforcing LDA compliance and any efforts it has made to improve that enforcement.

To determine the extent to which lobbyists can demonstrate compliance, we examined a stratified random sample of 99 quarterly lobbying disclosure (LD-2) reports with income and expenses of $5,000 or more filed during the third and fourth quarters of calendar year 2017, and the first and second quarters of calendar year 2018.[4] We selected the randomly sampled reports from the publicly downloadable database maintained by the Clerk of the House of Representatives (Clerk of the

---

[1] Pub. L. No. 110-81, 121 Stat. 735 (Sept. 14, 2007) *codified at* 2 U.S.C. §§ 1601-1614.

[2] 2 U.S.C. § 1614.

[3] A complete list of our prior related reports is included at the end of this chapter.

[4] Our original sample included 108 randomly selected LD-2 reports. After notification of our review, one lobbyist amended an LD-2 report to no lobbying activity. During our review, we identified three reports that were not associated with any lobbying activity, and additionally two lobbyists declined to participate in our survey. Each of these six cases was excluded from our review. Lastly, we excluded one report due to hardship experienced by the firm owner, and two reports that had been additional reports selected in case of significant nonresponse, which we determined that we did not need to include.

House).[5] This methodology allows us to generalize some elements to the population of LD-2 reports. We then surveyed and interviewed each lobbyist or lobbying firm in our sample.[6] Our questionnaire asked lobbyists about their lobbying income and expenses and accompanying supporting documentation. In our follow-up interviews, we asked them to provide written documentation for key elements of their LD-2 reports. This documentation included the amount of income reported for lobbying activities, the amount of expenses reported, the houses of Congress or federal agencies lobbied, lobbying issue areas, and the names of lobbyists listed in the report. We also reviewed whether lobbyists listed on the LD-2 reports properly disclosed prior covered official positions, and whether the lobbyists filed the semiannual report of federal political contributions.

Two lobbying firms in our sample, Fierce Government Relations and Hawk International, declined to meet with us following our initial letters, sent in August 2018, and follow-up contacts in September and November 2018. We informed both firms that because they declined to meet, we would supply their names to Congress, as provided for in HLOGA.[7] Both acknowledged understanding this provision. Appendix I contains a list of lobbyists and clients whose LD-2 reports we randomly selected for our review.

To determine whether lobbyists reported their federal political contributions as required by the LDA, we analyzed stratified random samples of year-end 2017 and midyear 2018 semiannual political

---

[5] Our sample is only one of a large number of samples that we might have drawn. Because each sample could have provided different estimates, we express our confidence in the precision of our estimate as a 95-percent confidence interval. This interval would contain the actual population value for 95 percent of the samples we could have drawn. Unless otherwise stated, all percentage estimates have a maximum 95-percent confidence interval of within 12 percentage points or less of the estimate. For prior LD-2 reviews, we have drawn stratified random samples of 25 to 27 cases per quarter, to attain 80-100 completed cases each review.

[6] Although we contacted each lobbying firm, lobbying sole proprietorship, and organization with in-house lobbyists in our sample, we did not always meet with the lobbyists identified as the point of contact or with the actual lobbyists. We sometimes met with individuals representing the lobbyists in our sample. For the purposes of this review, we use the term lobbyists to refer to lobbyists, lobbying firms, organizations with in-house lobbyists, and individuals representing the lobbyists who were present during the interview.

[7] 2 U.S.C. § 1614(c).

contributions (LD-203) reports. The samples contain 80 LD-203 reports that have contributions listed and 80 LD-203 reports that list no contributions. We selected the randomly sampled reports from the publicly downloadable contributions database maintained by the Clerk of the House (see appendix II for a list of lobbyists and lobbying firms randomly selected for our review of LD-203 reports). We then checked the contributions reported in the Federal Election Commission's (FEC) database against the contributions identified in our sample reports.[8] This helped us determine whether all contributions reported in the FEC database were also reported on the LD-203s as required. We contacted lobbyists and asked them to provide documentation to clarify differences we observed. This methodology allows us to generalize to the population of LD-203 reports both with and without contributions.

To determine whether lobbyists were meeting the requirement to file an LD-2 report for the quarter in which they registered, we compared new registrations (LD-1) filed in the third and fourth quarters of 2017, and the first and second quarters of 2018 to the corresponding LD-2 reports on file with the Clerk of the House.

To assess the reliability of the data used, we reviewed available documentation and interviewed knowledgeable officials about the process of collecting, entering, and storing data, and mechanisms to ensure validity, reliability, and consistency of data. We found the data to be sufficiently reliable for our purposes.

To identify challenges and potential improvements to compliance, we used a structured web-based survey to obtain views from lobbyists included in our sample of reports. In general, we asked lobbying firms whether it was easy or difficult to comply with the LD-2 disclosure requirements.

---

[8] FEC is the independent regulatory agency charged with administering and enforcing the federal campaign finance law that covers (1) public disclosure funds raised and spend to influence federal elections; (2) restrictions on contributions and expenditures made to influence federal elections; and (3) the public financing of Presidential campaigns. FEC has jurisdiction over the financing of campaigns for the U.S. House, Senate, Presidency and the Vice Presidency.

Specifically, we asked in our survey whether they understood lobbying terms such as lobbying activities, terminating lobbyists, lobbying issues codes, and covered positions.

To describe the resources and authorities available to USAO and any efforts to improve LDA enforcement, we interviewed USAO officials and obtained information about their system's capabilities to track enforcement and compliance trends and referral data that it receives from the Secretary of the Senate and the Clerk of the House.[9] A more detailed description of our methodology is provided in appendix III.

The mandate does not require us to identify lobbyist organizations that failed to register and report in accordance with LDA requirements. The mandate also does not require us to determine whether reported lobbying activity or political contributions represented the full extent of lobbying activities that took place.

We conducted this performance audit from May 2018 to March 2019 in accordance with generally accepted government auditing standards. Those standards require that we plan and perform the audit to obtain sufficient, appropriate evidence to provide a reasonable basis for our findings and conclusions based on our audit objectives. We believe that the evidence obtained provides a reasonable basis for our findings and conclusions based on our audit objectives.

BACKGROUND

The LDA defines a lobbyist as an individual who is employed or retained by a client for compensation for services that include more than one lobbying contact (written or oral communication to covered officials, such as a high ranking agency official or a Member of Congress made on behalf of a client), and whose lobbying activities represent at least 20

---

[9] When a lobbyist or lobbying firm fails to provide an appropriate response to the Secretary of the Senate's or the Clerk of the House's' written notice that the individual or firm may be in noncompliance with the LDA, the Secretary of the Senate and the Clerk of the House are required to notify USAO that the lobbyist or lobbying firm may be in noncompliance. 2 U.S.C. § 1605 (a)(8).

percent of the time that he or she spends on behalf of the client during the quarter.[10] Lobbying firms are persons or entities that have one or more employees who lobby on behalf of a client other than that person or entity.[11]

The LDA requires lobbyists to register with the Secretary of the Senate and the Clerk of the House, and to file quarterly reports disclosing their respective lobbying activities. Lobbyists are required to file their registrations and reports electronically with the Secretary of the Senate and the Clerk of the House through a single entry point. Registrations and reports must be publicly available in downloadable, searchable databases from the Secretary of the Senate and the Clerk of the House. No specific statutory requirements exist for lobbyists to generate or maintain documentation in support of the information disclosed in the reports they file. However, guidance issued by the Secretary of the Senate and the Clerk of the House recommends that lobbyists retain copies of their filings and documentation supporting reported income and expenses for at least 6 years after they file their reports. Figure 1 provides an overview of the registration and filing process.

---

[10] 2 U.S.C. § 1602(10). The LDA defines a covered executive branch official as the President, Vice President, an officer or employee, or any other individual functioning in the capacity of such an officer or employee, in the Executive Office of the President; an officer or employee serving in levels I through V of the Executive Schedule; members of the uniformed services whose pay grade is at or above O-7; and any officer or employee serving in a position of a confidential, policy-determining, policy-making or policy-advocating character who is excepted from competitive service as determined by the Office of Personnel Management (commonly called Schedule C employees). 2 U.S.C. § 1602(3). The LDA defines a covered legislative branch official as a member of Congress, an elected officer of either house of Congress, or any employee or any other individual functioning in the capacity of an employee of a member, a committee of either house of Congress, the leadership staff of either house of Congress, a joint committee of Congress, or a working group or caucus organized to provide legislative services or other assistance to members. 2 U.S.C. § 1602(4). Lobbying activities include not only direct lobbying contacts but also efforts in support of such contacts, such as preparation and planning activities, research, and other background work that is intended for use in contacts. 2 U.S.C. §1602(7).

[11] 2 U.S.C. § 1602(9).

Sources: GAO analysis of the Lobbying Disclosure Act of 1995, as amended. | GAO-19-357.

Figure 1. Lobbying Disclosure Process.

Lobbying firms are required to register with the Secretary of the Senate and the Clerk of the House for each client if the firms receive or expect to receive more than $3,000 in income from that client for lobbying activities.[12] Lobbyists are also required to submit an LD-2 quarterly report for each registration filed. The LD-2s contain information that includes:

- the name of the lobbyist reporting on quarterly lobbying activities;
- the name of the client for whom the lobbyist lobbied;
- a list of individuals who acted as lobbyists on behalf of the client during the reporting period;
- whether any lobbyists served in covered positions in the executive or legislative branch, such as high-ranking agency officials or congressional staff positions, in the previous 20 years;
- codes describing general lobbying issue areas, such as agriculture and education;
- a description of the specific lobbying issues;

---

[12] Organizations employing in-house lobbyists file only one registration. An organization is exempt from filing if total expenses in connection with lobbying activities are not expected to exceed $13,000. Amounts are adjusted for inflation and published in LDA guidance.

- houses of Congress and federal agencies lobbied during the reporting period; and
- reported income (or expenses for organizations with in-house lobbyists) related to lobbying activities during the quarter (rounded to the nearest $10,000).

The LDA requires lobbyists to report certain political contributions semiannually in the LD-203 report. These reports must be filed 30 days after the end of a semiannual period by each lobbying firm registered to lobby and by each individual listed as a lobbyist on a firm's lobbying report. The lobbyists or lobbying firms must:

- list the name of each federal candidate or officeholder, leadership political action committee, or political party committee to which he or she contributed at least $200 in the aggregate during the semiannual period;
- report contributions made to presidential library foundations and presidential inaugural committees;
- report funds contributed to pay the cost of an event to honor or recognize an official who was previously in a covered position, funds paid to an entity named for or controlled by a covered official, and contributions to a person or entity in recognition of an official, or to pay the costs of a meeting or other event held by or in the name of a covered official; and
- certify that they have read and are familiar with the gift and travel rules of the Senate and House, and that they have not provided, requested, or directed a gift or travel to a Member, officer, or employee of Congress that would violate those rules.

The LDA also requires that the Secretary of the Senate and the Clerk of the House guide and assist lobbyists with the registration and reporting requirements and develop common standards, rules, and procedures for LDA compliance.

The Secretary of the Senate and the Clerk of the House review the guidance annually. It was last revised January 31, 2017, to (among other issues), revise the registration threshold to reflect changes in the Consumer Price Index, and clarify the identification of clients and covered officials and issues related to rounding income and expenses.[13] The guidance provides definitions of LDA terms, elaborates on registration and reporting requirements, includes specific examples of different disclosure scenarios, and provides explanations of why certain scenarios prompt or do not prompt disclosure under the LDA. The offices of the Secretary of the Senate and the Clerk of the House told us they continue to consider information we report on lobbying disclosure compliance when they periodically update the guidance. In addition, they told us they email registered lobbyists quarterly on common compliance issues and reminders to file reports by the due dates.

The Secretary of the Senate and the Clerk of the House, along with USAO, are responsible for ensuring LDA compliance. The Secretary of the Senate and the Clerk of the House notify lobbyists or lobbying firms in writing that they are not complying with the LDA reporting. Subsequently, they refer those lobbyists who fail to provide an appropriate response to USAO. USAO researches these referrals and sends additional noncompliance notices to the lobbyists or lobbying firms, requesting that they file reports or terminate their registration. If USAO does not receive a response after 60 days, it decides whether to pursue a civil or criminal case against each noncompliant lobbyist. A civil case could lead to penalties up to $200,000 for each violation, while a criminal case—usually pursued if a lobbyist's noncompliance is found to be knowing and corrupt—could lead to a maximum of 5 years in prison.

---

[13] An organization employing in-house lobbyists is exempt from registration if its total expenses for lobbying activities does not exceed and is not expected to exceed $13,000 during a quarterly period. The $3,000 income threshold for lobbying firms remains unchanged.

Lobbyists Generally Demonstrate Compliance with Disclosure Requirements

Lobbyists Filed Disclosure Reports as Required for Most New Lobbying Registrations

Generally, under the LDA, within 45 days of being employed or retained to make a lobbying contact on behalf of a client, the lobbyist must register by first filing an LD-1 form with the Secretary of the Senate and the Clerk of the House.

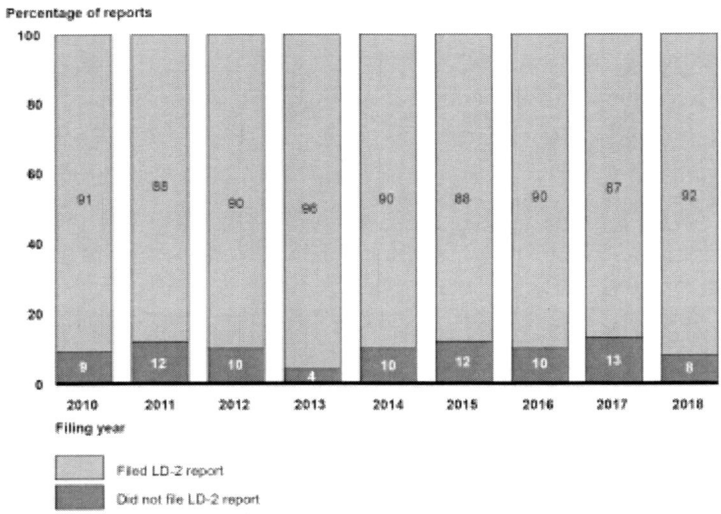

Source: GAO analysis. | GAO-19-357.

Figure 2. Comparison of Newly Filed Lobbying Registrations to Initial Lobbying Disclosure (LD-2) Reports from 2010 through 2018.

Thereafter, the lobbyist must file quarterly disclosure (LD-2) reports that detail the lobbying activities, including filing a first report for the quarter in which the lobbyist registered. Of the 3,618 new registrations we identified for the third and fourth quarters of 2017 and the first and second quarters of 2018, we matched 3,329 of them (92.01 percent) to corresponding LD-2 reports filed within the same quarter as the registration. These results are consistent with the findings we have reported in prior reviews. We used the House lobbyists' disclosure database as the source of the reports. We also used an electronic matching algorithm that allows for misspellings and other minor inconsistencies between the registrations and reports. Figure 2 shows lobbyists filed disclosure reports as required for most new lobbying registrations from 2010 through 2018.

As part of their regular enforcement procedures, the Clerk of the House and the Secretary of the Senate are to follow up with newly filed registrations where quarterly reports were not filed. If the Clerk of the House and the Secretary of the Senate are unsuccessful in bringing the lobbyist into compliance, they may refer those cases to USAO as described earlier in Figure 1.

For Most LD-2 Reports, Lobbyists Provided Documentation for Key Elements, Including Documentation for Their Income and Expenses

For selected elements of lobbyists' LD-2 reports that can be generalized to the population of lobbying reports, our findings have generally been consistent from year to year.[14] Most lobbyists reporting $5,000 or more in income or expenses provided written documentation to varying degrees for the reporting elements in their disclosure reports. Figure 3 shows that for most LD-2 reports, lobbyists provided documentation for income and expenses for sampled reports from 2010 through 2018, and our 2018 estimate does not represent a statistically significant change from 2017.[15]

---

[14] To assess the statistical significance of change over time, we used statistical tests that adjusted for multiple comparisons across the 9 years included in our analysis. The percentage estimates of the LD-2 analysis have a maximum 95 percent confidence interval of within 12 percentage points or fewer.

[15] However, in recent years, our findings showed some variation in the estimated percentage of lobbyists who have reports with documentation for income and expenses supporting lobbying activities. Specifically, our estimate for 2017 (99 percent) represented a statistically significant increase from 2016 (83 percent). While the results provide some

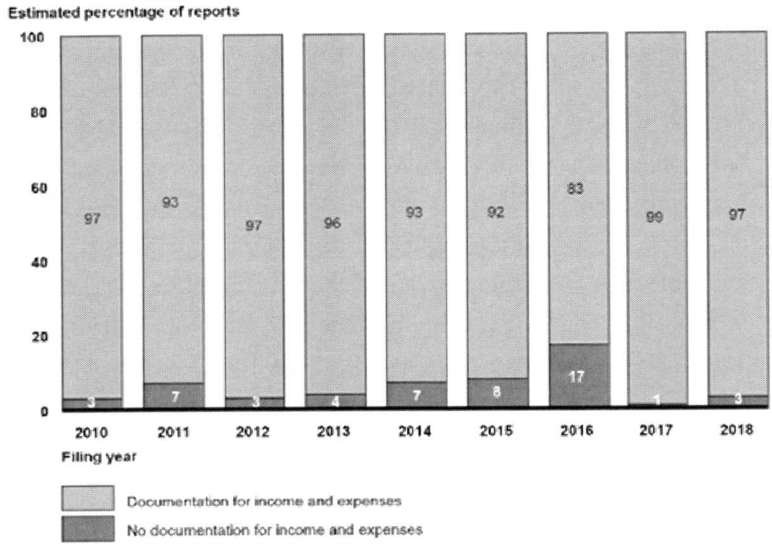

Source: GAO analysis. | GAO-19-357.

Note: Estimated percentages have a margin of error of 12 percentage points or fewer.

Figure 3. Estimated Percentage of Quarterly Lobbying Disclosure (LD-2) Reports with Documentation for Income and Expenses from 2010 through 2018.

Figure 4 shows that in 2018, 10 percent of lobbyists' reported income or expenses differed by $10,000 or more. Additionally, for some LD-2 reports, lobbyists did not round their income or expenses as the guidance requires. In 2018, we estimate 20 percent of reports did not round reported income or expenses according to the guidance. We have found that rounding difficulties have been a recurring issue on LD-2 reports from 2010 through 2018.[16] As we previously reported, several lobbyists who listed expenses told us that based on their reading of the LD-2 form, they believed they were required to report the exact amount. While this is not

confidence that apparent fluctuations in our results across years are likely attributable to sampling error, the inability to detect significant differences may also be related to the nature of our sample, which was relatively small and designed only for cross-sectional analysis.

[16] Under the LDA guidance, both the lobbying firm reporting income and the organizations reporting expenses are to provide a good faith estimate of the actual dollar amount rounded to the nearest $10,000. Our estimate of the number of reports with rounding errors includes reports that disclosed the exact amount of income from or expenditures on lobbying activities, but failed to round to the nearest $10,000 as required.

consistent with the LDA and the guidance, this may be a source of some of the confusion regarding rounding errors. In 2016, the guidance was updated to include an additional example about rounding expenses to the nearest $10,000.

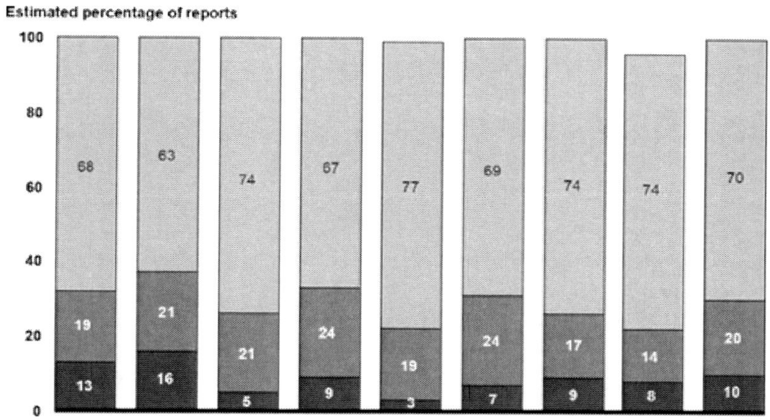

Source: GAO analysis. | GAO-19-357.

Note: Estimated percentages have a margin of error of 12 percentage points or fewer. In 2014 and 2017, percentages do not total 100 due to rounding.

Figure 4. Estimated Percentage of Lobbying Disclosure (LD-2) Reports with Differences in Reported and Documented Amount of Income and Expenses from 2010 through 2018.

The LDA requires lobbyists to disclose lobbying contacts made with federal agencies on behalf of the client for the reporting period. This year, of the 99 LD-2 reports in our sample, 46 reports disclosed lobbying activities at federal agencies. Of those, lobbyists provided documentation for all disclosed lobbying activities at the federal agencies for 29 LD-2 reports. Figure 5 shows that lobbyists for most LD-2 reports provided documentation for selected elements of their LD-2 reports that include general issue area codes for lobbying activities, lobbying the House and the Senate, and individual lobbyists listed from 2010 through 2018. In 2017 and 2018, there was an improvement of compliance with documentation for lobbying the House and the Senate over the previous 7 years.

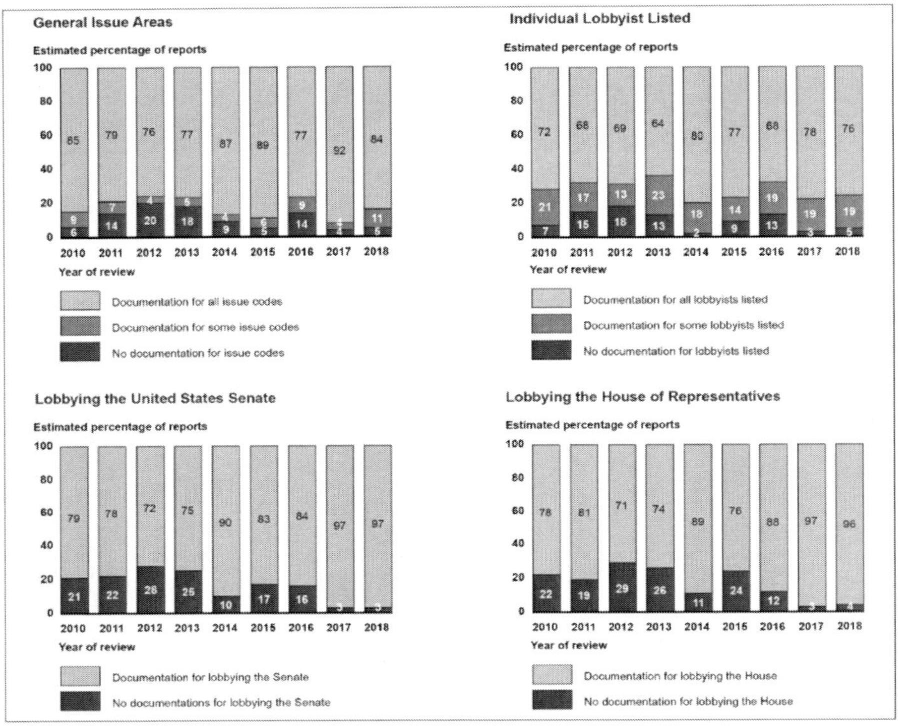

Source: GAO analysis of survey results. | GAO-19-357.

Note: Estimated percentages have a margin of error of 12 percentage points or fewer.

Figure 5. Extent to Which Lobbyists Provided Documentation for Various Reporting Requirements from 2010 through 2018.

For Most Lobbying Disclosure Reports (LD-2), Lobbyists Filed Political Contribution Reports (LD203) for All Listed Lobbyists

Figure 6 shows that lobbyists for most lobbying firms filed contribution reports as required in our sample from 2010 through 2018. All individual lobbyists and lobbying firms reporting lobbying activity are required to file political contribution (LD-203) reports semiannually, even if they have no contributions to report, because they must certify compliance with the gift and travel rules.

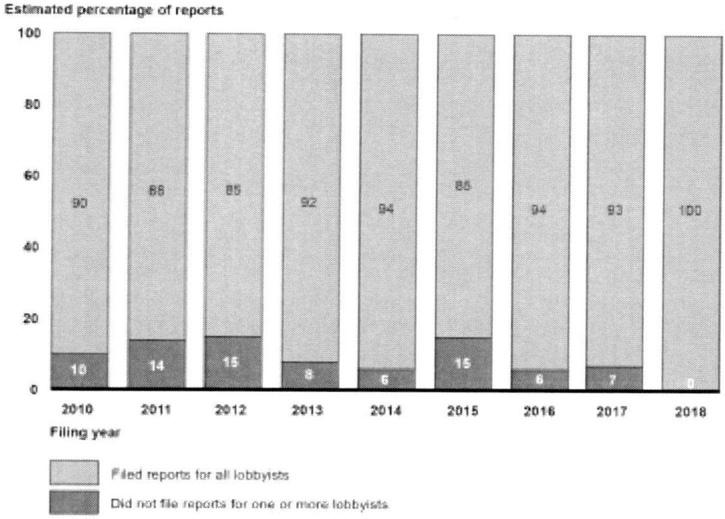

Source: GAO analysis. | GAO-19-357.

Note: Estimated percentages have a margin of error of 12 percentage points or fewer.

Figure 6. Extent to Which Lobbyists on Lobbying Disclosure (LD-2) Reports Filed Contribution Reports for All Listed Lobbyists from 2010 to 2018.

For Some LD-2 Reports, Lobbyists May Have Failed to Disclose Previously Held Covered Positions

The LDA requires a lobbyist to disclose previously held covered positions in the executive or legislative branch, such as high-ranking agency officials and congressional staff, when first registering as a lobbyist for a new client. This can be done either on a new LD-1 or on the quarterly LD2 filing when added as a new lobbyist. This year, we estimate that 19 percent of all LD-2 reports may not have properly disclosed previously held covered positions as required.[17] As in our other reports, some lobbyists were still unclear about the need to disclose certain covered

[17] Prior to each interview, we reviewed the lobbyists' previous work histories by searching lobbying firms' websites, LinkedIn, Leadership Directories, Legistorm, and Google to determine whether lobbyists properly disclosed their covered positions as required by the LDA.

positions, such as paid congressional internships or certain executive agency positions. Figure 7 shows the extent to which lobbyists may not have properly disclosed one or more covered positions as required from 2010 through 2018.

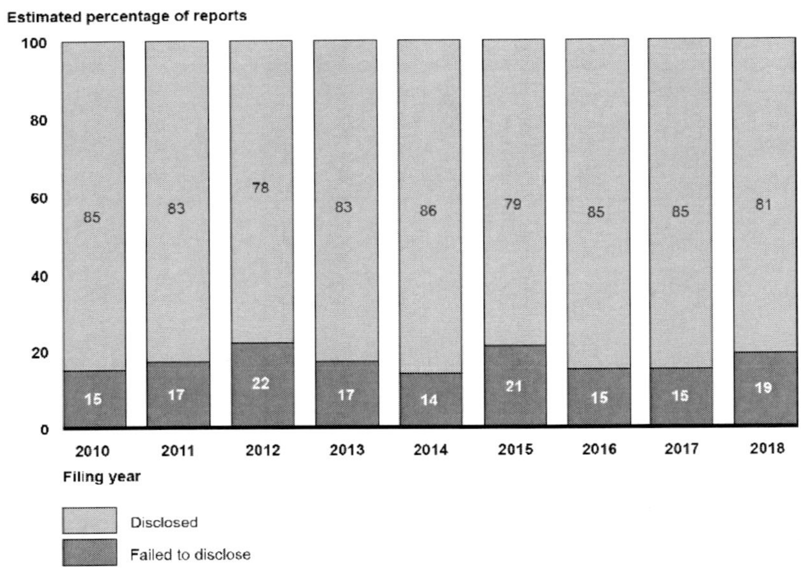

Source: GAO analysis. | GAO-19-357.

Note: Estimated percentages have a margin of error of 12 percentage points or fewer. Lobbying disclosure requires reporting on two types of positions: covered executive branch and legislative branch positions. The term covered executive branch position refers to an officer or an employee serving in: (1) a position of the Executive Schedule; (2) a position of a confidential, policy-determining, policy-making, or policy-advocating character, among others. The term covered legislative branch position refers to: (1) a Member of Congress; (2) an elected officer of either House of Congress; and (3) any employee of a Member of Congress, a committee, or the leadership staff of either House of Congress, among others.

Figure 7. Estimated Percentage of Lobbying Disclosure (LD-2) Reports Where Lobbyists May Not Have Properly Disclosed One or More Covered Positions from 2010 through 2018.

Some Lobbyists Amended Their Disclosure Reports after We Contacted Them

Lobbyists amended 23 of the 99 LD-2 disclosure reports in our original sample to change previously reported information after we contacted them. Of the 23 reports, 10 were amended after we notified the lobbyists of our review, but before we met with them. An additional 13 of the 23 reports were amended after we met with the lobbyists to review their documentation. We consistently find a notable number of amended LD-2 reports in our sample each year following notification of our review. This suggests that sometimes our contact spurs lobbyists to more closely scrutinize their reports than they would have without our review. Table 1 lists reasons lobbying firms in our sample amended their LD-2 reports.

Table 1. Reasons Lobbyists in Our Sample Amended Their Disclosure Reports

	Number of times reason was selected
Updated covered position	10
Updated income or expenses	7
Changed House, Senate or executive branch agency lobbying activity	6
Individual lobbyist	2
No lobbying activity	1
General issues	1

Source: GAO analysis. | GAO-19-357.

Note: Some reports were amended for more than one reason.

Most LD-203 Contribution Reports Disclosed Political Contributions Listed in the Federal Election Commission Database

As part of our review, we compared contributions listed on lobbyists' and lobbying firms' LD-203 reports against those political contributions reported in the Federal Election Commission (FEC) database to identify whether political contributions were omitted on LD-203 reports in our sample. The samples of LD-203 reports we reviewed contained 80 reports with contributions and 80 reports without contributions. We estimate that overall in 2018, lobbyists failed to disclose one or more reportable contributions on 33 percent of reports.[18] Additionally, eight LD203 reports were amended in response to our review. Table 2 shows our results from 2010 to 2018; estimates in the table have a maximum margin of error of 11 percentage points. For this year's review, the estimated change in the percent of LD-203 reports missing one or more FECreportable contributions was a statistically significant increase compared to each of the prior 9 years.

Table 2. Percentage of Lobbying Disclosure (LD-203) Reports That Omitted One or More Political Contributions from 2010- 2018

Year of Review	2010	2011	2012	2013	2014	2015	2016	2017	2018
Number of reports with contributions that had one or more omissions	7	12	14	10a	8	11	9	18	42
Number of reports without contributions that had one or more omissions	1	2	4	0	1	0	1	6	11
Estimated percentage of all reports with one or more omissions	4%	9%	9%	4%	4%	4%	5%	12%	33%

Source: GAO analysis. | GAO-19-357.

Note: N = 80, except where noted [a]N = 79.

[18] We did not estimate the percentage of other non-FEC political contributions that were omitted because they tend to constitute a small minority of all listed contributions and cannot be verified against an external data source.

MOST LOBBYING FIRMS REPORTED SOME LEVEL OF EASE IN COMPLYING WITH DISCLOSURE REQUIREMENTS AND UNDERSTOOD LOBBYING TERMS

As part of our review, we conducted interviews with 97 different lobbying firms in the 2018 sample of LD-2 disclosure reports.[19] Consistent with prior reviews, most lobbying firms reported that they found it "very easy" or "somewhat easy" to comply with reporting requirements. Of the 97 different lobbying firms interviewed, 24 reported that the disclosure requirements were "very easy," 61 reported them "somewhat easy," and 11 reported them "somewhat difficult" or "very difficult." One lobbying firm did not respond to this question (see Figure 8).

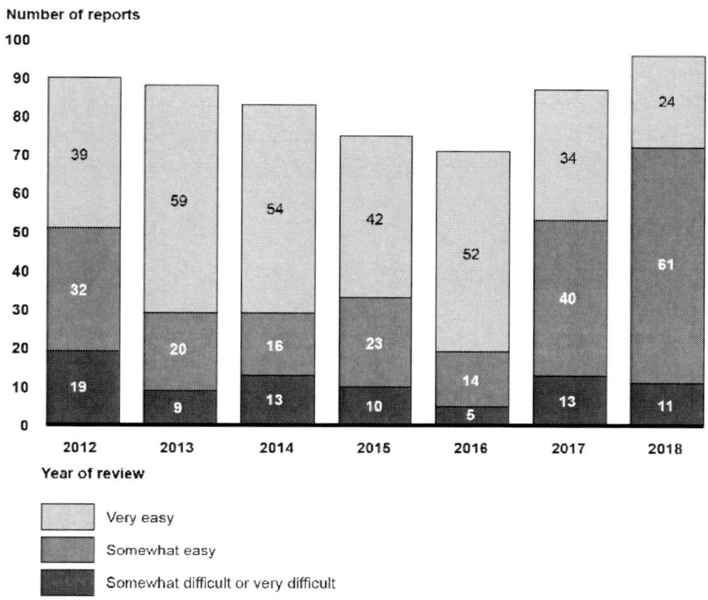

Source: GAO analysis of survey results. | GAO-19-357.

Figure 8. Ease of Complying with Lobbying Disclosure Requirements 2012 through 2018.

---

[19] The use of the term "lobbying firms" in this context includes organizations with in-house lobbyists.

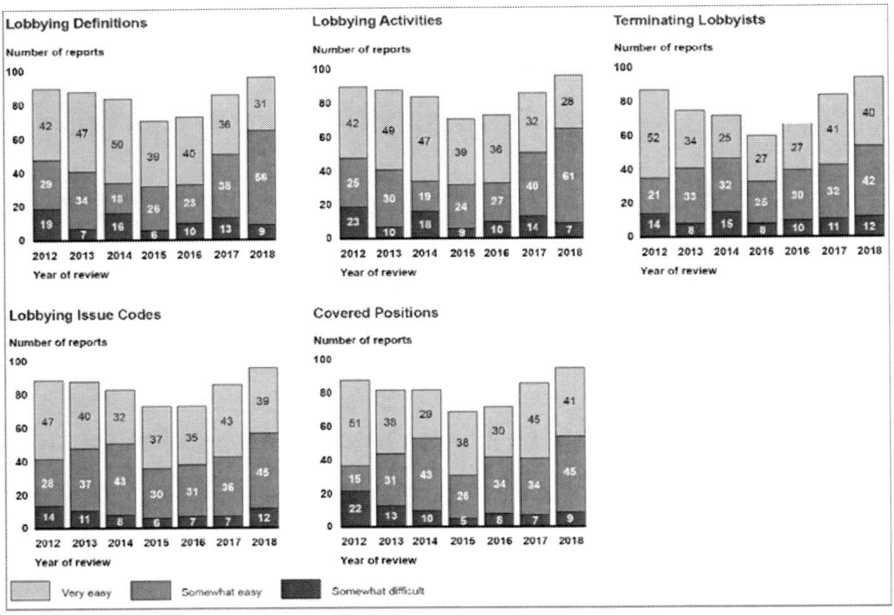

Source: GAO analysis of survey results. | GAO-19-357.

Note: The number of possible responses varies because in 2015 and 2016, the sample size was reduced from 100 firms to 80 and only one response per firm is included. In 2017, the sample size increased to 100 because a reduced sample size did not give us enough power to detect and report on a change in the estimate of the percentage of reports that had documentation (83 percent down from 92 percent in 2015), or whether it was a statistically significant change. In 2018, the sample size remained 100.

Figure 9. Ease of Understanding Key Lobbying Terms Definitions from 2012 through 2018.

Most lobbying firms we surveyed rated the definitions of terms used in LD-2 reporting as “very easy” or “somewhat easy” to understand with regard to meeting their reporting requirements. This is consistent with prior reviews. Figure 9 shows what lobbyists reported as their ease of understanding the terms associated with LD-2 reporting requirements from 2012 through 2018.[20]

[20] Some lobbying firms may not have responded to all of the questions about their ease of understanding the terms associated with LD-2 reporting requirements. Therefore, the

THE U.S. ATTORNEY'S OFFICE FOR THE DISTRICT OF COLUMBIA CONTINUES TO ENFORCE THE LDA

The U.S. Attorney's Office Has Resources and Authorities to Enforce LDA Compliance

The U.S. Attorney's Office for the District of Columbia (USAO) officials stated that they continue to have sufficient personnel resources and authority under the LDA to enforce reporting requirements. This includes imposing civil or criminal penalties for noncompliance. Noncompliance refers to a lobbyist's or lobbying firm's failure to comply with the LDA. However, USAO noted that due to attrition the number of the assigned personnel has changed from 2017 as indicated in Table 3.

Table 3. USAO Staffing Levels, 2017-2018

2017	2018
• one contract paralegal specialist assigned full time • two paralegal specialists assigned part time	• one contract paralegal specialist assigned full time • one paralegal specialist assigned part time
• two civil attorneys – part time	• one civil attorney assigned part time
• one civil investigator as needed • one criminal attorney assigned part time • additional attorneys assigned as needed	• one civil investigator as needed • criminal and civil Assistant U.S. Attorneys are available as needed

Source: U.S. Attorney's Office for the District of Columbia. | GAO-19-357.

USAO officials stated that lobbyists resolve their noncompliance issues by filing LD-2, LD-203, or LD-2 amendments, or by terminating their registration, depending on the issue. Resolving referrals can take anywhere from a few days to years, depending on the circumstances.[21]

---

number of responses may be inconsistent with the number of different lobbying firms in Figure 9.

[21] Referrals are the notifications that USAO receives from the Secretary of the Senate or the Clerk of the House about a possible noncompliance of a lobbyist or lobbying firm with the LDA.

During this time, USAO creates summary reports from its database to track the overall number of referrals that are pending or become compliant as a result of the lobbyist receiving an email, phone call, or noncompliance letter. Referrals remain in the pending category until they are resolved. The pending category is divided into the following areas: "initial research for referral," "responded but not compliant," "no response /waiting for a response," "bad address," and "unable to locate." USAO officials noted that they attempt to review and update all pending cases every six months.

USAO focuses its enforcement efforts primarily on the "responded but not compliant" and the "no response/waiting for a response" groups. Officials told us that, if after several attempts, it cannot contact the noncompliant firm or its lobbyist, it confers with both the Secretary of the Senate and the Clerk of the House to determine whether further action is needed.

In the cases where the lobbying firm is repeatedly referred for not filing disclosure reports but does not appear to be actively lobbying, USAO suspends enforcement actions. USAO officials reported they will continue to monitor these firms and will resume enforcement actions if required.

Status of LD-2 Enforcement Efforts

USAO received 3,798 referrals from both the Secretary of the Senate and the Clerk of the House for failure to comply with LD-2 reporting requirements cumulatively for filing years 2009 through 2018. Figure 10 shows the number and status of the referrals received, and the number of enforcement actions taken by USAO to bring lobbying firms into compliance. Enforcement actions include USAO attempts to bring lobbyists into compliance through letters, emails, and calls.[22] About 40 percent (1,533 of 3,798) of the total referrals received are now compliant

[22] Referrals can include multiple parts, such as LD-2s that were not filed for several clients or LD-203s that were not filed for several lobbyists. A referral cannot be in compliance unless all the parts have been resolved. Enforcement actions reflect attempts to bring each part of the referral into compliance.

because lobbying firms either filed their reports or terminated their registrations. In addition, some of the referrals were found to be compliant when USAO received the referral, so no action was taken. This may occur when lobbying firms respond to the contact letters from the Secretary of the Senate and the Clerk of the House after USAO received the referrals. About 59 percent (2,250 of 3,798) of referrals are pending further action because USAO could not locate the lobbying firm, did not receive a response from the firm after an enforcement action, or plans to conduct additional research to determine if it can locate the lobbying firm. The remaining 15 referrals did not require action or were suspended because the lobbyist or client was no longer in business or the lobbyist was deceased.

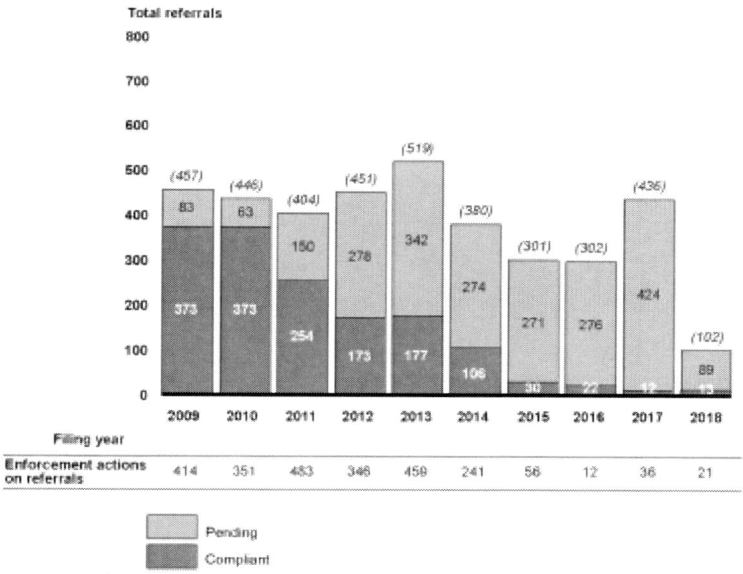

Source: U.S. Attorney's Office for the District of Columbia. | GAO-19-357.

Note: Referrals may be received by the USAO months or years after the filing period to which they relate.

Figure 10. Status of Lobbying Disclosure Act Referrals for Lobbying Disclosure (LD-2) Reporting.

Status of LD-203 Referrals

LD-203 referrals consist of two types: (1) LD-203(R) referrals represent lobbying firms that have failed to file LD-203 reports for their lobbying firm; and (2) LD-203 referrals represent the lobbyists at the lobbying firm who have failed to file their individual LD-203 reports as required. USAO received 2,629 LD-203(R) referrals from lobbying firms (cumulatively from 2009 through 2018) and 5,897 LD-203 referrals for individual lobbyists (cumulatively from 2009 through 2017) from the Secretary of the Senate and the Clerk of the House for noncompliance with reporting requirements). LD-203 referrals are more complicated than LD-2 referrals because both the lobbying firm and the lobbyists within the firm are each required to file an LD-203. Lobbyists employed by a lobbying firm typically use the firm's contact information and not the lobbyists' personal contact information. This makes it difficult to locate a lobbyist who is not in compliance and may have left the firm.

In 2018, USAO officials confirmed that, while many firms have assisted USAO by providing contact information for lobbyists, they are not required to do so. According to officials, USAO has difficulty pursuing LD-203 referrals for lobbyists who have departed a firm without leaving forwarding contact information with the firm. While USAO utilizes web searches and online databases, including social media, to find these missing lobbyists, it is not always successful. Figure 11 shows the status of LD-203(R) lobbying firm referrals received and the number of enforcement actions taken by USAO to bring lobbying firms into compliance. About 42 percent (1,093 of 2,629) of the lobbying firms referred by the Secretary of the Senate and the Clerk of the House for noncompliance from calendar years 2009 through 2018 are now considered compliant because firms either filed their reports or terminated their registrations. About 58 percent (1,523 of 2,629) of the referrals are pending further action. The remaining 13 referrals did not require action or were suspended because the lobbyist or client was no longer in business or the lobbyist was deceased.

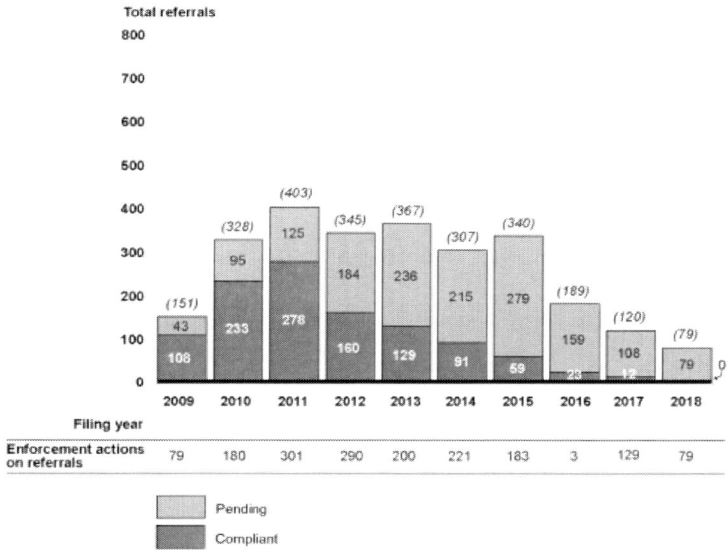

Source: U.S. Attorney's Office for the District of Columbia. | GAO-19-357.

Note: Referrals may be received by the USAO months or years after the filing period to which they relate.

Figure 11. Status of Lobbying Disclosure Act Referrals for Lobbying Disclosure (LD-203(R)) Lobbying Firms Only.

USAO received 5,897 LD-203 individual lobbyists referrals from the Secretary of the Senate and the Clerk of the House for lobbyists who failed to comply with LD-203 reporting requirements for calendar years 2009 through 2017. Figure 12 shows the status of the referrals received and the number of enforcement actions taken by USAO to bring lobbyists into compliance. In addition, Figure 12 shows that about 32 percent (1,880 of 5,897) of the lobbyists had come into compliance by filing their reports or no longer being registered as a lobbyist. About 68 percent (4,003 of 5,897) of the referrals are pending further action because USAO could not locate the lobbyist, did not receive a response from the lobbyist, or plans to conduct additional research to determine if it can locate the lobbyist. The remaining 14 referrals did not require action or were suspended because the lobbyist or client was no longer in business or the lobbyist was deceased.

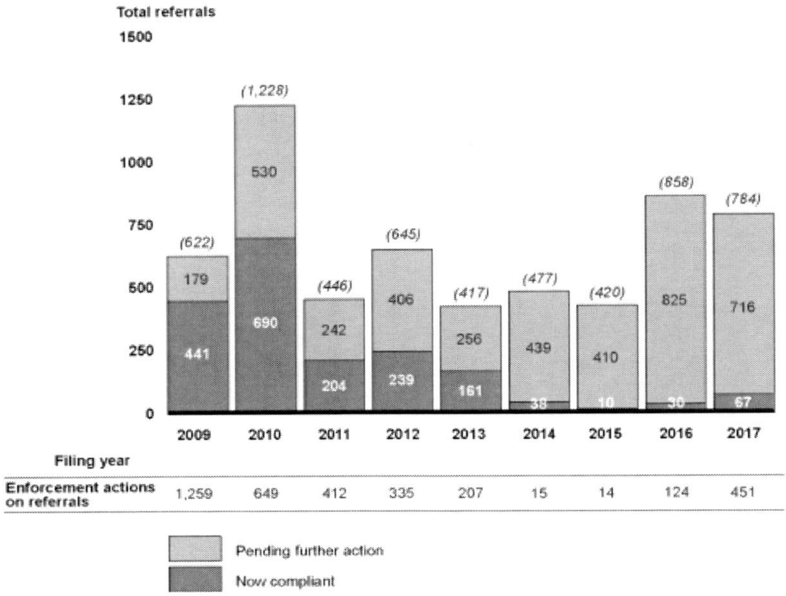

Source: U.S. Attorney's Office for the District of Columbia. | GAO-19-357.

Note: No referrals have been received for 2018. Referrals may be received by the USAO months or years after the filing period to which they relate.

Figure 12. Status of Lobbying Disclosure Act Referrals for Lobbying Disclosure (LD-203) Lobbyists Only.

USAO received LD-203 referrals from the Secretary of the Senate and the Clerk of the House for 7,617 individual lobbyists who failed to comply with LD-203 reporting requirements for any filing year from 2009 through 2017. Figure 13 shows the status of compliance for individual lobbyists listed on referrals to USAO. About 36 percent (2,706 of 7,617) of the lobbyists had come into compliance by filing their reports or by not being registered as a lobbyist. About 65 percent (4,911 of 7,617) of the referrals are pending action because USAO could not locate the lobbyists, did not receive a response from the lobbyists, or plans to conduct additional research to determine if it can locate the lobbyists.

USAO officials said that many of the pending LD-203 referrals represent lobbyists who no longer lobby for the lobbying firms affiliated with the referrals, even though these lobbying firms may be listed on the lobbyist's LD-203 report.

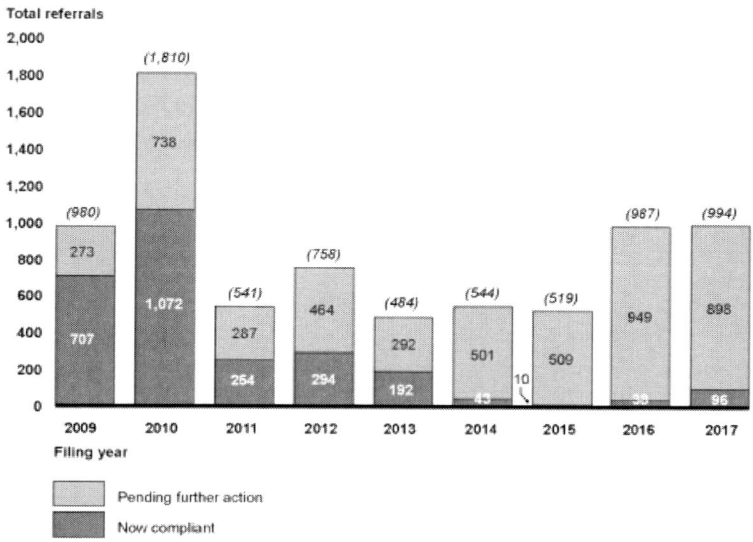

Source: U.S. Attorney's Office for the District of Columbia. | GAO-19-357.

Note: No referrals have been received for 2018. Referrals may be received by the USAO months or years after the filing period to which they relate.

Figure 13. Status of Compliance for Lobbying Disclosure (LD-203) Lobbyists Only Referrals.

Status of Enforcement Settlement Actions

According to USAO officials, lobbyists and lobbying firms who repeatedly fail to file reports are labeled chronic offenders and referred to one of the assigned attorneys for follow-up. USAO also receives complaints regarding lobbyists who are allegedly lobbying but never filed an LD-203. USAO officials added that USAO monitors and investigates chronic offenders to ultimately determine the appropriate enforcement actions, which may include settlement or other civil actions.

Additionally, USAO officials reported that they are working to resolve an active case involving a chronic offender firm and lobbyist that was pending as of 2018. USAO officials noted that the agency is continuing settlement discussions with the company that failed to respond to required LDA violation notices and its lobbyist did not respond to individual violations for semiannual reporting. The company is now current on filing its reports and USAO is working with the Secretary of the Senate and the Clerk of the House on settling past violations. USAO continues to review its records to identify additional chronic offenders for further action due to noncompliance.

AGENCY COMMENTS

We provided a draft of this chapter to the Department of Justice for review and comment. The Department of Justice did not have comments.

Yvonne D. Jones
Director, Strategic Issues

List of Committees

The Honorable Ron Johnson
Chairman

The Honorable Gary C. Peters
Ranking Member
Committee on Homeland Security and Governmental Affairs
United States Senate

The Honorable Lindsey Graham
Chairman

The Honorable Dianne Feinstein
Ranking Member
Committee on the Judiciary
United States Senate

The Honorable Roy Blunt
Chairman

The Honorable Amy Klobuchar
Ranking Member
Committee on Rules and Administration
United States Senate

The Honorable Zoe Lofgren
Chairman

The Honorable Rodney Davis
Ranking Member
Committee on House Administration
House of Representatives

The Honorable Jerrold Lewis Nadler
Chairman

The Honorable Doug Collins
Ranking Member
Committee on the Judiciary
House of Representatives

The Honorable Elijah E. Cummings
Chairman

The Honorable James D. Jordan
Ranking Member
Committee on Oversight and Reform
House of Representatives.

APPENDIX I: LIST OF LOBBYISTS AND CLIENTS FOR SAMPLED LOBBYING DISCLOSURE REPORTS

The random sample of lobbying disclosure reports we selected was based on unique combination of House ID, lobbyist, and client names (see Table 4).

Table 4. Names of Lobbyist and Clients Selected in Random Sampling of Lobbyist Disclosure Reports Filed in the Third and Fourth Quarters of 2017 and First and Second Quarters of 2018

Lobbyists	Clients
Airbnb, Inc.	Airbnb, Inc.
Akerman LLP	Port of Palm Beach
Akerman LLP	Scotts Valley Band of Pomo Indians
Akin Gump Strauss Hauer & Feld	TerreStar Corporation
Alcalde & Fay	City of Riviera Beach, Florida
Alliance of Community Health Plans, Inc.	Alliance of Community Health Plans, Inc.
Alpine Group, Inc.	Grassland Water District
Alston & Bird LLP	CHE Senior Psychological Services
Alzheimer's Association	Alzheimer's Association
American Association for Clinical Chemistry	American Association for Clinical Chemistry
American Continental Group	The Jockey Club
American Defense International, Inc.	Xtreme Concepts, Inc.
American Horse Council	American Horse Council
American Kidney Fund	American Kidney Fund
American Public University System	American Public University System
Anndyl Policy Group, LLC	Renew Financial
Arnold & Porter Kaye Scholer LLP	Verisign, Inc.
BGR Government Affairs	American Family Mutual Insurance Company S.I.
Bracewell LLP	Pier 1 Imports, Inc.
Brooks Bawden, LLC	Major County Sheriffs' Association
Brownstein Hyatt Farber Schreck, LLP	Ardent Health Services

Lobbyists	**Clients**
Brownstein Hyatt Farber Schreck, LLP	Guaranteed Asset Protection Alliance
Cannae Policy Group LLC	Veterans Assembled Electronics, LLC
Capitol Hill Partners	Western Alliance of Farmworker Advocates
Capitol Legislative Strategies LLC	Home Builders Association of Central Arizona
Capitol Tax Partners, LLP	H & R Block Management, LLC
Card & Associates, LLC	PillPack
Cassidy & Associates, Inc.	University of Southern Mississippi
Center for Individual Freedom	Center for Individual Freedom
CF Industries, Inc.	CF Industries, Inc.
Comcast Corporation	Comcast Corporation
Cornerstone Government Affairs, Inc.	Catholic Health Association
Corus Federal Strategies	Deep Springs Technology, LLC
Covington & Burling LLP	Unisys Corporation
Crossroads Strategies, LLC	Salesforce.Com, Inc.
Crossroads Strategies, LLC	Spotify USA Inc.
Crossroads Strategies, LLC	Northrop Grumman Corporation
CSL Behring LLC	CSL Behring LLC
Lobbyists	Clients
Faegre Baker Daniels Consulting	Global Down Syndrome Foundation
Federal Science Partners LLC	Vaisala, Inc.
Fierce Government Relationsa	Kindred Healthcare
Fonterra Cooperative Group Limited	Fonterra Cooperative Group Limited
Foresight Law + Policy PLLC	Consortium for School Networking
General Electric Company (Including Subsidiaries)	General Electric Company (Including Subsidiaries)
Grizzle Company	Regional Airport Authority of Louisville & Jefferson County
Harbinger Strategies, LLC	Facebook, Inc.
Hawk International, LLCa	International Chiropractors Association
Health and Medicine Counsel of Washington	U.S. Hereditary Angioedema Association
Hobart Hallaway & Quayle Ventures, LLC	SF Motors, Inc.
Hogan Lovells US LLP	Credit Suisse Securities (USA)
Hollier & Associates	National Shooting Sports Foundation
ImmigrationWorks USA	ImmigrationWorks USA
Invariant LLC	ChowNow, Inc.
J.A. Green & Company (Formerly LLC)	Electron Energy Corporation
K&L Gates LLP	Velocys Inc
K&L Gates LLP	Coalition for Energy Efficient Jobs & Investment
K&L Gates LLP	Gulf of Mexico Reef Fish Shareholders' Alliance
K&L Gates LLP	Trans-Atlantic Business Council
Kelley Drye & Warren LLP	Outdoor Amusement Business Association
King & Spalding LLP	BioScrip, Inc.
Lewis-Burke Associates, LLC	California Institute of Technology
Lewis-Burke Associates, LLC	University of Cincinnati

Table 4. (Continued)

Lobbyists	Clients
Lord Corporation	Lord Corporation
Lyondell Chemical Company	Lyondell Chemical Company
Marcus G. Faust, PC	Clark County Water Reclamation District
Mercury	Movement Mortgage
Michael Best Strategies LLC	Plains All American Pipeline, L.P.
Ml Strategies, LLC	PriceSmart, Inc.
Monument Policy Group, LLC	Target Logistics Management LLC (Formerly Known as Target Lodging Management LLC
Mr. Alan Reuther	UAW Retiree Medical Benefits Trust
Mr. James Edwards	National Association of Small Trucking Companies
Mr. Marshall Brachman	Physicians Realty Trust
Ms. Marla Grossman	American Continental Group on Behalf of the Songwriters Guild of America
NAIOP	NAIOP
Nathanson+Hauck	Pew Charitable Trusts
National Association of Electrical Distributors, Inc.	National Association of Electrical Distributors, Inc.
O'Neill And Associates	Alaska Airlines
Polaris-Hutton Group, LLC	General Motors Company
Policy Matters, LLC (Formerly Known As TKB Consulting, LLC)	The Community Reach Center
Porterfield, Fettig & Sears, LLC	Prudential Financial
Potomac Partners DC	9/11 Memorial
Powers, Pyles, Sutter & Verville, PC	ID Experts Corp
Prime Policy Group	New Hanover County
Prime Policy Group	New Hanover County
Raffaniello & Associates	American Institute of Certified Public Accountants
Roberti Global (F/K/A Roberti White, LLC)	General Motors, LLC
S-3 Group	Arise Virtual Solutions
SBL Strategies, LLC	Santa Rosa County, FL
Signal Group Consulting, LLC	Microsoft Corporation
Stanton Park Group	ScribeAmerica
Strategic Health Care	Gaylord Hospital
Subject Matter (fka Elmendorf Ryan)	Davita Inc.
Taylor Strategies	Intrexon Corporation
The American Public Gas Association	The American Public Gas Association
The Colwell Group, LLC	USI Insurance Services
The FGA Group LLC	American E-Liquids Manufacturing Standards Association

Lobbyists	Clients
The Livingston Group, L.L.C.	Sasol Chemicals (USA) LLC
The Livingston Group, L.L.C.	TenCate Protective Fabrics North America
The Margolin Group	County of Santa Clara
The McManus Group	Achaogen
The Russell Group, Inc.	National Association of Clean Water Agencies
The Simmons & Russell Group, LLC	Google Inc.
Thomas Walters & Associates, Inc.	County of Santa Barbara
Thorsen French Advocacy LLC	Beer Institute
Van Scoyoc Associates	Corporate Friends of CDC, Inc.
Venable LLP	State Street Bank and Trust Company
Venn Strategies	Lifetouch
Williams And Jensen, PLLC	Plasma Protein Therapeutics Association

Source: Lobbying disclosure database of the Clerk of the House of Representatives for the third and fourth quarters of 2017 and the first and second quarters of 2018. | GAO-19-357.

[a]Firms did not participate in GAO's lobbying disclosure survey.

APPENDIX II: LIST OF SAMPLED LOBBYING CONTRIBUTION REPORTS WITH AND WITHOUT CONTRIBUTIONS LISTED

Table 5. Lobbyists and Lobbying Firms in Sample of Lobbying Contribution Reports with Contributions Listed, Filed Year-End 2017 and Midyear 2018

Lobbyist or lobbying firm	Reporting period
Act For America	Year-end 2017
Air Line Pilots Association Inc. PAC	Midyear 2018
American Lung Association	Midyear 2018
American Society for Radiation Oncology	Midyear 2018
American Traffic Safety Services Association	Midyear 2018
Andrew Howell	Year-end 2017
Atlantic Strategies Group	Midyear 2018
Bryce L. Harlow	Midyear 2018
Building and Construction Trades Dept., AFL-CIO	Year-end 2017
Carlos Becerra	Midyear 2018
Catherine Finley	Year-end 2017
Celgene Corporation	Year-end 2017
Charles Garrison	Year-end 2017

Table 5. (Continued)

Lobbyist or lobbying firm	Reporting period
Chet Thompson	Midyear 2018
Clint Hackney	Midyear 2018
David Anderson	Year-end 2017
David C. Rich	Midyear 2018
Dora Hughes	Year-end 2017
Elizabeth Reicherts	Midyear 2018
Erik Robert Olson	Year-end 2017
Erika Nijenhuis	Year-end 2017
Gary Michael Hall	Midyear 2018
George Cooper	Midyear 2018
Intel Corporation PAC	Year-end 2017
Jacqueline S. Glassman	Midyear 2018
James Hall	Year-end 2017
James Heimbach	Midyear 2018
Jamie Gregorian	Midyear 2018
Janice Kupiec	Year-end 2017
Jason Hill	Midyear 2018
Javier DeJesus Martinez	Midyear 2018
Jeffrey McMillen	Midyear 2018
Jerry "Jay" Driscoll	Year-end 2017
Jesse Barba	Midyear 2018
Jessica Lawrence-Vaca	Year-end 2017
Jessica Woolley	Midyear 2018
John Tolman	Midyear 2018
Jonathan Paone	Midyear 2018
Katherine Cullen	Midyear 2018
Kevin Allis	Midyear 2018
Kristin Welsh	Midyear 2018
Laurence Lane	Midyear 2018
Lucas Tomanelli	Year-end 2017
Manuel Ortiz	Year-end 2017
Mark Eugene Kinney	Year-end 2017
Marti Thomas	Midyear 2018
Matthew Lee Johnson	Year-end 2017
Michael A. Andrews	Year-end 2017
Michael A. Brairton	Year-end 2017
Michael Mattoon	Midyear 2018
Michael Rapelyea	Year-end 2017
Mike Biagi	Midyear 2018
Miranda Franco	Year-end 2017

Lobbyist or lobbying firm	Reporting period
Nancy Dorn	Year-end 2017
National Multifamily Housing Council, Inc.	Midyear 2018
National Nurses United: a Fund for a Healthy America	Year-end 2017
National Organization for The Reform of Marijuana Laws	Year-end 2017
Navient Solutions, LLC	Midyear 2018
Nina Ozlu Tunceli	Year-end 2017
Owens-Illinois, Inc. Employees Good Citizenship Fund	Year-end 2017
Paul T. Donovan	Year-end 2017
Peter Haller	Year-end 2017
Peter Haller	Midyear 2018
Princeton University	Year-end 2017
Ricky Le	Midyear 2018
Robert Flock	Midyear 2018
SSA Marine	Midyear 2018
SSAB Americas PAC	Year-end 2017
Stanley G. Fendley	Midyear 2018
Steve Glaze	Year-end 2017
Stuart P. Ingis	Year-end 2017
Susan Esserman	Midyear 2018
Beef PAC of Texas Cattle Feeders Association	Midyear 2018
Lobbyist or lobbying firm	Reporting period
The Velasquez Group, LLC	Year-end 2017
Tiahrt Enterprises, LLC	Year-end 2017
Valero Energy Corporation	Year-end 2017
Vanguard Group	Year-end 2017
Wiley Rein LLP	Year-end 2017
William Piper	Midyear 2018
William Simpson	Year-end 2017

Source: Lobbying contributions database of the Clerk of the House of Representatives. Year-end reports for calendar year 2017 and midyear reports for calendar year 2018. | GAO-19-357.

Table 6. Lobbyists and Lobbying Firms in Random Sample of Lobbying Contribution Reports without Contributions Listed, Filed Year-End 2017 or Midyear 2018

Lobbyist or lobbying firm	Reporting period
60 Plus Association	Year-end 2017
American Financial Services Association PAC	Year-end 2017
American Small Manufacturers Coalition	Midyear 2018
Andrew Saelens	Midyear 2018
Barbara G. Broussard	Year-end 2017
Bartlett Naylor	Midyear 2018

Table 6. (Continued)

Lobbyist or lobbying firm	Reporting period
Billy Howe	Midyear 2018
Carolina L. Mederos	Year-end 2017
Carolyn B. Gleason	Year-end 2017
Carrie Hunt	Midyear 2018
Christopher LaGrone	Year-end 2017
Courtney Piron	Midyear 2018
Da Vinci Group	Year-end 2017
Daniel Bryant	Year-end 2017
Danielle Burr	Midyear 2018
Deborah Saxon	Year-end 2017
Denise B. Muha	Midyear 2018
Eric Dixon	Year-end 2017
Erik Schneider	Year-end 2017
Evan Rachkovsky	Midyear 2018
Feng-Yen Li	Year-end 2017
Fernando Gomez	Year-end 2017
Geoffrey Plague	Midyear 2018
GRQ, LLC	Midyear 2018
Harbinger Strategies, LLC	Year-end 2017
Heather McNatt Hennessey	Midyear 2018
Jack Thompson	Midyear 2018
Jacqueline Ball	Midyear 2018
Jane Starke	Midyear 2018
Jeffery Fluck	Midyear 2018
Jennifer Rachel Kefer	Midyear 2018
Jessica Carlton	Midyear 2018
John D. Van Etten	Year-end 2017
John Ladd	Year-end 2017
John Scott Gray	Year-end 2017
Jose Ceballos	Year-end 2017
Joseph Kuklis	Year-end 2017
Joseph Mondello	Year-end 2017
Joshua Habursky	Year-end 2017
Karl Brooma	Midyear 2018
Kenneth A. Brown	Midyear 2018
Maile L. Wilson	Midyear 2018
Mark Cothran	Year-end 2017
Martin Frost	Midyear 2018
Matthew Schafle	Midyear 2018
Medical Group Management Association	Year-end 2017

Lobbyist or lobbying firm	**Reporting period**
Michael F. Scanlon	Year-end 2017
Morna Willens	Midyear 2018
Mrs. Holly Stevens	Year-end 2017
Ms. Diane O'Toole	Midyear 2018
Ms. Rebecca Halkias	Year-end 2017
Nokia of America Corporation	Midyear 2018
Nydia Bonnin	Midyear 2018
Patricia Davitt Long	Midyear 2018
Patrick Arness	Midyear 2018
Paul T. Kelly	Year-end 2017
Phillip Lovell	Year-end 2017
Robert Kappelmann	Midyear 2018
Ronald Bird	Year-end 2017
Ryan D. Flickner	Year-end 2017
S-3 Group	Year-end 2017
Scott Olson	Year-end 2017
Sean Peter Devery	Year-end 2017
Shaun Sahlhoff	Midyear 2018
Slover & Loftus	Midyear 2018
Spiegel & McDiarmid, LLP	Midyear 2018
Stephanie Gupta	Year-end 2017
Stephen G. Wood	Year-end 2017
Lobbyist or lobbying firm	Reporting period
Suzanne C. Sterner	Midyear 2018
Thair Phillips	Year-end 2017
Anesthesia Service Medical Group Advocacy Fund	Midyear 2018
The Lambos Firm, LLP (Formerly Known as The Lambos Firm)	Year-end 2017
The Shelburne Group	Year-end 2017
The Trade Partnership	Year-end 2017
Thomas Lindsley	Midyear 2018
Thomas Paris	Midyear 2018
TJS III Holdings LLC	Midyear 2018
Ultra Electronics Advanced Tactical Systems	Year-end 2017
University of Central Florida	Midyear 2018
Zachary Scott	Midyear 2018

Source: Lobbying contributions database of the Clerk of the House of Representatives. Year-end reports for calendar year 2017 and midyear reports for calendar year 2018. | GAO-19-357.

APPENDIX III: OBJECTIVES, SCOPE, AND METHODOLOGY

Our objectives were to determine the extent to which lobbyists are able to demonstrate compliance with the Lobbying Disclosure Act of 1995, as amended (LDA) by providing documentation (1) to support information contained on registrations and reports filed under the LDA; (2) to identify challenges or potential improvements to compliance, if any; and (3) to describe the resources and authorities available to the U.S. Attorney's Office for the District of Columbia (USAO), its role in enforcing LDA compliance, and any efforts it has made to improve LDA enforcement.

We used information in the lobbying disclosure database maintained by the Clerk of the House of Representatives (Clerk of the House). To assess whether these disclosure data were sufficiently reliable for the purposes of this chapter, we reviewed relevant documentation and consulted with knowledgeable officials. Although registrations and reports are filed through a single web portal, each chamber subsequently receives copies of the data and follows different data-cleaning, processing, and editing procedures before storing the data in either individual files (in the House) or databases (in the Senate). Currently, there is no means of reconciling discrepancies between the two databases caused by the differences in data processing. For example, Senate staff told us during previous reviews they set aside a greater proportion of registration and report submissions than the House for manual review before entering the information into the database. As a result, the Senate database would be slightly less current than the House database on any given day pending review and clearance.

House staff told us during previous reviews that they rely heavily on automated processing. In addition, while they manually review reports that do not perfectly match information on file for a given lobbyist or client, staff members approve and upload such reports as originally filed by each lobbyist, even if the reports contain errors or discrepancies (such as a variant on how a name is spelled). Nevertheless, we do not have reason to believe that the content of the Senate and House systems would vary substantially. Based on interviews with knowledgeable officials and a review of documentation, we determined that House disclosure data were sufficiently reliable for identifying a sample of quarterly disclosure reports (LD-2) and for assessing whether newly filed lobbyists also filed required reports. We used the House database for sampling LD-2 reports from the third and fourth quarters of 2017 and the first and second quarters of 2018, as well as for sampling year-end 2017 and midyear 2018 political contributions reports (LD-203). We also used the database for matching quarterly registrations with filed reports. We did not evaluate the Offices of the Secretary of the Senate or the Clerk of the House, both of which have key roles in the lobbying disclosure process. However, we did consult with officials from each office. They provided us with general background information at our request.

To assess the extent to which lobbyists could provide evidence of their compliance with reporting requirements, we examined a stratified random sample of 99 LD-2 reports from the third and fourth quarters of 2017 and the first and second quarters of 2018.[23] We excluded reports with no lobbying activity or with income or expenses of less than $5,000 from our sampling frame.[24] We drew our sample from 49,918 activity reports filed for the third and fourth quarters of 2017 and the first and second quarters of 2018 available in the public House database, as of our final download date for each quarter.

Our sample of LD-2 reports was not designed to detect differences over time. However, we conducted tests of significance for changes from 2010 to 2018 for the generalizable elements of our review. We found that results were generally consistent from year to year and there were few

---

[23] Our original sample included 108 randomly selected LD-2 reports. After notification of our review, one lobbyist amended an LD-2 report to no lobbying activity. During our review, we identified three reports that were not associated with any lobbying activity, and additionally two lobbyists declined to participate in our survey. Each of these six cases were excluded from our review. Lastly, we excluded one report due to hardship experienced by the firm owner and two additional reports selected in case of significant nonresponse.

[24] LD-2 activity reports with "no lobbying issue activity" and reports with less than $5,000 in reported income or expenses are filtered out because they do not contain verifiable information on income, expenses, or activity.

statistically significant changes (as noted in our report) after using a Bonferroni adjustment to account for multiple comparisons.[25] For this year's review, we estimated that 97 percent of LD-2 reports provided written documentation for the lobbying income and expenses.

Our sample is based on a stratified random selection and is only one of a large number of samples that we may have drawn. Because each sample could have provided different estimates, we express our confidence in the precision of our particular sample's results as a 95-percent confidence interval. This interval would contain the actual population value for 95 percent of the samples that we could have drawn. The percentage estimates for LD-2 reports have 95-percent confidence intervals of within plus or minus 12 percentage points or fewer of the estimate itself.

We contacted all the lobbyists and lobbying firms in our sample and, using a structured web-based survey, asked them to confirm key elements of the LD-2 and whether they could provide written documentation for key elements in their reports, including:

- the amount of income reported for lobbying activities;
- the amount of expenses reported on lobbying activities;
- the names of those lobbyists listed in the report;
- the houses of Congress and the federal agencies that they lobbied, and
- the issue codes listed to describe their lobbying activity.

After reviewing the survey results for completeness, we interviewed lobbyists and lobbying firms to review the documentation they reported as having on their online survey for selected elements of their respective LD2 report.

Prior to each interview, we conducted a search to determine whether lobbyists properly disclosed their covered position as required by the LDA.

[25] A Bonferroni adjustment is a statistical adjustment designed to reduce the chance of making a type-1 inferential error that is concluding that a difference exists when it is instead an artifact of sampling error. The adjustment raises the threshold for concluding that any single difference is "statistically significant" so that overall the chance of making at least one type-1 error when making multiple comparisons does not exceed a specified level.

We reviewed the lobbyists' previous work histories by searching lobbying firms' websites, LinkedIn, Leadership Directories, Legistorm, and Google. Prior to 2008, lobbyists were only required to disclose covered official positions held within 2 years of registering as a lobbyist for the client. The Honest Leadership and Open Government Act of 2007 amended that time frame to require disclosure of positions held 20 years before the date the lobbyists first lobbied on behalf of the client. Lobbyists are required to disclose previously held covered official positions either on the client registration (LD-1) or on an LD-2 report. Consequently, those who held covered official positions may have disclosed the information on the LD-1 or a LD-2 report filed prior to the report we examined as part of our random sample. Therefore, where we found evidence that a lobbyist previously held a covered official position, and that information was not disclosed on the LD-2 report under review, we conducted an additional review of the publicly available Secretary of the Senate or Clerk of the House database to determine whether the lobbyist properly disclosed the covered official position on a prior report or LD-1. Finally, if a lobbyist appeared to hold a covered position that was not disclosed, we asked for an explanation at the interview with the lobbying firm to ensure that our research was accurate.

In previous reports, we reported the lower bound of a 90-percent confidence interval to provide a minimum estimate of omitted covered positions and omitted contributions with a 95-percent confidence level. We did so to account for the possibility that our searches may have failed to identify all possible omitted covered positions and contributions. As we have developed our methodology over time, we are more confident in the comprehensiveness of our searches for these items. Accordingly, this chapter presents the estimated percentages for omitted contributions and omitted covered positions rather than the minimum estimates. As a result, percentage estimates for these items will differ slightly from the minimum percentage estimates presented in prior reports.

In addition to examining the content of the LD-2 reports, we confirmed whether the most recent LD-203 reports had been filed for each firm and lobbyist listed on the LD-2 reports in our random sample. Although this review represents a random selection of lobbyists and firms, it is not a direct probability sample of firms filing LD-2 reports or lobbyists listed on LD-2 reports. As such, we did not estimate the likelihood that LD-203 reports were appropriately filed for the population of firms or lobbyists listed on LD-2 reports.

To determine if the LDA's requirement for lobbyists to file a report in the quarter of registration was met for the third and fourth quarters of 2017 and the first and second quarters of 2018, we used data filed with the Clerk of the House to match newly filed registrations with corresponding disclosure reports. Using an electronic matching algorithm that includes strict and loose text matching procedures, we identified matching disclosure reports for 3,329, or 92.01 percent, of the 3,618 newly filed registrations. We began by standardizing client and lobbyist names in both the report and registration files (including removing punctuation and standardizing words and abbreviations, such as "company" and "CO"). We then matched reports and registrations using the House identification number (which is linked to a unique lobbyist-client pair), as well as the names of the lobbyist and client.

For reports we could not match by identification number and standardized name, we also attempted to match reports and registrations by client and lobbyist name, allowing for variations in the names to accommodate minor misspellings or typos. For these cases, we used professional judgment to determine whether cases with typos were sufficiently similar to consider as matches. We could not readily identify matches in the report database for the remaining registrations using electronic means.

To assess the accuracy of the LD-203 reports, we analyzed stratified random samples of LD-203 reports from the 29,798 total LD-203 reports. The first sample contains 80 reports of the 9,502 reports with political contributions and the second contains 80 reports of the 20,296 reports listing no contributions. Each sample contains 40 reports from the yearend 2017 filing period and 40 reports from the midyear 2018 filing period. The samples from 2018 allow us to generalize estimates in this chapter to either the population of LD-203 reports with contributions or the reports without contributions to within a 95-percent confidence interval of within plus or minus 11 percentage points or fewer. Although our sample of LD203 reports was not designed to detect differences over time, for this year's review, the estimated change in percentage of LD-203 reports missing one or more reportable contributions was a statistically significant increase compared to each of the prior 9 years.[26]

While the results provide some confidence that apparent fluctuations in our results across years are likely attributable to sampling error, the inability to detect significant differences may also be related to the nature of our sample, which was relatively small and designed only for cross-sectional analysis. We analyzed the contents of the LD-203 reports and compared them to contribution data found in the publicly available Federal Elections Commission's (FEC) political contribution database. We consulted with staff at FEC responsible for administering the database. We determined that the data are sufficiently reliable for the purposes of our reporting objectives.

We compared the FEC-reportable contributions on the LD-203 reports with information in the FEC database. The verification process required text and pattern matching procedures so we used professional judgment when assessing whether an individual listed is the same individual filing an LD-203. For contributions reported in the FEC database and not on the LD-203 report, we asked the lobbyists or organizations to explain why the contribution was not listed on the LD-203 report or to provide documentation of those contributions. As with covered positions on LD-2 disclosure reports, we cannot be certain that our review identified all cases of FEC-reportable contributions that were inappropriately omitted from a lobbyist's LD-203 report. We did not estimate the percentage of other non-FEC political contributions that were omitted because they tend to constitute a small minority of all listed contributions and cannot be verified against an external source.

---

[26] We used a Bonferroni adjustment to adjust for multiple comparisons to account for the pairwise tests for each item examined.

To identify challenges to compliance, we used a structured web-based survey and obtained the views from 97 different lobbying firms included in our sample on any challenges to compliance. The number of different lobbying firms is 97, which is less than our original sample of 99 reports because some lobbying firms had more than one LD-2 report included in our sample. We calculated responses based on the number of different lobbying firms that we contacted rather than the number of interviews. Prior to our calculations, we removed the duplicate lobbying firms based on the most recent date of their responses. For those cases with the same response date, the decision rule was to keep the cases with the smallest assigned case identification number. To obtain their views, we asked them to rate their ease with complying with the LD-2 disclosure requirements using a scale of "very easy," "somewhat easy," "somewhat difficult," or "very difficult." In addition, using the same scale, we asked them to rate the ease of understanding the terms associated with LD-2 reporting requirements.[27]

To describe the resources and authorities available to the U.S. Attorney's Office for the District of Columbia (USAO) and its efforts to improve its LDA enforcement, we interviewed USAO officials. We obtained information on the capabilities of the system officials established to track and report compliance trends and referrals and on other practices established to focus resources on LDA enforcement. USAO provided us with reports from the tracking system on the number and status of referrals and chronically noncompliant lobbyists and lobbying firms.

The mandate does not require us to identify lobbyists who failed to register and report in accordance with the LDA requirements, or determine for those lobbyists who did register and report whether all lobbying activity or contributions were disclosed. Therefore, this was outside the scope of our audit.

---

[27] One lobbying firm did not respond to the questions about their ease of understanding the terms associated with LD-2 reporting requirements.

We conducted this performance audit from May 2018 to March 2019 in accordance with generally accepted government auditing standards. Those standards require that we plan and perform the audit to obtain sufficient, appropriate evidence to provide a reasonable basis for our findings and conclusions based on our audit objectives. We believe that the evidence obtained provides a reasonable basis for our findings and conclusions based on our audit objectives.

In: Government Reports …
Editor: Evie Boan
ISBN: 978-1-53615-928-8

Chapter 2

ARCHITECT OF THE CAPITOL: A FORMALIZED PROCESS COULD IMPROVE MANAGEMENT OF THE CONSTRUCTION DIVISION'S WORKFORCE AND WORKLOAD*

United States Government Accountability Office

ABBREVIATIONS

AOC	Architect of the Capitol
CDMS	Construction Division Management System
PPM	Planning and Project Management

* This is an edited, reformatted and augmented version of United States Government Accountability Office; Report to Congressional Requesters, Publication No. GAO-19-343, dated March 2019.

WHY GAO DID THIS STUDY

AOC is organized into 10 jurisdictions that operate and maintain the buildings and grounds of the U.S. Capitol complex. For projects such as renovations and repairs, the jurisdictions can use their own employees, a contractor, or AOC's Construction Division, which is staffed with trade workers such as electricians and plumbers. Most of the Division's staff are employed on a temporary basis and paid with funds the Division receives from the jurisdictions for projects it executes on their behalf. In March 2017, AOC laid off 30 of the Division's approximately 190 temporary employees, citing a lack of work from the jurisdictions.

GAO was asked to review the Division's operations. This chapter examines the jurisdictions' use of the Division and the Division's management of its workforce, among other issues. GAO analyzed information on projects the Division completed during fiscal years 2014 through 2018, reviewed AOC policies, visited the sites of six projects that are illustrative of the work the Division performs for the jurisdictions, and interviewed AOC staff, including officials from AOC's 10 jurisdictions and five of the employees AOC laid off in 2017.

WHAT GAO RECOMMENDS

GAO recommends that AOC formalize the process the Division uses for collecting information on the jurisdictions' construction priorities each month, such as through developing written procedures. AOC concurred with GAO's recommendation.

WHAT GAO FOUND

The Architect of the Capitol's (AOC) Construction Division (hereafter the Division) is designed to serve as a flexible option that the 10 operational jurisdictions that comprise AOC can use to meet their facility needs. In their efforts to manage the buildings and grounds of the U.S. Capitol complex, AOC's jurisdictions have used the Division for projects that vary widely in cost, complexity, and duration (see figure). For example, over the last 5 fiscal years, the jurisdictions have used the Division for projects ranging in cost from about $1,000 to about $10 million and in scope from hazardous material testing to multiyear lighting-system upgrades. Jurisdiction officials cited the Division's flexibility in adjusting to scope and other changes to keep a project on schedule as one of the reasons they may decide to use the Division instead of an outside contractor. While jurisdiction officials said they were generally satisfied with the Division's services, officials from two jurisdictions suggested that the Division consider changing how it operates—for example, by transferring some positions to its parent organization in an effort to lower what it charges the jurisdictions. According to AOC officials, making changes such as this one to the Division's operations could have varying effects, such as increasing how much funding AOC would require from other sources beyond the jurisdictions.

Work on a new child care center for the House of Representatives.

Work at the Library of Congress to reverse the swing of doors to allow for the more orderly evacuation of occupants in the event of an emergency.

Repairs to the steps of a Senate office building.

Source: GAO. | GAO-19-343.

Examples of Construction Division Projects.

The Division has taken steps to strategically manage its workforce to help ensure that it has the right number and composition of staff to meet the jurisdictions' needs but has not formalized the process it uses for collecting information on the jurisdictions' construction priorities each month. Because the Division's workload is driven by projects the jurisdictions hire it to perform, such things as changes in projects' priorities and work to be performed make determining future workforce needs challenging. The Division's approach to managing its workforce generally aligns with practices that GAO has previously identified that help agencies strategically manage their human capital. This approach includes having strategies to address gaps if the size and composition of an agency's workforce are not aligned with its workload requirements. However, because the Division has not formalized the process it uses to collect information each month on the jurisdictions' construction priorities it may miss opportunities to obtain information that is critical to making informed decisions. The Division also cannot provide reasonable assurance to AOC management and Congress that it is taking the steps necessary to manage its workload and that it is basing its workforce projections on the most current information available.

The Honorable Amy Klobuchar
Ranking Member
Committee on Rules and Administration
United States Senate

The Honorable Chris Murphy
Ranking Member
Subcommittee on the Legislative Branch
Committee on Appropriations
United States Senate

The Architect of the Capitol (AOC) is responsible for the maintenance, operation, and preservation of more than 18.4-million square feet of building space and more than 570 acres of grounds in Washington, D.C., Maryland, and Virginia.[1] This responsibility includes a number of buildings that comprise the U.S. Capitol complex, including the U.S. Capitol, House and Senate office buildings, the Library of Congress, the Supreme Court,

[1] In addition to Washington, D.C., AOC is also responsible for buildings at Fort Meade and in Landover, Maryland, and in Culpeper and Manassas, Virginia.

and the U.S. Botanic Garden. AOC is organized into 10 operational jurisdictions,[2] each of which is managed by a superintendent (or equivalent), who oversees that jurisdiction. For renovations, repairs, and new construction, the superintendents can use their own employees, a private contractor, or AOC's Construction Division (hereafter the Division). The Division is designed to be a flexible option for the jurisdictions and operates in response to their needs. It is comprised primarily of trade workers such as electricians, plumbers, and masons that it employs on a temporary basis.[3] In March 2017, AOC laid off 30 of the Division's approximately 190 temporary employees, citing a lack of work from the jurisdictions. While the number and types of temporary employees within the Division are continually changing based on the work it is performing, the magnitude of this layoff raised questions about how AOC manages its workload and workforce.

You asked us to review the Division's role in supporting AOC's jurisdictions, as well as the circumstances surrounding the March 2017 layoff of 30 of the Division's temporary employees. This chapter:

- describes how the jurisdictions use the Division and the factors they reported considering when deciding whether to use the Division,
- assesses how the Division manages its workforce given the variability of its workload, and
- assesses whether AOC's appointment and subsequent March 2017 layoff of temporary employees from the Division complied with applicable policy.

---

[2] The term "operational jurisdiction" refers to an organization within AOC that is responsible for building operations. For example, the Senate Office Buildings jurisdiction is responsible for the buildings and grounds under control of the U.S. Senate. For the purposes of this chapter, we use the term "jurisdiction" to refer to those organizations.

[3] Unlike permanent federal employees, temporary employees are hired for a specified period of time. For the purposes of this chapter, the term "temporary" refers to nonpermanent federal employment status.

To describe how the jurisdictions use the Division and the factors affecting this use, we obtained and analyzed available data on projects the Division completed for the jurisdictions during fiscal years 2014 through 2018.[4] In addition, we visited the sites of six projects that the Division was executing at the time of our review. The projects we visited were selected to enable us to understand the nature of the work the Division performs for the jurisdictions; accordingly, the information we provide regarding those projects is not generalizable to all projects the Division performs for the jurisdictions. We also interviewed Division officials and each of the jurisdictions' superintendents. During the interviews, we asked superintendents what suggestions they had to change the Division's operations and discussed with Division officials the potential implications of those changes. We did not independently evaluate the superintendents' suggestions or the implications of implementing the superintendents' suggestions.

To assess how the Division manages its workforce, we reviewed pertinent documents, such as the Division's Organization and Operating Plan,[5] obtained and analyzed payroll data for the Division for fiscal years 2014 through 2018, and interviewed Division officials. We compared the Division's efforts to manage its workforce to strategic-human capital management activities or practices identified in our prior work[6] and standards for internal control in the federal government.[7]

To assess whether AOC's appointment and subsequent March 2017 layoff of 30 temporary employees from the Division followed applicable practices and policy, we reviewed relevant federal laws, AOC policy, and agency personnel documents. We also interviewed AOC's Chief Human Capital Officer and other officials within the Human Capital Management Division about AOC's appointment and layoff of the Division's temporary

---

[4] Comparable data for projects where the jurisdictions used their own employees or a contractor instead of the Division were not available; as a result, a comparison of data among these options was not possible.

[5] AOC, *Construction Division Organization and Operating Plan* (December 2017).

[6] GAO, *Human Capital: Key Principles for Effective Strategic Workforce Planning*, GAO-04-39 (Washington, D.C: Dec. 11, 2003).

[7] GAO, *Standards for Internal Control in the Federal Government*, GAO-14-704G (Washington, D.C.: September 2014).

employees. In addition, we interviewed five of the nine laid off temporary employees, who were subsequently rehired by AOC, to obtain their perspective on AOC's processes for appointing and laying off temporary employees.[8]

We assessed the reliability of the Division's project and payroll data that we used in our analysis by reviewing available documentation and interviewing agency officials. We found these data to be sufficiently reliable for the purposes of this chapter, which includes describing the type and cost of projects the Division completed for the jurisdictions over the last 5 fiscal years, identifying illustrative examples of those projects and describing the size and composition of the Division's workforce. For more details on our scope and methodology, see appendix I.

We conducted this performance audit from March 2018 to March 2019 in accordance with generally accepted government auditing standards. Those standards require that we plan and perform the audit to obtain sufficient, appropriate evidence to provide a reasonable basis for our findings and conclusions based on our audit objectives. We believe that the evidence obtained provides a reasonable basis for our findings and conclusions based on our audit objectives.

BACKGROUND

AOC is responsible for the maintenance, operation, and preservation of the buildings that comprise the U.S. Capitol complex, as shown in Figure 1.

AOC is organized into the following 10 jurisdictions, each of which is funded by a separate appropriation:

1. Capitol Building,
2. Capitol Grounds and Arboretum (hereafter the Capitol Grounds),

[8] We contacted nine individuals and five agreed to meet with us.

3. Capitol Police Buildings, Grounds, and Security (hereafter the Capitol Police),
4. Capitol Power Plant,
5. House Office Buildings (hereafter the House),
6. Library Buildings and Grounds (hereafter the Library),
7. Planning and Project Management (PPM),[9]
8. Senate Office Buildings (hereafter the Senate),
9. Supreme Court Building and Grounds, and
10. U.S. Botanic Garden (hereafter the Botanic Garden).

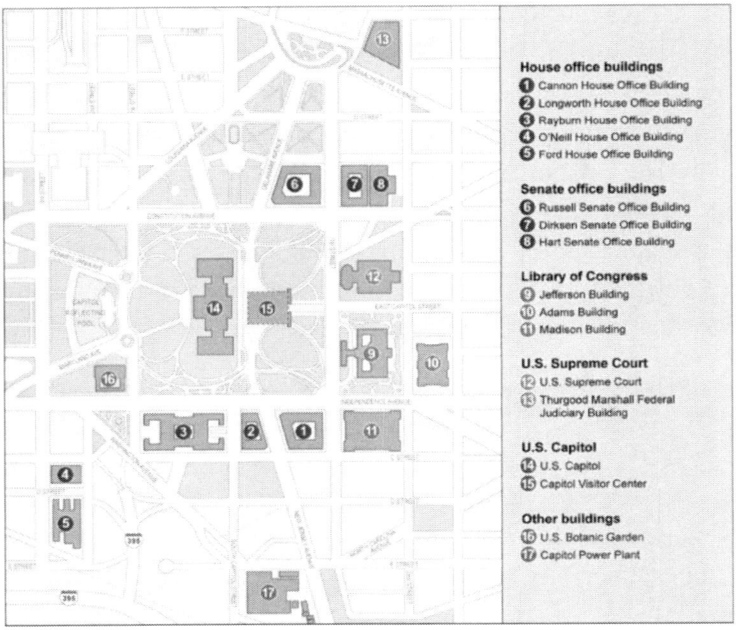

Sources: National Park Service and GAO. | GAO-19-343.

Note: The Architect of the Capitol is responsible for additional buildings not included in this map.

Figure 1. The U.S. Capitol Complex in Washington, D.C.

---

[9] PPM is funded through AOC's appropriation for Capital Construction and Operations, which provides for certain centrally managed, mission-oriented construction and utility functions, such as the maintenance of emergency generators. That appropriation also covers common operational and mission-support services, such as safety, environment, procurement, and legal support serving all of the jurisdictions.

PPM provides consolidated services to all of AOC's jurisdictions, such as long-range facility planning, historic preservation, and architectural and engineering design services. In addition, PPM manages systems that span jurisdictions including electrical distribution and emergency generators. PPM is also the parent organization of the Division, which provides construction and facility management support to all of AOC's jurisdictions.

Established in the 1970s, the Division's mission is to "support AOC jurisdictions serving their Congressional and Supreme Court clients by providing high quality construction and craftsmanship with seamless flexibility, best value, and extraordinary customer service, while protecting our national treasures." The Division's operations are funded through a mix of appropriations and project funding from the jurisdictions. Specifically, according to AOC officials, the agency's appropriation for Capital Construction and Operations provides the salaries and expenses of up to 13 permanent staff. The salaries and expenses of the remaining staff, as well as other costs (such as materials) are covered by the project funding the Division receives from the jurisdictions. According to AOC officials, essentially, the jurisdictions hire the Division to execute work on their behalf, and the Division charges the jurisdictions for its expenses.[10]

As a result, the number and type of temporary employees the Division employs at any given time is directly related to the projects it is performing for the jurisdictions. As of October 2018, of the Division's 162 employees, 12 were permanent employees responsible for executive management and administrative functions. The remaining 150 were temporary employees—124 trade workers and 26 construction support employees—that it hired under temporary (e.g., 13- or 24-month) appointments. The trade workers include electricians, plumbers, masons, woodcrafters and carpenters, cement finishers, sheet metal mechanics, painters and plasterers, hazardous material abaters and insulators, laborers, and warehouse and material handlers. The construction support employees include personnel who

---

[10] The jurisdictions use appropriations made available to them for construction to fund their projects. These appropriations have varying periods of availability (e.g., 1-year, multiple years, or an indefinite period), depending upon the specific language of each appropriation.

perform activities such as construction management, purchasing, and timekeeping.

The Division's temporary employees are eligible for benefits. By law, AOC is generally required to provide all temporary employees with "the same eligibility for life insurance, health insurance and other benefits" to temporary employees who are hired for periods exceeding one year.[11] The benefits AOC's temporary employees receive may differ from what other federal temporary employees in the executive branch receive since these benefits vary depending on the type of temporary appointment and the employing agency, among other things. For example, employees serving under an appointment limited to 1 year or less are generally not eligible for the Federal Employees' Group Life Insurance program.

Source: GAO presentation of Architect of the Capitol information. | GAO-19-343.
Note: This figure depicts how the total hourly rate of a trade worker that hypothetically costs the Construction Division $45 an hour is calculated.

Figure 2. Calculating the Hourly Rate the Construction Division Charges Jurisdictions for a Trade Worker.

As previously stated, the Division pays for the salaries and expenses of its temporary employees with project funding from the jurisdictions. That project funding covers both the Division's direct and indirect costs. Direct costs are those directly attributed to and expended on a project, such as labor (i.e., trade workers) and materials. In contrast, indirect costs are necessary costs that are not directly attributable to a specific project, such as employee leave and training, as well as salaries for construction support

[11] See the Congressional Operations Appropriations Act, 2002, Pub. L. No. 107-68, § 133, 115 Stat. 560, 581-82 (2001), as amended by the Legislative Branch Appropriations Act, 2004, Pub. L. No. 108-83, § 1101, 117 Stat. 1007, 1027 (2003) (codified at 2 U.S.C. § 1831 note).

employees, such as supervisors and purchasing agents. To pay for its indirect costs, the Division charges the jurisdictions what it calls an "indirect rate." As of October 2018, the Division's indirect rate was 0.85. The Division applies this rate to every direct labor-hour associated with a project it executes for the jurisdictions. For example, for a trade worker with a hypothetical hourly cost of $45, the Division charges the jurisdictions about $83, as shown in Figure 2.

For more information on the Division's direct and indirect costs, see appendix II.

JURISDICTIONS USED THE DIVISION FOR A WIDE RANGE OF PROJECTS, CITING FLEXIBILITY AND CAPACITY AS KEY FACTORS, AND WERE GENERALLY SATISFIED WITH THE DIVISION'S SERVICES

Jurisdictions Used the Division for a Wide Range of Projects

Based on our analysis of the Division's data for projects completed during fiscal years 2014 through 2018, the jurisdictions used the Division to varying degrees for projects that ranged widely in terms of cost, complexity, and duration.

- Cost: There was a wide range in the nominal cost of individual projects the Division completed during fiscal years 2014 through 2018. The smallest individual project cost about $1,100 in 2017 dollars to perform hazardous materials testing in the Ford Office Building for the House jurisdiction in fiscal year 2016. Larger projects may be done in phases and when combined can cost millions of dollars. For example, in 2015 the Division completed a lighting project at the James Madison Building for the Library jurisdiction in two phases at a total cost of about $9.8 million in 2017 dollars.

- Complexity: During this period, the Division's projects ranged from work involving one type of activity or trade to work involving several phases or many trades. For example, the Capitol Power Plant jurisdiction used the Division for paint projects and a door replacement. Other projects included the construction of a lactation suite at the Ford House Office Building. For this 4-month project, the Division performed carpentry, electrical work, hazardous materials abatement, and other tasks in order to demolish an existing women's restroom and build a lactation suite with an adjacent, smaller women's restroom (see Figure 3).

Source: Architect of the Capitol. | GAO-19-343.

Figure 3. New Lactation Suite in the Ford House Office Building.

- Duration: During this period, the jurisdictions used the Division for projects that varied from quick turnaround projects that took a few days to complete to longer, multi-year projects. Most (about 88 percent) of the projects were completed within one year, while about 4 percent were completed between 1 and 2 years, and about 8 percent took 2 or more years to complete. For example, the Senate jurisdiction used the Division for an elevator repair project in 2016 at the Russell Office Building that took one day to complete while smoke detector upgrades in the James Madison Building for the Library jurisdiction took over 5 years and were completed in 2014. We also identified several examples of projects that the Division did for jurisdictions in phases. Sometimes the duration of the phases were less than one year but when combined the work spanned multiple years. For example, the Division built additional office spaces for staff displaced by the House jurisdiction's renovation of the Cannon Office Building. Each phase of the work was completed within one year, but the work spanned almost 2 years from November 2014 to August 2016.

The extent to which each of the jurisdictions used the Division also varied. Based on our analysis of the Division's data and discussions with the jurisdictions, the Library, House, and Senate jurisdictions were the primary users of the Division during fiscal years 2014 through 2018, comprising more than 90 percent of the total work by cost for completed projects, as shown in Figure 4. The Division completed projects exceeding $1 million for each of these jurisdictions.

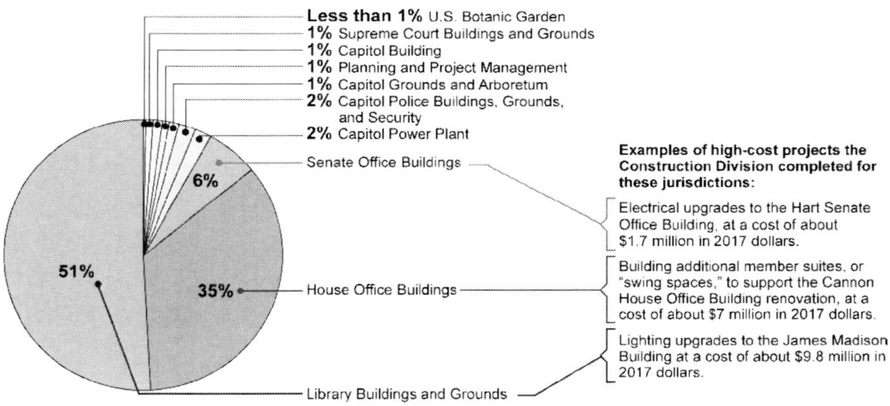

Source: GAO analysis of Architect of the Capitol data. | GAO-19-343.

Note: This figure shows the percentages of the total cost of projects the Construction Division completed for the jurisdictions over fiscal years 2014 and 2018 and does not include the cost of projects that were ongoing as of October 1, 2018. Values represented in the figure have been adjusted for inflation to reflect fiscal year 2017 dollars. Percentages may not add to 100 due to rounding.

Figure 4. Construction Division's Workload by Jurisdiction Based on the Cost of Projects, Fiscal Years 2014 to 2018.

Jurisdiction Officials Cited the Division's Flexibility and Capacity as Factors That Influence Decisions to Use the Division

Flexibility

While jurisdictions have the option to use their own staff or a contractor for projects, jurisdiction officials said they consider a range of factors when determining whether to use the Division. They most frequently cited the Division's flexibility in responding to scheduling and scoping changes and the jurisdictions' own internal capacity to execute a project. They less frequently cited other factors, such as the availability of appropriations.

Schedule

Jurisdiction officials said the Division provided scheduling flexibility at no extra charge compared to using outside contractors. According to jurisdiction officials, when projects require a great deal of flexibility, the jurisdictions may be more likely to choose the Division over a contractor because the Division can start and stop work as needed and can work nights or on weekends if necessary to keep a project on schedule without charging extra fees. For example, work on projects may need to be stopped or delayed for a variety of reasons, such as for security purposes if there is a protest near the worksite, or during a presidential visit.

Jurisdiction officials also noted that the Division can typically mobilize faster than a contractor, a consideration that can be an important factor in determining whether to use the Division. For example, jurisdiction officials noted that the Division's employees can begin work faster than an outside contractor because they have employee identification badges that authorize access to most buildings across the Capitol complex without an escort. 'Contractors must obtain a badge prior to accessing a work site and require escorts in instances when they do not have an AOC or site-specific badge, and the process of obtaining a badge adds time to when a contractor can begin work. As another example, jurisdiction officials also told us that using a contractor requires that AOC develop full design specifications for a project, a process that takes time and resources. In contrast, the Division can execute work without full design specifications. For example, Capitol Power Plant officials told us they used the Division for renovations to their Administration Building because, according to the officials, the Division started the work sooner, without design specifications and thereby completed the project faster than a contractor likely could have. Capitol Power Plant officials explained that the work— which included new carpet and painting—was agreed upon with the Division without spending time developing detailed design specifications that would have been required to obtain a contractor for the work.

Scope Changes

According to jurisdiction officials, the Division is typically more flexible than a contractor when dealing with issues that arise from unforeseen site conditions or changes to a project's scope. For example, during the construction of the lactation suite discussed above, the Division uncovered lead paint in the walls, requiring the work to stop until the lead paint was removed. According to officials, contractors typically charge for making changes to a project's scope, such as removing hazardous materials uncovered during construction or associated delays. The Division does not charge for making changes or associated delays. This flexibility is because the Division charges based on direct labor hours spent on a project, meaning its expenses are charged as they are incurred. Accordingly, while a project's costs may increase if more labor is charged to a project, the Division also has the option of having its employees work on other projects if work on a particular project has to stop.

Jurisdiction officials told us that the Division also works with the jurisdictions to save money on projects. According to officials, such savings were the case during a 2-year project that the Division completed at the Library jurisdiction's Jefferson Building in 2018 with a cost of $3.5 million in 2017 dollars. The project involved reversing the direction of doors in high-occupancy areas to allow for more orderly evacuation of occupants in the event of an emergency, as shown in Figure 5. It also involved replacing some of the building's historic doors and associated hardware with replicas that meet modern safety standards. Officials told us the Division helped the jurisdiction save about $1.2 million (in current dollars) during the course of the project by identifying less expensive materials for the project than originally planned for.

Signage at the Jefferson Building identifying the scope of work of a project.

Architect of the Capitol employees demonstrating the nature of safety improvements the Construction Division executed for the Library of Congress.

Source: GAO. | GAO-19-343.

Figure 5. Safety Improvements at the Library of Congress.

Capacity

Internal Staff

Jurisdiction officials also told us that they use the Division for projects when they lack the internal capacity to do so. Most of the jurisdictions have some trade workers, such as electricians and plumbers, on staff to handle their daily operations and maintenance needs. Jurisdictions may execute smaller projects with their own employees but may use the Division for projects beyond routine maintenance work that their own employees cannot fit into their schedules. For example, officials with the Senate jurisdiction told us that they have staff capable of performing cabinetry work but have used the Division in the past for cabinetry work so that their staff could focus on more routine maintenance work. Senate jurisdiction officials also told us that they primarily use their own staff for construction work, but will use the Division as an option to supplement their staff when the volume of the Senate jurisdiction's own workload is higher than what can be handled internally.

Skill and Equipment

Jurisdictions may use the Division if they lack the skills or equipment to execute a particular project. Officials from five of the jurisdictions told us that they have staff within their jurisdiction who can execute small projects involving hazardous materials, such as lead paint abatement under 2 square feet in size. Larger projects have additional abatement requirements, and the jurisdictions have used the Division for these projects. As another example, the Capitol Grounds jurisdiction used the Division in 2016 to install the annual Christmas tree on the Capitol lawn because the jurisdiction lacked the necessary equipment to do so. The Botanic Garden jurisdiction, which does not employ any masons, used the Division for a project at its Conservatory in 2016 because of the Division's masonry expertise. Officials with the Senate jurisdiction also cited the Division's masonry expertise among other factors, such as the Division's familiarity with the jurisdiction's buildings, in selecting the Division to repair the steps at the Russell Senate Office Building in 2017, as shown in Figure 6.

In 2017, the Construction Division began executing a project at the Russell Senate Office Building that involves dismantling, cleaning, and reinstalling exterior steps and a terrace.

Source: GAO. | GAO-19-343.

Figure 6. Repairs to the Steps of the Russell Senate Office Building.

Additional Considerations

Availability of Appropriations

Jurisdiction officials told us that they might not use the Division if the work cannot be completed by the time the jurisdiction's appropriations expire. Specifically, because the jurisdictions pay for the Division's services as work is executed rather than upfront when the work is initiated, the jurisdictions must ensure that work by the Division can be completed before their appropriations expire. Jurisdiction officials told us that as a result, the Division may not be a realistic option when using 1-year appropriations near the end of the fiscal year.[12] In contrast, when using a contractor, jurisdictions may obligate fixed period appropriations prior to the end of the fiscal year for work that will continue into the following fiscal year.

Cost

Most jurisdiction officials said that a project's cost was not a key factor they considered when determining whether to use the Division for a project. When the jurisdictions are considering using a contractor they are not required to obtain cost estimates from the Division first and generally do not do so. As a result, comprehensive information on the relative costs of using the Division compared to a contractor was not available. However, in cases where the jurisdictions told us they did obtain estimates from both the Division and a contractor, they said the cost to use the Division was sometimes more expensive than a contractor and sometimes less expensive, as illustrated in the following examples.

- Officials with the Supreme Court Building and Grounds jurisdiction told us they used the Division to install a new heating, ventilation, and air-conditioning system in one of its buildings

---

[12] As previously stated, the jurisdictions use appropriations made available to them for construction to fund their projects. These appropriations have varying periods of availability (e.g., 1-year, multiple years, or an indefinite period), depending upon the specific language of each appropriation.

after it obtained an estimate from a contractor. According to officials, the project required specialized skills that the Division's trade workers did not have. However, once they received the contractor's estimate, the jurisdiction officials determined it was cheaper to pay for the Division's employees to get trained to do the project than using a contractor.

- Officials with the Senate jurisdiction told us they obtained cost estimates for lead abatement work from both the Division and a contractor several years ago. According to officials, the contractor's estimate was less than that of the Division because the contractor proposed using different equipment for the project than the Division, and the jurisdiction used the contractor for the abatement.

Jurisdiction Officials Reported They Were Generally Satisfied with the Division's Services; A Few Suggested Making Changes to Its Operations

The jurisdiction officials we interviewed said they were generally satisfied with the Division's services, including the quality of its work, and were particularly satisfied with the flexibility the Division offers. Officials from seven of the nine jurisdictions we interviewed also told us they would not suggest making changes to how the Division currently operates.[13]

Officials from two of the jurisdictions suggested the organizational and cost-allocation changes discussed below. According to Division officials, implementing those suggestions would have implications for its operations and structure, and would require additional research and evaluation to determine if they are feasible.

---

[13] As part of our review, we asked 9 of AOC's 10 jurisdictions whether they would suggest changing anything to their current arrangement with the Division or to its operations. We did not ask PPM because the Division is a component of PPM.

- Transfer positions from the Division to its parent organization, PPM: Officials from one jurisdiction suggested that the Division could lower its indirect rate by transferring payroll responsibility for some supervisory positions, such as its construction or safety managers, from the Division to PPM. As discussed above, because the Division does not receive an appropriation for the salaries and expenses of its temporary construction support employees, it pays for those costs by charging the jurisdictions for direct labor hours and also an "indirect rate."

Division officials told us that payroll responsibility for some construction support positions could be transferred to PPM and that this transfer would reduce the Division's indirect rate because that rate increases by about 1.1 percent for each employee captured in the rate. Because PPM is the parent organization of the Division, this step would not reduce the total costs of projects to AOC as an organization; rather, it would transfer the responsibility for paying certain costs from the jurisdictions to PPM. According to AOC officials, this could have several effects. First, PPM would need to find a way to fund those positions, which would likely require an increase in its appropriations to cover additional positions. Second, transferring supervisory positions to PPM could mean those personnel could be tasked to support other AOC-wide efforts, rather than supervising and managing the day-to-day execution of the Division's projects. Similarly, Division officials told us that transferring supervisory positions or support personnel such as purchasing agents to PPM could reduce the Division's flexibility, such as its ability to hire additional supervisors or support personnel if its workload increases in the future.

- Make the Division's indirect rate variable: Officials with that same jurisdiction suggested that the Division consider making its indirect rate (which as of October 2018 was a fixed rate of 0.85) a variable rate. Under a variable rate approach, projects would have different rates depending on their needs. For example, a project requiring only labor would be charged one rate, but a project requiring labor and additional services, such as the purchasing of materials, would be charged a higher rate. According to Division officials, charging the jurisdictions varying rates depending on the extent to which a project utilizes the Division's resources could reduce the cost for some jurisdictions but increase it for others since the Division must charge enough to recover all of its costs. Division officials told us AOC evaluated this option in 2017 but decided against it. AOC determined that making the Division's indirect rate variable would result in increased administrative burden because the Division would have to determine which projects and workhours would be variable and which would not. It would then need to track and assess them differently for each project.

- Provide additional on-site supervisors for complex multi-trade projects: For most projects, the Division provides supervisors who manage the day-to-day execution of multiple projects. However, jurisdictions have the option to pay, as a direct cost, for dedicated, on-site supervisors to oversee and manage their projects exclusively. Officials with one jurisdiction suggested that the Division make it standard practice for complex, multi-trade projects to have a dedicated, on-site supervisor. Division officials told us that having a dedicated, on-site supervisor works best for complex, multi-trade projects such as the East Phase of the House jurisdiction's 13-month, $15 million child care center project that the Division completed in December 2018 (see Figure 7).[14]

According to Division officials, having dedicated, on-site supervisors day and night during construction enabled the project to remain on schedule and below budget because the supervisors were responsible for overseeing all construction activities and could immediately address questions or concerns that arose, thereby resulting in increased efficiency and cost savings. Division officials told us that while the project's scope

---

[14] According to AOC officials, the Division's portion of the project cost $8.6 million in 2017 dollars.

increased during execution, the Division was able to work additional nights and weekends to meet the project's deadline. Even with additional scope, Division officials estimated that they have saved the House jurisdiction about $500,000 (in current dollars) on the project through increased oversight and by identifying areas of cost savings, such as purchasing less expensive lighting fixtures than called for in the design.

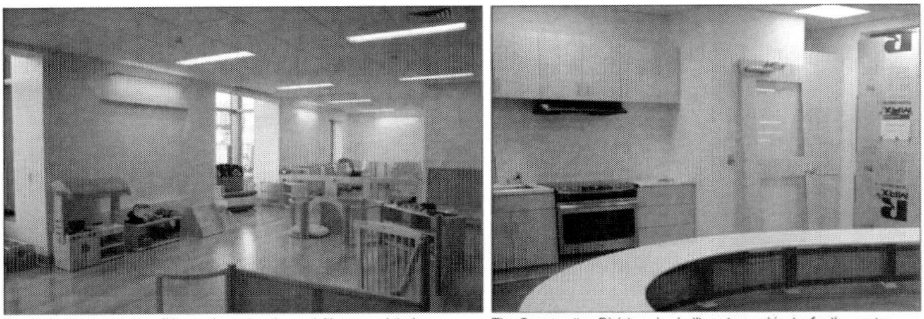

The project included demolition and construction activities associated with new classrooms, as well as supporting infrastructure and utilities.

The Construction Division also built custom cabinetry for the center, as shown in a seating area for activities.

Source: GAO. | GAO-19-343.

Figure 7. New Child Care Center for the House of Representatives.

The Division Has Taken Steps to Strategically Manage Its Workforce but Does Not Have a Formalized Process for Collecting Some Information

Uncertainties Make Anticipating the Division's Workforce Needs Challenging

The variability of the Division's workload makes anticipating the necessary size (number of employees) and composition (mix of trades and number of employees within each trade) of its workforce challenging. AOC has reported to Congress that the primary drivers behind the size and composition of the Division's workforce have been project demand and the availability of funding.[15] As previously discussed, the Division's workload is driven by projects the jurisdictions hire it to perform. Without projects to execute for the jurisdictions, the Division does not have funding to pay the salaries and expenses of most of its employees. Accordingly, the size of the Division's workforce expands and contracts in response to the jurisdictions' demand for work. For example, over the last 5 fiscal years, the size of the Division's trade workforce has fluctuated between a high of 191 in fiscal year 2016 and a low of 121 in fiscal year 2018. During that period, the number of employees the Division employed within each trade also fluctuated.

Several factors contribute to the variability of the Division's workload and make determining its future workforce needs challenging. First, officials told us that the Division has no control over whether the jurisdictions use the Division for their projects. Second, even if a jurisdiction decides to use the Division, Division officials told us that projects are notional or uncertain until that jurisdiction signs a project agreement, among other things.[16] Third, even with a signed agreement, jurisdictions can reduce a project's scope or cancel it all together, a situation that can leave the Division searching to find work for the trade workers it planned to use for the project. Finally, differing project priorities also come into play, as both Division officials and representatives from three of the jurisdictions acknowledged that some projects and work for certain jurisdictions are a higher priority than others. According to officials, when priority or emergency projects arise, the timing and work for ongoing projects can be affected as trade workers are shifted to the priority or emergency. In some cases, the on-going project may continue at a slower pace with fewer workers and in other cases all work might be stopped for a period of time.

---

[15] AOC, *Report to Congress* (Aug. 4, 2017).

[16] A project agreement defines the scope, cost, and duration of activities for a project.

The Division Has Taken Steps to Anticipate Its Workforce Needs but Lacks a Formalized Process for Collecting Information on the Jurisdictions' Construction Priorities

Over the last several years the Division has made efforts to strategically manage its workforce to help ensure that it has the right number and composition of employees to meet the jurisdictions' needs. Our prior work has identified certain practices that, when implemented, can help federal agencies strategically manage their human capital.[17] These practices include: (1) involving managers and stakeholders in decision-making, (2) basing workforce decisions on current needs and future projections, (3) having strategies to address workforce gaps, and (4) monitoring progress. As discussed below, we found that the Division has taken steps that generally align with those practices. However, it does not have a formalized process for collecting information that it uses to project future workforce needs, and we note that several of the steps it has taken date to the time of the March 2017 layoffs or more recently.

Involve Managers and Stakeholders in Decision-Making

The Division has taken steps to involve AOC's management, including the superintendents of the jurisdictions, in managing its workforce given the variability of its workload. According to Division officials, its staff are in frequent contact with the jurisdictions and meet periodically with the jurisdictions to discuss the status of ongoing and future projects. The officials said that Division staff meet bi-weekly with the larger jurisdictions—such as the Senate, House, and Library—and monthly or as needed with others as well as with PPM on a weekly basis to discuss the status of projects and workforce needs. According to Division officials, this regular communication with the jurisdictions is their primary and most important method of identifying and addressing workload issues or concerns. Jurisdiction officials echoed the Division's comments, noting that they are in frequent contact with staff from the Division or as needed.

---

[17] GAO-04-39.

Base Workforce Decisions on Current Needs and Future Projections

Over the last several years, the Division has taken steps to improve how it collects and tracks information from the jurisdictions upon which to base its future workforce projections. Prior to 2015, the Division used a paper-based process to collect information on the jurisdictions' work requests and tracked information on a spreadsheet. In 2015, the Division implemented a software tool called the Construction Division Management System (CDMS) to streamline that process, making it easier for the jurisdictions to submit requests for work. For example, using CDMS, the Division can now electronically collect information for ongoing projects from the jurisdictions, such as change orders and schedule updates, and the jurisdictions can electronically submit requests for cost or schedule information for future projects. According to Division officials, Construction Managers, who are familiar with the resource needs of individual projects, are responsible for updating and validating the information in CDMS—typically bi-weekly—and the information in CDMS is available to the jurisdictions to review and verify.

More recently, in July 2017, the Division hired a scheduler to develop resource-loaded schedules for ongoing projects. This involves assigning labor, materials, equipment, and other resources to a project's schedule. According to Division officials, currently, the Division develops resource-loaded schedules for about 70 percent of its workload as the projects that comprise its remaining workload are too small or short-term for such schedules. In addition, in October 2017, the Division began collecting additional information on the jurisdictions' construction priorities through a monthly data call. As part of this data call, which the Division performs via email, the Division requests updated information from the jurisdictions on their current projects, such as the expected start date or whether minor tasks remain, and the status of potential future projects. Using the information the Division collects from the jurisdictions, officials told us it then forecasts its workload and workforce needs out over the succeeding 12 months. According to officials, those projections are an "art, not a science," because of the uncertainties surrounding the Division's workload. However, the Division has not formalized the process it uses to collect information about the jurisdictions' construction priorities. Specifically, we found that the Division lacks a written set of procedures for the monthly data call discussed above to help ensure that staff understand who is responsible for collecting information, what information should be collected, and when that information should be collected. This lack of procedures led to a situation in July 2018 where, according to officials, the Division did not conduct that data call but has since set calendar reminders for key staff in an effort to help ensure they do not miss it again. While setting such reminders may have some benefit now, it does not ensure that others within AOC will execute that data call in the future. Formalized processes, such as written procedures, can help ensure that steps an agency is taking can be implemented in a predictable, repeatable, and accountable way. Such procedures are also a key component of internal control designed to provide reasonable assurance that an organization's operations are effective and efficient.[18] AOC officials agreed that a more formalized process for collecting information about the jurisdictions' construction priorities could help ensure the data is collected consistently. It would also better position AOC management to ensure that the Division's process will be implemented consistently and that the jurisdictions understand what information is expected of them. It could also provide reasonable assurance to AOC management and Congress that the Division is taking the steps necessary to manage its workload and basing its workforce projections on the most current information available.

Have Strategies to Address Workforce Gaps

The Division has a number of strategies it can employ if the size and composition of its workforce are not aligned with its workload requirements. For example, officials told us the Division can utilize direct-hire authority to quickly fill positions if there is a shortage of employees with specific skillsets to meet the jurisdictions' needs.[19] Officials told us

---

[18] GAO-14-704G.

[19] According to AOC's Career Staffing Plan, direct-hire is the authority to fill certain positions without the need for competition.

employees may also work overtime to meet the jurisdictions' needs if the Division's workload projections do not show a need to hire additional employees. In instances where there is a lack of work, officials told us the Division has the options of not renewing the appointments of its temporary employees; helping affected employees in finding positions in jurisdictions to the extent practicable; or, if necessary, lay off affected employees, as it did in March 2017.

Division officials told us they are also exploring additional strategies to help address potential instances where the size and composition of its workforce are not aligned with its workload requirements moving forward. One potential strategy involves using the Division to help address AOC's backlog of deferred maintenance and capital renewal, which AOC estimated in 2017 was about $1.4 billion.[20] Another potential strategy involves working with the jurisdictions to establish more large projects that provide a stable amount of work over a period of time. An example of a recent such project is the East Phase of the O'Neill Child Care Center project. According to Division officials, around 25–30 trade workers worked at the site at any given time, providing stability and work for multiple trades. When work on other projects was delayed or did not materialize, the Division was able to move the trade workers to the child care project.

Monitor Progress

Over the last several years the Division has taken steps to monitor the accuracy of its workload and workforce projections by discussing its projections with AOC management, including the Architect of the Capitol and the superintendents of the jurisdictions, each month. According to officials, the Division began these monthly briefings for AOC's management in December 2016, when its workload decreased due to the completion of work related to the renovation of the Cannon Office Building. During these briefings, Division staff provide the Architect of the

---

[20] In 2017, AOC reported that significant investments are needed for preservation and to ensure the future safety of AOC building occupants and visitors. See AOC, *Performance and Accountability Report 2017*, 2017.

Capitol and the superintendents with information on the Division's active, committed, and potential projects over the next several months. According to Division officials, these briefings provide an opportunity to discuss with AOC's management any issues or concerns they have with the Division's workload.

The Division employed the practices described above in the months leading up to the March 2017 layoff of the 30 temporary employees. Division officials told us that 5 to 6 months prior to March 2017, they anticipated a potential decline in the Division's workload and worked with the jurisdictions to identify potential projects that the Division could execute, but sufficient additional projects did not materialize. During this process, the Division involved PPM, the jurisdictions, and AOC's management, among others. The efforts to minimize the number of employees affected by any layoffs included identifying job openings within the jurisdictions that employees could apply for. According to officials, one employee was hired by the Senate jurisdiction, another by the Capitol Grounds jurisdiction, and a third by the Office of the Chief Administrative Officer in the House, prior to the layoff.

During the course of our review, we observed that the Division employed these strategies. Specifically, Division officials told us that they anticipated there might be a potential decline in the Division's workload in early 2019. The Division raised this potential with AOC's management during the summer of 2018, and officials told us the issue was resolved once the House and Library jurisdictions identified several projects that the Division could execute beginning in 2019.

AOC's Appointment and Subsequent Lay Off of Temporary Employees in March 2017 Followed Applicable Practices and Policy

AOC's authority to appoint and remove its employees is governed by title 2 of the U.S. Code and AOC has established various practices and policy related to their terms of employment. We found that AOC generally followed its practices when it appointed 30 temporary employees and adhered to its policy when it subsequently laid them off in March 2017.

AOC Generally Followed Its Practices in Appointing and Renewing the Terms of Employment for Temporary Employees

Our review of the appointment letters for 27 of the 30 temporary employees laid off in March 2017 found that the letters specified that the position was temporary and was for a term not-to-exceed 13-months.[21] We also found that 10 of the 27 appointment letters included language stating that the position was dependent on the availability of work or funding. As part of our review, we met with five of the nine employees that AOC rehired following the March 2017 layoffs, all five employees told us that they were aware of the temporary nature of their positions and of the fact that they could be laid off at any time due to lack of work. Human capital officials told us that in April 2017, they developed a standard appointment letter to communicate the terms of employment for temporary employees more consistently. This letter includes language explaining that temporary appointments may be terminated at any time due to a lack of work, lack of funds, or failure to meet management's expectations. For a copy of AOC's standard appointment letter for temporary employees, see appendix III.

AOC may renew the employment of temporary employees at the end of their 13-month appointment based on project needs and the availability of funding, according to human capital officials. We found that the 13 month appointments for 26 of the 30 temporary employees were routinely renewed prior to their March 2017 layoff.[22] Of the 26 temporary employees, 12 had been employed from 13 months to 5 years, 9 had been employed from 6 to 10 years, and 5 had been employed for more than 10 years. The remaining four had been employed for less than 13 months. Human capital officials told us that there is no limitation on the number of times an employee's appointment may be renewed. To ensure that

---

[21] AOC human capital officials told us the appointment letters were unavailable for the other three employees because there was a different process in place when they were hired.

[22] The other four temporary employees worked for the Division for less than 13 months prior to their layoff and did not have a Standard Form 50 (Notification of Personnel Action) showing an employment extension.

employees serving under temporary appointments understand the terms of their employment, human capital officials told us that since March 2014 employees who have had their appointments renewed sign a standard Extension of Temporary Appointment form. This form states the position is temporary, may be shorter or longer than 13 months, and may end at any time. For a copy of this extension form, see appendix IV.

AOC Generally Followed Applicable Policy When Laying Off the Division's Temporary Employees

AOC's layoff policy allows the Director of PPM, as delegated by the Architect of the Capitol, to lay off the Division's temporary employees for lack of work, lack of funds, or failure to meet management's expectations.[23] The policy does not specify which factors AOC should consider in selecting employees to be laid off, thereby allowing the agency discretion in this area.

Our review of the layoff letters for the 30 temporary employees laid off in March 2017 confirmed that AOC communicated to the employees that the layoff was due to a lack of work. In this particular situation, the Division officials said they determined the number of temporary employees needed to carry out its projected workload and considered two factors equally: (1) the employees' performance and skillset and (2) the employees' ability to work independently and as part of a team. Human capital officials told us that AOC's offices of Employee and Labor Relations and its General Counsel reviewed the Division's request, and found no human-capital or legal concerns. The human capital officials drafted letters notifying the 30 employees of their layoff, effective upon receipt. Division supervisors provided the letters to employees at the start of their shifts on March 21, 2017. Figure 8 provides summary information by trade on the 30 temporary employees that AOC laid off in March 2017.

At the time of the March 2017 layoff, AOC did not have a policy that required the Division to notify the Division's temporary employees of an impending layoff. Human capital officials told us that they did not provide

---

[23] AOC, *Policy Memorandum 316-1, Delegation of Architect's Final Decision Making Authority—Separation of Non-Permanent Employees* (April 2016).

the Division's temporary employees with advance notice of their layoff because of concerns that such advance notice could result in an unproductive and disruptive work environment. In terms of notifying relevant employee unions, human capital officials said they provided 12-hour advance notification of the layoff to one employee union, in accordance with that union's collective-bargaining agreement. The five rehired employees we interviewed told us they were caught off guard by the March 2017 layoffs. None of the 30 temporary employees filed grievances related to the layoff, according to human capital officials.

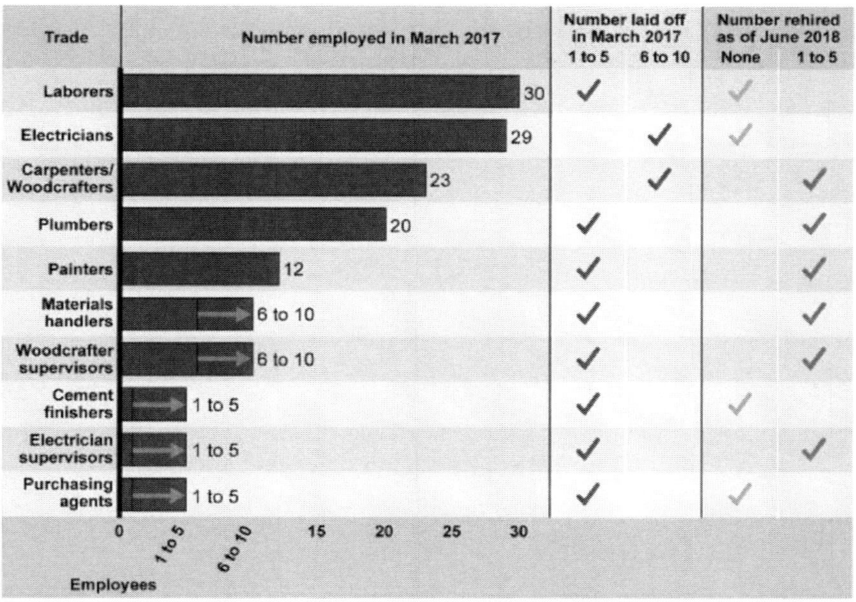

Source: GAO analysis of Architect of the Capitol personnel information. | GAO-19-343.

Note: To protect individuals' privacy we have consolidated cells with 5 or fewer individuals.

Figure 8. Summary Information on the Temporary Employees the Architect of the Capitol Laid Off in March 2017.

Since the layoff, human capital officials told us they recognized that AOC did not have a consistent policy for providing advance notice of layoffs to temporary employees across AOC's 10 jurisdictions. According to AOC's Chief Human Capital Officer, some jurisdictions provided advance notice of layoffs to temporary employees while others did not. To provide consistency with such notification and in response to our inquiries, in October 2018 AOC issued guidance standardizing the notification period for temporary employees laid off due to lack of work or lack of funds across all jurisdictions. This guidance directs jurisdictions to provide all temporary employees with a notification period of 2-weeks prior to the effective date of being laid off for these reasons. It also provides jurisdictions the option to request administrative leave so that the temporary employee may stop work immediately and be paid during the two week notification period.

CONCLUSION

The Division was created to serve as a flexible option that the jurisdictions can use to meet the facility needs of their congressional and Supreme Court clients. By design, the Division can hire employees if there is demand for its services and lay off employees, as it did in March 2017, if there is insufficient demand or project funding to pay them. In recent years, the Division has taken steps to more strategically manage its workforce and minimize disruptions to that workforce in part by increasing its communication with the jurisdictions. However, formalizing the process the Division uses to collect information on the jurisdictions' construction priorities, such as by providing staff with a written set of procedures, which specifies what is required of staff and when, could help ensure that those staff consistently collect and use the best information to make decisions about the appropriate number of employees and the mix of trades. Formalizing that process in this manner could also help the Division provide reasonable assurance to AOC management and Congress that it is taking the steps necessary to manage its workload and basing its workforce projections on the most current information available.

RECOMMENDATION FOR EXECUTIVE ACTION

The Architect of the Capitol should formalize the process the Construction Division uses to collect information on the jurisdictions' construction priorities each month, such as through developing written procedures. (Recommendation 1)

AGENCY COMMENTS

We provided AOC with a draft of this chapter for review and comment. AOC responded with a letter in which it concurred with our recommendation and said it intended to address our recommendation later this year. AOC's letter is reprinted in appendix V. AOC also provided technical comments, which we incorporated in the report as appropriate.

Lori Rectanus
Director, Physical Infrastructure Issues

Chelsa Gurkin
Acting Director, Education, Workforce, and Income Security Issues

APPENDIX I: OBJECTIVES, SCOPE, AND METHODOLOGY

Our objectives were to: (1) describe how the Architect of the Capitol's (AOC) jurisdictions use the Construction Division (hereafter the Division) and the factors they reported considering when deciding whether to use the Division, (2) assess how the Division manages its workforce given the variability of its workload, and (3) assess whether AOC's appointment and subsequent March 2017 layoff of temporary employees from the Division complied with applicable policy.

To describe how the jurisdictions use the Division and the factors affecting this use, we obtained and analyzed data on projects the Division completed for the jurisdictions during fiscal years 2014 through 2018. We focused our discussion of these data to the cost, scope, and duration of projects and do not present information on the number of completed projects because of differences in how the jurisdictions identify projects. To assess the reliability of the Division's data, we reviewed available documentation and interviewed agency officials. We determined that the Division's project data were sufficiently reliable for the purposes of this chapter, which includes describing the type and cost of projects the Division completed for the jurisdictions over the last 5 fiscal years and identifying illustrative examples of those projects. For appropriate comparison, the costs of completed projects we present in our report have been adjusted for inflation and converted to 2017 dollars using the fiscal-year gross domestic product index, which is compiled by the U.S. Department of Commerce, Bureau of Economic Analysis. We attempted to obtain comparable data for projects where the jurisdictions used their own employees or a contractor, but these data were not readily available. With respect to the jurisdictions' use of their own employees, the Capitol Building jurisdiction attempted to obtain this data for us, but the data that were available did not include the cost of all labor spent on projects. Further, according to AOC, the jurisdictions do not capture data on employees' time spent on construction work so this data also included projects that were considered routine maintenance. With respect to the jurisdictions' use of contractors, the data that were available also included purchase card transactions, among other unrelated costs. According to AOC, identifying just the contract costs of the jurisdictions' construction projects would require that AOC conduct significant research and review every transaction associated with its contracts.

To provide illustrative examples, we visited the sites of six projects that the Division was executing at the time of our review.[24] To select these projects, we asked the agency to provide us with projects that would enable us to understand the nature of the work the Division performs for the jurisdictions. In addition to the 4 projects the agency provided, we selected 2 additional sites based on projects that were discussed during our interviews. During our visits, we met with Division officials and representatives from the jurisdictions to discuss the projects in detail. We visited the following projects:

- an abatement and insulation project at the Russell Senate Office Building,
- repairs to the drainage system at the Russell Senate Office Building,
- the replacement of doors at the Library of Congress,
- demolition and construction activities associated with the construction of a new lactation suite at the Ford House Office Building,
- demolition and construction activities associated with the construction of a new child care center at the O'Neill House Office Building, and
- the replacement of light poles across the U.S. Capitol complex.

We also interviewed officials from the Division and AOC's 10 jurisdictions, including their respective superintendents. Except Planning and Project Management, we asked the jurisdictions if they had any suggestions for changing the Division's operations. We did not ask Planning and Project Management because the Division is a component of that jurisdiction. We then discussed with Division officials the potential implications of making those changes. We did not independently evaluate the implications of implementing the superintendents' suggestions as part of this review.

[24] The information we provide regarding those projects is not generalizable to all projects the Division performs for the jurisdictions.

To assess how the Division manages its workforce, we reviewed pertinent documents, such as AOC's August 2017 report to Congress on the Division,[25] the Division's Organization and Operating Plan,[26] user guides for the Construction Division Management System, and prior GAO reports. We also obtained and analyzed payroll data for the Division for fiscal years 2014 to 2018 and interviewed Division officials. To assess the reliability of the Division's data, we interviewed agency officials. We determined that the Division's payroll data were sufficiently reliable for the purposes of this chapter, which includes describing the size and composition of the Division's workforce over the last 5 fiscal years. We compared the Division's efforts to manage its workforce to strategic human capital-management activities or practices identified in our prior work[27] and standards for internal control in the federal government.[28]

To assess whether AOC's layoff of temporary employees from the Division in March 2017 complied with applicable policy, we reviewed relevant federal laws and agency policy, such as the Separation of Non-Permanent Employees Policy Memorandum (AOC Order 316-1). We also reviewed pertinent personnel documents, such as appointment letters, layoff letters, and Standard Form 50 personnel documentation. We compared AOC's policy with AOC's implementation during the March 2017 layoff of 30 temporary employees. We did not independently verify AOC's application of the criteria used to determine which employees to lay off in March 2017. In addition, we interviewed officials from both AOC's Human Capital Management Division and the Division. As part of our work, we requested interviews with the nine temporary employees that AOC subsequently rehired and interviewed the five who responded in order to obtain their perspective on AOC's processes for laying off temporary employees. This information is not generalizable to all rehired temporary employees.

---

[25] AOC, *Report to Congress* (Aug. 4, 2017).

[26] AOC, *Construction Division Organization and Operating Plan* (December 2017).

[27] GAO, *Human Capital: Key Principles for Effective Strategic Workforce Planning*, GAO-04-39 (Washington, D.C: Dec. 11, 2003).

[28] GAO, *Standards for Internal Control in the Federal Government*, GAO-14-704G (Washington, D.C.: September 2014).

We conducted this performance audit from March 2018 to March 2019 in accordance with generally accepted government auditing standards. Those standards require that we plan and perform the audit to obtain sufficient, appropriate evidence to provide a reasonable basis for our findings and conclusions based on our audit objectives. We believe that the evidence obtained provides a reasonable basis for our findings and conclusions based on our audit objectives.

APPENDIX II: THE CONSTRUCTION DIVISION'S DIRECT AND INDIRECT COSTS

The Construction Division's (hereafter the Division) costs include both direct and indirect costs. Direct costs are costs directly attributed to and expended on a project, such as labor (i.e., trade workers) and materials. Indirect costs are costs that cannot be directly attributed to a single project, such as costs associated with employee leave and training. Table 1 shows the components of the Division's direct and indirect costs.

To pay for its indirect costs, the Division charges the jurisdictions what it calls an "indirect rate" as part of the work it performs. As of October 2018, the Division's indirect rate was 0.85. The Division applies this rate to every direct labor-hour associated with a project it performs for the jurisdictions. For example, a trade worker that the Division employs who has a hypothetical hourly cost of $45 also has an indirect cost of about $38. Accordingly, that trade worker's total hourly cost, which the Division charges the jurisdictions, is about $83.

The Division developed the methodology for its indirect rate in 2012, in consultation with the Architect of the Capitol's (AOC) Chief Financial Officer and the jurisdictions, after it determined that its funding model at that time did not adequately recover costs that were not directly attributable to projects.

Table 1. Components of the Construction Division's Costs

Direct costs—attributable to a specific project	
Trade workers: project labor[a]	
Equipment rental	
Expended equipment	
Project materials	
Project-specific training	
Waste disposal	
Indirect costs—not attributable to a specific project or used across multiple projects	
Trade workers:	annual leave
	holidays
	sick leave
	other leave (e.g., administrative days-off, snow days, State of the Union shutdown-time)
	other activities (e.g., medical surveillance appointments, preconstruction activities,[b] safety and training activities, uniform-fitting activities)
Project support and all other time for inspectors, purchasing agents, supervisors, and timekeepers	
Equipment purchases, maintenance, and repairs	
Gas cylinder leases	
Support contracts	
Tools	
Vehicle leases, operating expenses, and repair	

Source: GAO analysis of Architect of the Capitol information. | GAO-19-343.

[a]Includes travel time to and from the jobsite and the cost of employee benefits that the agency is responsible for.

[b]Includes labor expended prior to having an agreement and funding for a project.

According to the Division, the primary driver for developing this indirect rate was employee leave. Specifically, the Division's employees earn about 11 hours of leave per pay period, and funds to cover that leave need to be recovered because they cannot be obligated and charged to a project at the time the leave is earned but prior to its being taken by the employee. The Division allocates its indirect costs among the jurisdictions, using statutory authorities available to the Architect of the Capitol.[29]

---

[29] For further information on how the Division allocates the costs of construction projects for individual areas of Capitol Hill that receive separate appropriations, see GAO, *Architect of*

According to AOC officials, historically, the Division's indirect rate was determined by staff within the Division. The rate was determined by looking at historical cost and project data over the two prior fiscal years. As of fiscal year 2019, AOC established a steering committee to determine the Division's indirect rate. This committee is comprised of five members: AOC's Chief Financial Officer, the Director of the Division, the superintendent of the House Office Buildings jurisdiction, and a superintendent from another large jurisdiction and a small jurisdiction. According to AOC officials, the Division's indirect rate is now based on projected costs and projects for the current fiscal year, and this rate will be monitored and may be adjusted throughout the year to address potential gaps or overages in funding for the Division's annual indirect costs.

APPENDIX III: ARCHITECT OF THE CAPITOL'S STANDARD TEMPORARY APPOINTMENT LETTER

ARCHITECT OF THE CAPITOL

Architect of the Capitol
U.S. Capitol, Room SB 15
Washington, DC 20515

www.aoc.gov

Date

New Employee Name
Street Address
City, State, Zip Code

Dear (Name):

Congratulations on your selection for the position of **(Position Title)** with the Architect of the Capitol (AOC). This letter confirms your acceptance of our offer of employment. Important information related to your appointment is described below.

Position Title:	XXX
Pay Plan, Series, Grade/Step:	XXX
Salary:	XXX
Location:	Architect of the Capitol, (Jurisdiction, Division, Branch)
Type of Appointment:	Temporary Appointment Not to Exceed (Date)
Effective Date:	XXX
Probationary Period Required:	No

---

the Capitol--Proposal for Establishment of a Working Capital Fund, GAO B-328065 (Washington, D.C. Oct. 27, 2016).

You are required to report to the *United States Capitol Visitor Center (CVC), Room (Number)*, located at First and East Capitol Streets, N.E., Washington, D.C., for Day 1 of the AOC Welcome Experience on **(Day, Date), at 8:30 am.** Please arrive approximately 20 minutes early to allow for entry into the building. *Important information regarding access to the CVC is enclosed. Please read it carefully to avoid delays or denied entry.*

In addition to this session, you must also attend the two-day AOC Welcome Experience on (Day, Date), in Room (Number) and (Day, Date), in Room (Number) at 8:30 a.m. at the Capitol Visitor Center.

Enclosed with this letter is an information package that includes directions to the U.S. Capitol Visitor Center.

Please note that this position is temporary in nature and is not to exceed_____months. This is strictly a temporary appointment where there is no permanent need or permanent funding available for the work involved. The duration of this temporary appointment is limited and may be shorter or longer depending on the extent of the work or project. This temporary position may also be terminated at any time without advance notice due to lack of work and/or lack of funds. As a non-permanent employee, you may also be separated without advance notice for failure to meet management's expectations.

If you desire to have your paycheck directly deposited into a bank account, it is recommended that you bring a voided check along with you on the first day of AOC Welcome Experience. You will be completing the Direct Deposit Sign-Up Form at this time. If you do not elect direct deposit, your paycheck will be mailed to your designated address.

You will complete designation of beneficiary forms which require the name(s), address(es), and social security number(s) of those you designate as beneficiary. Please ensure that you have the required information with you.

If you are new to the Federal Government, you will be eligible to participate in the Federal Employee Health Benefits Program. There are many plans to choose from and health benefits information will be provided during orientation. However, if you have access to the internet, you can review available plans at https://www.opm.gov/healthcare-insurance/healthcare/plan-information/guides. Other Federal Employee Benefits for which you are eligible will be discussed during orientation.

It is AOC's policy to provide reasonable accommodation for employees with qualified disabilities. If you would like to request a reasonable accommodation for the AOC Welcome Experience, please let me know at your earliest convenience so that the necessary arrangements can be made.

In case of an unforeseen emergency, such as inclement weather, please call [redacted] to hear a recorded message that will give you AOC's operational status. If the status indicates that we are on a delayed arrival, closed, or unscheduled leave, the AOC Welcome Experience will be rescheduled for the next business day. Staff from the Human Capital Management Division, Employment and Classification Branch, will contact you via telephone or email to provide further instructions.

I wish you success in your new position and if you have any questions regarding your appointment, please contact me on [redacted]. Welcome to the Architect of the Capitol!

Sincerely,

(Specialist's Name)
Human Resources Specialist

Enclosures
Employment Package Forms

Appendix IV: Architect of the Capitol's Acknowledgement Form for the Extension of Temporary Appointment

ARCHITECT OF THE CAPITOL

Architect of the Capitol
U.S. Capitol, Room SB-15
Washington, DC 20515

www.aoc.gov

Acknowledgement Form

Extension of Temporary Appointment

(Name: Last, First, Middle) ____

(Current Position Title, Series and Grade) ______________________________

Name of Jurisdiction/Division____

- I understand that my temporary appointment is being extended for another limited period of time.
- I understand that this is a strictly a temporary appointment where there is no permanent need or permanent funding available for the work involved and that the temporary appointment is limited in duration.
- I understand that the not-to-exceed date (NTE) of this temporary appointment may be shorter or longer, depending on the duration of the work.
- I understand that the temporary appointment can be terminated at any time based on the decision of Management.

Employee Signature: ________________________________

Date: ________________________

Appendix V: Comments from the Architect of the Capitol

ARCHITECT OF THE CAPITOL

Architect of the Capitol
U.S. Capitol, Room SB-16
Washington, DC 20515
202.228.1793

www.aoc.gov

March 12, 2019

Ms. Chelsa Gurkin
Director, Education, Workforce, and Income Security Issues
U.S. Government Accountability Office
Washington, DC 20548

Ms. Lori Rectanus
Director, Physical Infrastructure Issues
U.S. Government Accountability Office
Washington, DC 20548

Dear Ms. Gurkin and Ms. Rectanus:

Thank you for providing the Architect of the Capitol (AOC) the opportunity to comment on the Government Accountability Office (GAO) draft report entitled: *Architect of the Capitol: A Formalized Process Could Help Better Manage the Construction Division's Workforce and Workload* (GAO-19-343). The AOC concurs with GAO's findings and recommendation to formalize the process the Construction Division (CD) uses to collect information on the jurisdictions' construction priorities each month, such as, through written procedures. The director of Planning and Project Management will issue a formal written process consistent with your recommendation by May 31, 2019. Although not specifically addressed in your recommendation, for the longer term, the AOC will also evaluate the need for the development of an AOC-wide policy and/or process for further stabilizing the volatility of CD's workload.

The AOC is pleased that GAO found CD's approach to (1) managing its workforce generally aligns with practices GAO previously identified that help agencies strategically manage their human capital; and (2) the appointments and subsequent layoffs of temporary employees in March 2017 generally followed applicable practice and policy.

Sincerely,

Christine A. Merdon, P.E.
Acting Architect of the Capitol

In: Government Reports …
Editor: Evie Boan
ISBN: 978-1-53615-928-8

Chapter 3

FEDERAL ETHICS PROGRAMS: GOVERNMENT-WIDE POLITICAL APPOINTEE DATA AND SOME ETHICS OVERSIGHT PROCEDURES AT INTERIOR AND SBA COULD BE IMPROVED*

United States Government Accountability Office

ABBREVIATIONS

DAEO	Designated Agency Ethics Official
DOJ	Department of Justice
EHRI	Enterprise Human Resources Integration
EOP	Executive Office of the President
FOIA	Freedom of Information Act

* This is an edited, reformatted and augmented version of United States Government Accountability Office, Report to Congressional Requesters, Publication No. GAO-19-249, dated March 2019.

HHS	Department of Health and Human Services
Interior	Department of the Interior
OIG	Office of Inspector General
OGE	Office of Government Ethics
OMB	Office of Management and Budget
OPM	Office of Personnel Management
PAS	Presidential Appointee with Senate confirmation
Plum Book	*United States Government Policy and Supporting Positions*
PPO	Office of Presidential Personnel
SBA	Small Business Administration
SES	Senior Executive Service

WHY GAO DID THIS STUDY

Federal agencies' ethics programs seek to prevent conflicts of interest and safeguard the integrity of governmental decision-making.

GAO was asked to review compliance with ethics requirements for political appointees in the executive branch. This chapter examines the extent to which (1) existing data identify political appointees serving in the executive branch, and (2) selected agencies use internal controls to reasonably ensure that their ethics programs are designed and implemented to meet statutory and regulatory requirements.

GAO reviewed available data on political appointees. GAO also reviewed three case study agencies selected to provide a range in agency size and number of political appointees. GAO reviewed ethics documentation for a nongeneralizable sample of political appointees at the three agencies at any point between January 2017 and 2018 and interviewed officials from the agencies and two non-governmental organizations.

What GAO Recommends

Congress should consider legislation requiring the publication of political appointees serving in the executive branch. GAO also recommends three actions: SBA should document that training was completed; Interior should conduct more strategic planning for its ethics workforce and document ethics program policies and procedures. SBA neither agreed nor disagreed with GAO's recommendation, but provided documentation that partially addresses the recommendation. Interior agreed with GAO's recommendations.

What GAO Found

There is no single source of data on political appointees serving in the executive branch that is publicly available, comprehensive, and timely. Political appointees make or advocate policy for a presidential administration or support those positions. The Office of Personnel Management (OPM) and two nongovernmental organizations collect, and in some cases, report data on political appointees, but the data are incomplete. For example, the data did not include information on political appointee positions within the Executive Office of the President. The White House Office of Presidential Personnel (PPO) maintains data but does not make them publicly available.

The public has an interest in knowing the political appointees serving and this information would facilitate congressional oversight and hold leaders accountable. As of March 2019, no agency in the federal government is required to publicly report comprehensive and timely data on political appointees serving in the executive branch. OPM is positioned to maintain and make political appointee data publicly available on a timely basis but is limited in its ability to provide comprehensive data. PPO has more comprehensive data but may not be positioned to publish data on a recurring basis. Ultimately, it is a policy decision as to which agency is best positioned to report comprehensive and timely data on political appointees.

All three agencies GAO reviewed generally used appropriate internal controls to ensure they met basic ethics program requirements, though two of the agencies could take actions to strengthen their ethics programs.

- The Departments of Health and Human Services (HHS), and the Interior (Interior), and the Small Business Administration (SBA) all have procedures for administering their financial disclosure systems. HHS and Interior had procedures for providing initial ethics training as required beginning in January 2017. Prior to February 2019 SBA did not have written procedures for initial ethics training and did not adequately document political appointees' training dates. SBA's written procedures now reflect the requirements of initial ethics training and SBA developed a tracking sheet to indicate appointees completed training. GAO will assess the implementation of the tracking sheet to confirm the process is sufficient for documenting appointees' completion of initial ethics training.
- Interior's ethics program has human capital and workforce continuity challenges. Interior reported that four out of 14 full-time positions were vacant. Interior officials attributed the vacancies to a recent transformation of the ethics program and prioritizing the staffing at individual bureaus such as the National Park Service. However, vacancies affected the ethics program's ability to properly document policies and procedures as well as file and review financial disclosure forms. According to Interior officials, steps are being taken to address vacancies and document policies and procedures. However, GAO found that a more strategic and documented approach would enable Interior to better manage human capital, fill key positions, and maintain institutional knowledge.

March 14, 2019

The Honorable Gary C. Peters
Ranking Member
Committee on Homeland Security and Governmental Affairs
United States Senate

The Honorable Thomas R. Carper
Ranking Member
Permanent Subcommittee on Investigations
Committee on Homeland Security and Governmental Affairs
United States Senate

The Honorable Elijah E. Cummings
Chairman
Committee on Oversight and Reform
House of Representatives

The basic obligation of public service is to place loyalty to the Constitution, laws, and ethical principles above private gain. By acting ethically, government officials can increase public confidence in the integrity of the federal government. Federal agencies' ethics programs are to support ethical behavior by seeking to prevent conflicts of interest and safeguard the integrity of governmental decision-making. Ethics programs establish a foundation on which to build and sustain an ethical culture in the executive branch, including among the political appointees who can constitute the top management of executive branch agencies.[1]

You asked us to review compliance with ethics requirements as they relate to political appointees in the executive branch. This chapter examines the extent to which (1) existing data identify political appointees serving in the executive branch at any point in time, and (2) selected agencies use appropriate internal controls to reasonably ensure that their

---

[1] 5 C.F.R. § 2638.101.

ethics programs are designed and implemented to meet statutory and regulatory requirements. This chapter does not assess the overall objectives of federal agencies ethics programs and if those objectives are being effectively met.

For the first objective, we reviewed relevant laws and standards and the *United States Government Policy and Supporting Positions* (Plum Book).[2] We interviewed officials from the Office of Personnel Management (OPM) to understand the data they collect on political appointees. We also interviewed officials from two nongovernmental organizations, ProPublica and the Partnership for Public Service, which track political appointees serving in the executive branch at any point in time. We contacted the White House Office of Presidential Personnel (PPO) to discuss and request information on how it tracks, maintains, and uses data on political appointees. PPO redirected our request for information to the White House Counsel's Office. As of March 2019, the White House Counsel's Office had not responded to our requests for information. We interviewed two senior PPO officials from the two previous administrations to understand how they tracked and used data on political appointees. We assessed the information we gathered against principles for internal control regarding external communication and directives for the transparency and public availability of government data.[3]

For the second objective, we interviewed officials from the Office of Government Ethics (OGE), which sets policy for the executive branch ethics program and monitors ethics program compliance. We selected four agencies as case studies for review of their ethics programs. We selected the four agencies to provide a range in the number and type of political appointees in each agency,[4] a range in agency size, and a range in the

---

[2] Every 4 years, just after the Presidential election, the Plum Book is published, alternately, by the Senate Committee on Homeland Security and Governmental Affairs, and the House Committee on Oversight and Government Reform. The Plum Book lists civil service leadership and support positions that may be subject to noncompetitive status.

[3] GAO, *Standards for Internal Control in the Federal Government*, GAO-14-704G (Washington, D.C.: Sept. 2014); and Office of Management and Budget, *Open Government Directive*, M-10-06 (Washington, D.C.: Dec. 8, 2009).

[4] The four major types of political appointees include: presidential appointees with Senate confirmation, presidential appointees, noncareer Senior Executive Service, and Schedule

strength of their ethics programs, as determined by prior OGE program reviews.[5] We conducted case studies on three of the agencies we selected: the Departments of Health and Human Services (HHS), the Interior (Interior), and the Small Business Administration (SBA). The fourth agency selected was the Executive Office of the President (EOP). We contacted the White House Counsel's Office in February 2018 to solicit the EOP's perspective on the ethics program in place at the White House, and oversight of ethics compliance for political appointees in the executive branch. As of March 2019, the White House Counsel's Office had not responded to our requests for information. Therefore, we did not review the EOP ethics program.

To evaluate the extent to which the three case study agencies have and use appropriate internal controls, we reviewed selected principles from the Standards for Internal Control in the Federal Government (Standards for Internal Control). These standards call for management to design control activities, such as policies and procedures to achieve objectives. Based on our review, analysis, and professional judgment, we selected the internal control principles that were most relevant to effectively executing an executive branch ethics program. We provided each agency with an identical set of questions based on the selected internal control principles and components. We reviewed agency responses to our questions and supporting program and appointee documentation to evaluate whether agencies' policies and processes for overseeing ethics compliance for political appointees were consistent with these principles.

In addition, we acquired data from HHS, Interior, and SBA, on political appointees serving at any point between January 20, 2017 and January 28, 2018. To assess the reliability of the data, we asked each agency's officials about how the data were obtained, where the data came from, and what steps, if any, each agency took to assure the accuracy and

---

Cs. A Schedule C employee is an employee in a position that is excepted from the competitive service because of its policy-determining nature, or because it involves a close and confidential working relationship with the agency head or other top appointed official.

[5] OGE reviews assess individual agency compliance with executive branch ethics laws, regulations, and policies and evaluate the agency's systems, processes, and procedures for administering its ethics program. Reviews are generally conducted every 4 to 5 years.

completeness of the data. Based on responses provided by HHS, Interior, and SBA, we determined that those agencies' data were sufficiently reliable to indicate each agency's political appointees, with start and end dates, for use selecting a sample of appointees' at each agency. Next, we used a nongeneralizable random sampling method to select political appointees at each agency. We selected 12 political appointees at both HHS and Interior, and 10 political appointees at SBA.[6] We reviewed relevant documentation for these appointees to determine whether agency internal controls were sufficient to ensure that certain ethics program requirements, such as signing the ethics pledge, completing initial ethics training, and submitting a financial disclosure report, were met. In addition, we interviewed agency ethics officials, as needed, to discuss the documentation and information they provided. Our review of political appointees' documentation was limited to testing the agencies' ethics program processes and procedures. We did not review individual financial disclosure forms with the intent of identifying conflicts of interest nor did we perform a conflict of interest analysis. See appendix I for a more detailed description of our scope and methodology.

We conducted this performance audit from October 2017 to March 2019 in accordance with generally accepted government auditing standards. Those standards require that we plan and perform the audit to obtain sufficient, appropriate evidence to provide a reasonable basis for our findings and conclusions based on our audit objectives. We believe that the evidence obtained provides a reasonable basis for our findings and conclusions based on our audit objectives.

---

[6] To ensure we included certain types of political appointees in our review, we grouped the political appointees from each agency into three groups: (1) individuals in PAS positions, (2) individuals who left the agency during the time frame of our review, and (3) all remaining individuals. We randomly selected three appointees from the first group, three appointees from the second group, and six political appointees from the last group. At SBA, the total PAS appointees and total individuals who left the agency during our review time frame was less than six. As a result, there were fewer total appointees in our SBA sample compared to HHS and Interior.

BACKGROUND

Executive Branch Ethics Program

The Ethics in Government Act of 1978 was enacted to preserve and promote the accountability and integrity of public officials, and the institutions of the federal government.[7] The act requires political appointees and high-ranking government officials to complete a public financial disclosure report to help prevent and mitigate conflicts of interest for the purpose of increasing public confidence in the integrity of government. The act also established restrictions on postemployment activities of certain employees, and created OGE.

The primary mission of the executive branch ethics program is to prevent conflicts of interest on the part of executive branch employees.[8] The executive branch ethics program is a shared responsibility across government (see Figure 1).

- OGE is the supervising ethics office for the executive branch and sets policy for the entire executive branch ethics program.
- Executive branch agency heads are responsible for leading their agency's ethics program. Agency leaders are ultimately responsible for their organizations' ethical culture. Their actions can demonstrate the level of commitment to ethics and set a powerful example for their employees.[9]
- Designated Agency Ethics Officials (DAEO) and other agency ethics staff carry out ethics program responsibilities and coordinate with OGE.

---

[7] Pub. L. No. 95-521, 92 Stat. 1824 (1978), *codified, as amended at* 5 U.S.C. App. §§ 101– 505 and in scattered sections of titles 2, 5, 18, 28, United States Code.

[8] 5 C.F.R. § 2638.101(a).

[9] *OGE Memorandum, The Role of Agency Leaders in Promoting an Ethical Culture,* (Oct. 5, 2017).

- Inspectors General and the Department of Justice are authorized to investigate potential violations of criminal statutes pertaining to ethics.
- Executive branch employees are individually responsible for understanding and complying with the requirements of ethics laws and regulations, and are collectively responsible for making ethical conduct a standard of government service.

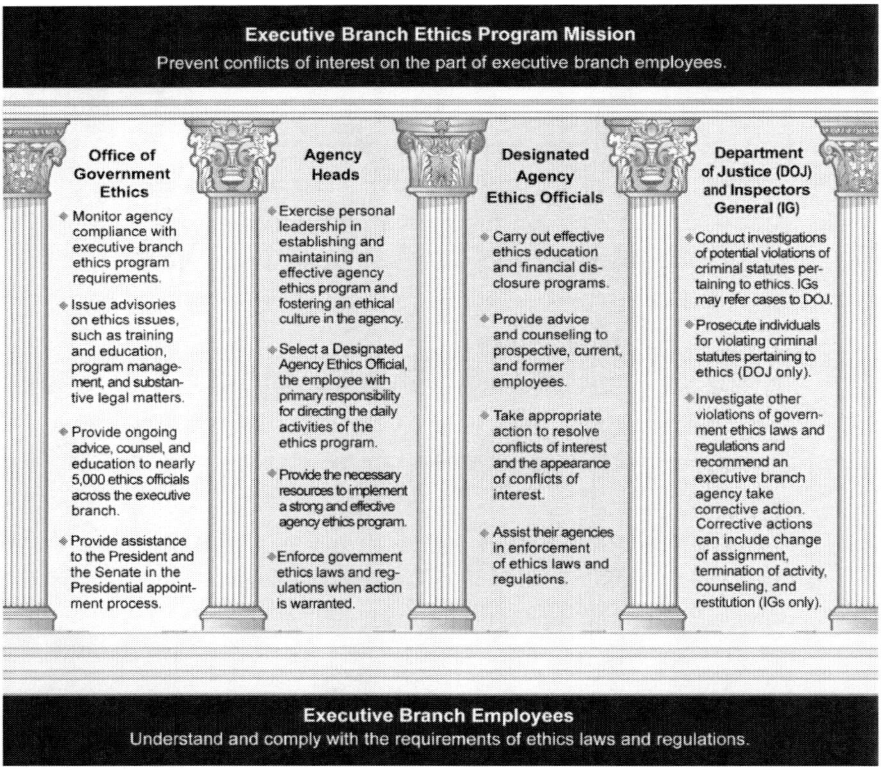

Source: GAO analysis of laws and regulations. | GAO-19-249.

Figure 1. Executive Branch Ethics Program Mission, Roles, and Selected Responsibilities.

Ethics Laws for Executive Branch Employees

Executive branch employees are ultimately responsible for understanding and abiding by the various ethics laws. Generally, executive branch employees are prohibited from working on government matters that will affect their personal financial interest or the financial interests of a spouse or minor child; general partner; any organization in which they serve as an officer, director, or trustee; and any person or organization with whom they are negotiating or have an arrangement for future employment.[10] Executive branch employees are also subject to

- criminal statutes prohibiting bribery and illegal gratuities;
- civil statutes requiring public financial disclosure; and
- employee standards of conduct, such as acting at all times in the public's interest, serving as good stewards of public resources, and refraining from misusing their office for private gain.[11]

Agency Offices of Inspectors General (OIG) have a responsibility to investigate potential ethics violations.[12] Among our three case study agencies, since January 2017, the HHS and Interior OIG have investigated potential travel and ethics issues involving political appointees while the SBA OIG did not initiate any similar investigations. The HHS OIG investigated the former Secretary of HHS's use of chartered and commercial aircraft and found that it did not always comply with applicable federal travel regulations and HHS policies and procedures.[13] In response to its OIG's findings, HHS implemented additional steps for political appointees' travel approval. Since January 2017, the Interior OIG has initiated five investigations into potential ethics violations involving

---

[10] 18 U.S.C. § 208; 5 C.F.R. § 2635.402(a), (b)(2).

[11] 5 C.F.R. § 2638.102.

[12] 5 C.F.R. § 2638.106.

[13] Office of the Inspector General, U.S. Department of Health and Human Services, *The Office of the Secretary of Health and Human Services Did Not Comply with Federal Regulations for Chartered Aircraft and Other Government Travel Related to Former Secretary Price* Report No.: A-12-17-00002 (July 2018).

the former Secretary of the Interior.[14] As of March 1, 2019, three investigations related to the former Secretary were completed. As a result of the first completed investigation, the Interior OIG found that "incomplete information" about the former Secretary's travel and use of chartered flights during 2017 was provided to the DAEO for review. The other two completed investigations found no evidence that the former Secretary violated ethics laws. Two investigations remained open as of March 2019. Interior's DAEO described multiple strategies that were implemented to address issues observed within the ethics program after he was hired in April 2018, such as establishing weekly meetings with the former Secretary of the Interior to discuss ethics matters.

Executive Branch Political Appointees

Executive Branch political appointees are subject to more ethics restrictions than other executive branch employees. Appointees make or advocate policy for a presidential administration or support those positions. Appointees generally serve at the pleasure of the appointing authority and do not have the civil service protections afforded to other federal employees.

There are four major categories of political appointees: Presidential Appointees with Senate confirmation (PAS); presidential appointees; noncareer employees in the Senior Executive Service (SES); and Schedule C employees. The most recent Plum Book, which was published on December 1, 2016, identified about 4,000 political appointee positions from these four major categories across the entire executive branch as of June 30, 2016 (see Figure 2). The Plum Book identifies presidentially appointed positions within the federal government using data from the Office of Personnel Management. It is published every 4 years just after the presidential election, alternately, by the Senate Committee on

[14] The Interior OIG initiated an investigation related to the unprofessional behavior of another political appointee at Interior. The OIG ended the investigation after the appointee resigned.

Homeland Security and Governmental Affairs and the House Committee on Oversight and Government Reform.

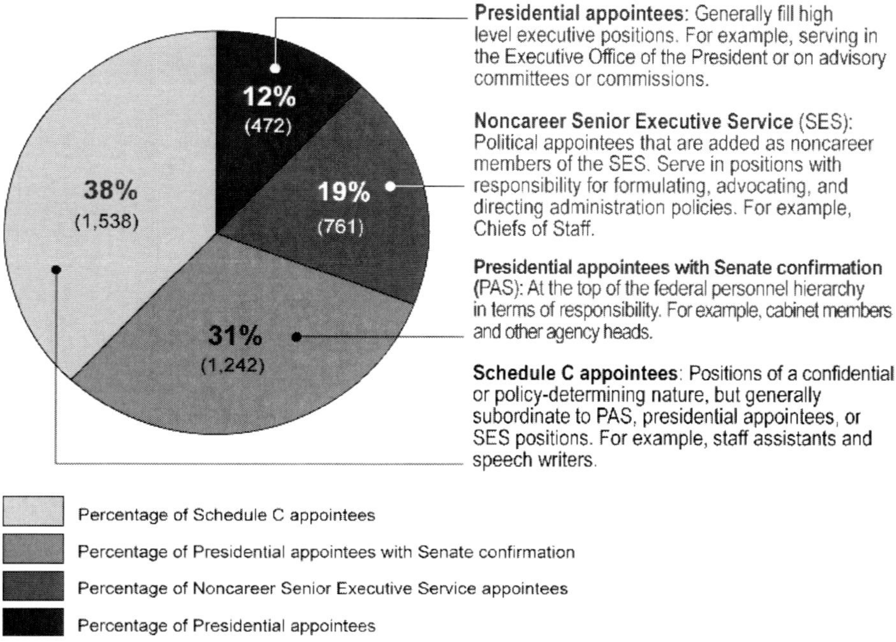

Source: GAO analysis of data from the 2016 Plum Book. | GAO-19-249.

Figure 2. Most Recently Published Data on the Number and Type of Political Appointees Positions, as of June 2016.

In addition to the ethics laws for executive branch employees, several recent presidential administrations have issued an order requiring political appointees in executive branch agencies to sign an ethics pledge.[15] Some of the restrictions in the ethics pledge relate to areas already covered under existing ethics provisions, such as restrictions on accepting gifts and

[15] President Trump issued Executive Order No. 13770 (EO 13770), "Ethics Commitments by Executive Branch Appointees," on January 28, 2017. 82 Fed. Reg. 9333 (Feb. 3, 2017). Prior administrations issued their own ethics pledges, including President Obama (EO 13490) and President Clinton (EO 12834). 74 Fed. Reg. 4673 (Jan. 26, 2009); 58 Fed. Reg. 5911 (Jan. 22, 1993). President Clinton revoked EO 12834 effective January 20, 2001, and President George W. Bush did not issue a new executive order with an ethics pledge. 66 Fed. Reg. 679 (Jan. 3, 2001).

postemployment restrictions. Political appointees may receive an ethics pledge waiver from the President or his designee of certain or all ethics restrictions and authorizations enabling them to participate in otherwise prohibited activities. Political appointees that sign the pledge are contractually bound to adhere to its restrictions. If violated, the restrictions in the pledge could only be enforced through civil actions.

Transparency and Ethics

To foster transparency, federal law permits members of the public to access various government records. OGE provides online access to certified copies of public financial disclosure reports for PAS and certain other executive branch employees, as well as any applicable ethics agreements, certification of compliance for the ethics agreement, and certificates of divestiture for PAS.[16] OGE also provides online access to copies of ethics pledge waivers for appointees at agencies.[17] Members of the public can use this information to assist in holding government officials accountable for carrying out their duties free from conflicts of interest.

No Single Source of Data on Political Appointees Exists That Is Comprehensive, Timely, and Publicly Available

OPM, PPO, and two nongovernmental organizations provide some data on political appointees serving in the executive branch, but the data

[16] Executive branch agencies or OGE can direct an employee to sell, or otherwise divest, an asset to avoid a conflict of interest or the appearance of one. If selling the asset will result in a capital gain, certain persons may be eligible for a certificate of divestiture to postpone the tax burden of complying with the government's conflict of interest requirements. 5 C.F.R. § 2635.402(e).

[17] Copies of ethics pledge waivers granted to Executive Office of the President and Office of the Vice President employees are available at https://www.whitehouse.gov/disclosures/, accessed Nov. 9, 2018.

have limitations that impede their usefulness. The Senate Homeland Security and Governmental Affairs Committee and the House Oversight and Government Reform Committee publish OPM data on political appointees after each presidential election in the Plum Book.[18] Data include name, title, type of appointment, salary, and location of employment. The data reflect the positions and the individuals who are filling the positions at a single point in time, about 5 months prior to the report's publication. While the data are comprehensive and publicly available, they are not timely. Because the Plum Book is a snapshot in time, it does not reflect changes that occur in between publications, such as changes to who is holding a certain position, the position title, and vacancies.

OPM also maintains more timely data on federal personnel; however, these data are not comprehensive or publicly accessible for identifying individuals serving in political appointee positions. OPM maintains data in the Executive and Schedule C System and the Enterprise Human Resources Integration (EHRI) system—the latter serves as OPM's primary repository for human capital data.[19] We found both systems have limitations, several of which were also identified by OPM officials.[20] The Executive and Schedule C System is not comprehensive. It includes data on Schedule C and noncareer SES political appointees, but generally does not include data on presidential appointees or PAS. Publicly available EHRI data do not identify political appointees, either at the individual or group level. In addition, the EHRI source data is not publicly available. Political appointees can be identified from a combination of multiple variables, but these combinations are not consistent within or across appointee types. OPM provided some data on political appointees serving in the executive branch as of June 2018 from the Executive and Schedule C System. We reviewed the data and found errors and omissions. For

---

[18] The Plum Book is generally published in December after the presidential election and is based on agency data reported to OPM as of the June prior to the election.

[19] According to OPM officials, the accuracy and timeliness of information in the Executive and Schedule C System and EHRI is largely based upon agency input.

[20] GAO, *Federal Human Resources Data: OPM Should Improve the Availability and Reliability of Payroll Data to Support Accountability and Workforce Analytics*, GAO-17-127 (Washington, D.C.: Oct. 7, 2016).

example, we found instances in which individuals appeared to be holding political appointee positions that they departed several months prior and individuals known to currently hold political appointee positions were not identified. We also found that the data are incomplete. For example, the data did not include information on political appointee positions within the EOP. The EOP provides data to OPM only every 4 years for inclusion in the Plum Book.

In addition to OPM, the White House maintains timely data on political appointees that are likely more comprehensive than OPM's data but are not publicly available. Historically, PPO maintained data on political appointees as part of its responsibilities to recruit, vet, and place political appointees in positions across the government. PPO data on political appointees have not been made publicly available by the Trump, Obama, or Bush administrations. According to former officials from the Bush and Obama administrations, PPO maintained and used data on political appointees to carry out its responsibilities. For example, during the Obama administration, PPO established a database to help with filling political appointee positions and managing the overall appointee process.

The database included preliminary information on candidates, such as names, application status, and where the applicant was in the vetting process. After a position was filled, the database tracked information such as the name of the appointee, position, federal department or agency, and start and departure dates. The primary limitation of the data was that departure dates of political appointees were unreliable. The former Obama administration official attributed this limitation to the lack of a process for agencies to formally notify PPO when an appointee left a position. To address this gap, PPO met regularly with staff in federal agencies to review data for accuracy.

There are requests by members of the public to obtain data on political appointees serving in the executive branch. For example, between January 2017 and November 2018, OPM received approximately 32 requests through the Freedom of Information Act (FOIA) for data on political appointments across federal agencies. According to OPM officials, requests for data on political appointees are common and tend to increase at the start of a new administration. Former PPO officials also stated that when they served at PPO they received requests for data on political appointees serving in the executive branch.

In the absence of comprehensive and timely data on political appointees serving in the executive branch, two nongovernmental organizations—the Partnership for Public Service and ProPublica—stated that they collect and report some data themselves.[21] The Partnership for Public Service primarily tracks and reports data on PAS appointments, which are compiled from publicly available sources such as Congress.gov and agency websites. According to the Partnership for Public Service, accurately tracking departure dates is the most significant limitation. Some PAS departures, such as cabinet level officials, are typically reported in the media; however, lower-level PAS departures may not be reported.

ProPublica collects and reports data on all types of political appointees serving in the executive branch. To obtain and compile its data, ProPublica makes FOIA requests to OPM and departments and agencies across the executive branch for political appointee staffing lists. ProPublica also makes requests for other data, such as financial disclosure forms through an administrative process required by the Ethics in Government Act of 1978. ProPublica said it has had more than 166,000 unique visitors to its database since it launched in March 2018. According to officials at ProPublica, one limitation is that they rely on agency responses to FOIA requests and therefore the data may not be comprehensive or timely.

The public has an interest in knowing who is serving in the government and making policy decisions. The Office of Management and Budget (OMB) stated that transparency promotes accountability by providing the public with information about what the government is doing. In a 2009 memorandum, OMB directed agencies to make information available online and to use modern technology to disseminate useful information, rather than waiting for specific requests under FOIA.[22]

---

[21] The Partnership for Public Service is a nonprofit, nonpartisan organization that seeks to improve government. ProPublica is an independent, nonprofit newsroom that produces investigative journalism.

[22] Office of Management and Budget *Open Government Directive*, M-10-06 (Dec. 8, 2009).

Although some data are publicly available on political appointees and FOIA requests can be used to varying effect to obtain data on political appointees, neither option results in comprehensive, timely, and publicly available data. Until the names of political appointees and their position, position type, agency or department name, start and end dates are publicly available at least quarterly, it will be difficult for the public to access comprehensive and reliable information.

Making such information available would promote transparency. The public, including independent researchers, the media, and nongovernmental organizations, can use these data to perform independent analyses to identify gaps and challenges for filling political appointee positions or to identify potential conflicts of interest. Such analyses would also facilitate congressional oversight of executive branch appointees by providing a comprehensive and timely source of information on political appointees.

As of March 2019, no agency in the federal government was required to publicly report comprehensive and timely data on political appointees serving in the executive branch. As the leader of human resources and personnel policy, OPM is positioned to collect, maintain, and make political appointee data publicly available on a frequent and recurring basis. However, OPM is limited in its ability to provide comprehensive data, in part because it does not regularly receive data from each agency that has political appointees, such as the EOP, which has approximately 225 political appointee positions based on the 2016 Plum Book. PPO is positioned to make more comprehensive data on political appointees publicly available. However, PPO is reestablished with each new presidential administration, which could be a barrier to establishing a consistent process for maintaining and publishing data on a recurring basis. Ultimately, it is a policy decision as to which agency is best positioned to report comprehensive and timely data on political appointees.

SBA AND INTERIOR ETHICS PROGRAMS DID NOT MEET ALL DOCUMENTATION REQUIREMENTS AND INTERIOR AND HHS HAD WORKFORCE CONTINUITY CHALLENGES

All three agencies we reviewed—HHS, Interior, and SBA—generally used appropriate internal controls to ensure they met basic ethics program requirements, such as financial disclosure, though two of the agencies—Interior and SBA—could do more to strengthen their ethics programs. SBA and Interior had not fully documented some of their procedures for ethics training and the ethics pledge, respectively. In implementing their ethics programs, each agency addressed human capital issues and workforce continuity challenges; however, we found that vacancies and staff turnover had negative effects on Interior's ethics program. For the full results of our assessment of agencies' internal controls, see appendix II.

Reviewed Agencies Generally Met Basic Requirements for Financial Disclosure and Ethics Training, but Interior and SBA Did Not Document Some Procedures

Financial Disclosure

All three agencies we reviewed met the minimum statutory and regulatory requirement to have written procedures for financial disclosure.[23] Federal law requires agencies to develop written procedures to collect, review, and evaluate financial disclosure reports (see sidebar).[24]

[23] We did not conduct an independent evaluation of the content of each agency's procedures to determine whether they comply with relevant requirements. OGE evaluates agencies' written procedures for financial disclosure during its program reviews to ensure that the agency procedures are in conformance with all relevant laws, regulations, and executive orders.

[24] 5 U.S.C. App. § 402(d)(1); 5 C.F.R. § 2638.104(c)(8)(i).

Table 1. Filing and Review Timeliness of Public Financial Disclosure Reports for a Nongeneralizable Sample of Political Appointees Serving between January 20, 2017 and January 28, 2018

	Department of Health and Human Services		**Department of the Interior**		**Small Business Administration**	
Type of report filed	New entrant or nominee	Termination	New entrant or nominee	Termination	New entrant or nominee	Termination
Number of political appointees required to file	10[a]	3	12	1	10	1
Number of reports filed timely	10	3	10[b]	0[b]	8	1
Number of reports filed 0-5 days late	0	0	1	0	2	0
Number of reports filed >5 days late	0	0	0	0	0	0
Number of reports reviewed timely by agency ethics official	10	3	10	0	9	1

Source: GAO analysis of timeliness of public financial disclosure report filing (Office of Government Ethics Form 278e). | GAO-19-249.

Note: In general, individuals nominated by the President to positions requiring Senate confirmation must file a nominee financial disclosure report within 5 days of transmittal of the President's nomination to the Senate for confirmation. Other appointees must file a new entrant report within 30 days of assuming their position. In general, all appointees must file a termination report within 30 days of leaving office. Reports must be reviewed by agency ethics officials within 60 days of receipt. 26 C.F.R. §§ 2634.201(b), (c), (e); 2634.605(a).

[a]Two of the political appointees in our HHS sample were incumbents from previous administrations. Due to records retention schedule, we were unable to evaluate the nominee financial disclosure reports filed by those two appointees.

[b]One appointee at Interior did not file a new entrant or a termination financial disclosure report. According to Interior ethics officials, the office mistakenly determined that the appointee was excluded from public filing requirements.

Each agency established financial disclosure processes in addition to what is required to reduce the risk of political appointees performing agency work while they may have conflicts of interest. For example, prior to an HHS political appointee's first day, the HHS process requires the appointee's financial disclosure report to be submitted and reviewed, and any potential conflicts be either resolved or identified, and an ethics agreement put in place with a timeline for conflict of interest resolution. This process aims to ensure that appointees are in compliance with ethics laws and regulations when they begin government service, rather than 30 days or more into their appointment.

Financial Disclosure Requirements Agencies:

- Administer public and confidential financial disclosure systems.
- Establish written procedures for collecting, reviewing, evaluating, and where applicable, making available to the public financial disclosure reports filed by the agency's employees.
- Political Appointees:
- File a new entrant public financial disclosure report within 30 days of assuming a public filing position.
- If appointed to a position requiring Senate confirmation, file a nominee report within 5 days of transmittal of the President's nomination to the Senate for confirmation.
- File a termination report within 30 days of leaving office.

Source: GAO analysis of financial disclosure statues and regulations. | GAO-19-249.

HHS and SBA have additional processes that include written procedures which reflect OGE's guidance for reviewing reports, such as following up with appointees when a financial disclosure report appears incomplete. OGE officials told us that engaging with an appointee during the review process allows agencies to confirm that the appointee understands and completes each required item. These interactions are also an opportunity to provide ethics counseling and establish a relationship with appointees who may be new to government service. Interior instituted a process in June 2018 that requires ethics officials to interview new appointees, review their financial disclosure report, and complete a financial disclosure checklist prior to certification.

In reviewing a nongeneralizable sample of political appointees at each of the three agencies, we found that nearly all political appointees filed financial disclosure reports on time, with four exceptions of non-PAS appointees from our Interior and SBA samples (see Table 1).[25] In one case, an Interior appointee who was required to file both a new entrant and termination report did not do so. According to Interior ethics officials, the

[25] For the complete results of our political appointee ethics requirement analysis, see appendix III.

office mistakenly determined that the appointee was excluded from public filing requirements. An individual who does not serve more than 60 days in a calendar year is not required to file a new entrant or a termination financial disclosure report; however, this political appointee served for 63 days.

Three appointees—two from SBA and one from Interior—filed new entrant reports past their due dates. Late filing heightens the risk of appointees performing agency work while having conflicts of interest; however, none of the three appointees filed more than 30 days after the due date or the last day of an extension, and therefore were not subject to a late filing fee.[26] For example, one Interior appointee received a 30-day extension to file a new entrant report, but filed it 4 days late. One SBA appointee received an extension exceeding the maximum time—90 days—that an agency may grant to any filer and consequently filed 2 days late.[27] According to SBA ethics officials, the appointee was given a 92-day extension because the due date was miscalculated. A second SBA appointee filed a report 1 day past the due date. We did not find timeliness issues with any reports filed by appointees at HHS or filed by PAS appointees at Interior or SBA.

Agency ethics officials generally reviewed appointees' financial disclosure reports in a timely manner. However, agencies followed up with non-PAS political appointees' to varying degrees when their financial disclosure reports were potentially missing information. For example, SBA followed up with an appointee to confirm that the appointee had not inadvertently omitted information, such as a retirement plan, from the financial disclosure report because the appointee reported having previous longterm employment. HHS asked for and received clarifying information from an appointee who reported compensation for legal work but did not report individual clients. However, Interior ethics officials told us they did

---

[26] Unless granted a waiver for "extraordinary circumstances," an official who files any public financial disclosure report more than 30 days after the due date, or more than 30 days after the last day of an extension, whichever occurs later, must pay the United States a $200 late filing fee. 5 U.S.C. App. § 104(d); 5 C.F.R. § 2634.704.

[27] An agency may grant any filer an extension to file a financial disclosure report for "good cause shown," provided such extensions do not exceed 90 days. 5 U.S.C. App. § 101(g)(1); 5 C.F.R. § 2634.201(f).

not follow up with two appointees in our sample who reported having no previous outside employment. Interior officials acknowledged that the reports were neither reviewed nor certified properly. According to Interior's new Designated Agency Ethics Official (DAEO), the June 2018 update to Interior's review process was implemented in response to deficiencies within its financial disclosure program.

Ethics Training

HHS and Interior had written procedures for initial ethics training as required, but SBA did not until February 2019. Federal regulation requires agencies to establish written procedures for providing initial ethics training beginning in January 2017 (see sidebar).[28]

Ethics Training Requirements Agencies:

- Carry out an ethics education program to teach employees how to identify government ethics issues and obtain assistance in complying with ethics laws and regulations.
- Establish written procedures, which the DAEO must review each year, for providing initial ethics training.
- Political Appointees:
- Complete initial ethics training within 3 months of appointment.
- If appointed to a position requiring Senate confirmation, complete an additional live ethics briefing on immediate ethics obligations within 15 days.

Source: GAO analysis of ethics training statutes and regulations. | GAO-19-249.

HHS's and Interior's written procedures reflect the requirements of initial ethics training. For example, both agencies' procedures describe time frames for providing initial ethics training to political appointees no later than 3 months after their appointment date, as well as the method for doing so. Prior to February 2019, SBA did not have adequate written procedures in place to address the requirement that became effective in January 2017. SBA's written procedures now reflect the requirements of initial ethics training. Now that SBA officials have formally documented procedures, they can have reasonable assurance that the procedures are

[28] On November 2, 2016, OGE published a final rule revising the elements and procedures of the executive branch ethics program, including establishing the requirement for agencies to develop written procedures for initial ethics training. These changes had an effective date of January 1, 2017. 5 C.F.R. § 2638.304(f); 81 Fed. Reg. 76,271 (Nov. 2, 2016).

implemented as intended and that all required appointees are provided initial ethics training.[29]

Interior's and HHS's ethics programs track and maintain documentation of dates that political appointees received initial ethics training. During the time of our review, SBA did not adequately document political appointees' training dates.[30] For example, ethics officials at Interior manually record training dates in a spreadsheet shared between Interior's ethics office, Office of Human Resources, and the White House Liaison. HHS requires appointees to confirm in writing that they completed initial ethics training. According to SBA ethics officials, the previous Alternate DAEO informally documented the dates that political appointees received training in her personal notes. Standards for internal control state that management should document significant events, and that documentation and records should be properly managed, maintained, and readily available for examination. Allowing one individual to control all key aspects of documenting an event puts the program at risk of errors.[31] As of February 2019, SBA officials had developed a tracking sheet and a certificate for appointees to sign that indicates they completed initial ethics training. We plan to assess the implementation of the tracking sheet to confirm that SBA is using the tracker to hold appointees accountable by documenting their completion of initial ethics training requirements. By developing and implementing a mechanism, such as a tracking sheet, SBA can have reasonable assurance that political appointees meet the requirement to take initial ethics training.

Our review of agency documentation, including SBA's informal documentation, found that political appointees completed required initial ethics training on time. Also, all three agencies provided the required

---

[29] Standards for internal control state that management should document its control policies and conduct periodic reviews to ensure controls are effective. See GAO-14-704G.

[30] Political appointees are also required to complete annual ethics training before the end of a given calendar year. Because the majority of appointees in our sample received initial ethics training in 2017, they were not required to receive annual ethics training until the end of calendar year 2018, which was outside the time frame of our review. Therefore, we did not assess compliance with annual training requirements. For the full results of our political appointee ethics documentation analysis, see appendix III.

[31] GAO-14-704G.

additional live ethics briefing for PAS appointees together with initial ethics training.

In addition to required training, all three agencies provided examples of other ways they have reminded appointees about their personal ethical responsibilities. For example:

- In advance of the holiday season, Interior provided supplementary training to political appointees on restrictions on accepting gifts.
- SBA used its agency-wide newsletter during the March Madness college basketball tournament to remind employees that they are prohibited from gambling in the workplace.
- HHS updated its ethics website to highlight Hatch Act rules in preparation for upcoming elections.[32]

Ethics Pledge

Political appointees we reviewed at each agency had signed the required ethics pledge prescribed in Executive Order 13770, "Ethics Commitments by Executive Branch Appointees." However, nine Interior appointees' and one HHS appointee's pledges were not timely signed.[33] For example, the former Secretary of the Interior signed the pledge 19 days after his appointment. According to an Interior ethics official, the political appointees were directed to sign the pledge at the start of their appointments, but did not do so. Interior's new DAEO told us in October 2018 that Interior now requires all appointees to sign the pledge on their first day as a condition of continuing their employment; however, this procedure has not been formally documented. The non-PAS HHS appointee signed the pledge 9 days after his permanent appointment date.

---

[32] The Hatch Act limits certain political activities of federal employees, as well as some state, D.C., and local government employees who work in connection with federally funded programs. 5 U.S.C. §§ 1501–1508, 7321–7326.

[33] OGE guidance states PAS appointees must sign ethics pledges between Senate confirmation and beginning their appointment. Non-PAS appointees are required to sign the pledge when they are appointed. According to OGE officials, ethics pledge signed by non-PAS appointees within a few days of the appointment are generally still considered timely signed. For the purpose of our analyses, we considered any pledge signed after the first 3 days of a non-PAS appointee's appointment to not be timely signed.

While the restrictions under the pledge are enforceable by civil action, there are no legal consequences, such as fines or penalties, for failing to timely sign the pledge.

Ethics Pledge Restrictions Political Appointees:

- President Trump issued Executive Order 13770, "Ethics Commitments by Executive Branch Appointees," which requires political appointees to sign an ethics pledge.
- Under the pledge, appointees are contractually bound to adhere to specified restrictions, including (but not limited to):
- for all appointees, a 2-year ban on involvement in "particular matters" involving former employers and clients;
- for former lobbyists, a 2-year ban on involvement on particular matters on which he or she lobbied; and
- for appointees who leave government service, a 5-year ban on lobbying agencies in which they served.

Source: GAO analysis of Executive Order 13770. | GAO-19-249.

The President or his designee may grant a waiver of any of the restrictions contained in the executive order. As of March 2019, 32 executive branch appointees—not including White House appointees—received limited waivers of the pledge.[34] Interior's then acting solicitor and principal deputy solicitor signed a limited waiver of certain restrictions on lobbying activities for one appointee in our sample upon the appointee's departure from the agency in July 2017.[35] However, according to Interior ethics officials, the official from the Solicitor's Office did not have authority to grant a waiver. Furthermore, Interior's ethics office was not included in the decision to grant the waiver, although Interior ethics officials ultimately notified the appointee when they became aware that the waiver was legally invalid. According to the DAEO, Interior is updating and documenting its ethics program processes and procedures, including new processes to sign ethics pledges and grant waivers, but did not provide a time frame for completion. We discuss Interior's efforts to document overall ethics program processes and procedures later in this chapter.

---

[34] Copies of any waivers granted to White House appointees pursuant to Executive Order 13770 are available on the White House website: https://www.whitehouse.gov/disclosures/.

[35] Paragraph 3 of the ethics pledge states that political appointees will not engage in any lobbying activities with respect to any covered executive branch official or noncareer Senior Executive Service appointee for the remainder of the administration.

Reviewed Agencies' Ethics Programs Face Human Capital and Workforce Continuity Challenges

We found that all of the agencies we reviewed are addressing human capital issues and workforce continuity challenges to varying extents to achieve the goals and objectives of the ethics program. Standards for internal control state that management can help ensure operational success by having the right personnel for the job on board and maintaining a continuity of needed skills and abilities. Standards for internal control also state that management has a responsibility to obtain the workforce necessary to achieve organizational goals. HHS and Interior reported challenges to recruiting and retaining ethics staff with the necessary knowledge, skills, and abilities. All of the reviewed agencies reported varying levels of effort to address vacancies, skills gaps, and succession planning.

HHS reported vacancies in its ethics program as well as challenges in recruiting and hiring; however ethics program officials took actions to mitigate negative effects of the vacancies. As of October 1, 2018, HHS's Ethics Division had six vacancies out of 32 full-time positions (a vacancy rate of approximately 19 percent), including the Alternate DAEO position. HHS officials told us that a senior attorney was assigned to assume the duties of the Alternate DAEO position for six months in 2018. HHS ethics officials told us that the 2017 government-wide hiring freeze and workforce reduction plan affected their efforts to fill vacancies.[36] However, ethics officials also told us that, as of October 1, 2018, four people had tentatively accepted offers to fill vacancies. HHS ethics officials told us that applicants for ethics attorneys and specialist positions generally do not have a background in federal government ethics laws. As a result, Ethics

[36] On January 23, 2017, the President issued a memorandum imposing a federal hiring freeze to halt the growth of the federal workforce until a "long-term plan to reduce the size of the federal government's workforce" is put in place. The freeze prohibited agencies to hire for vacant or new positions as of January 22, 2017, except in limited circumstances such as military or public safety personnel. On April 12, 2017, OMB issued guidance on implementing the hiring freeze as well as guidance for a government-wide reform plan that included reducing the federal workforce.

Division officials said that it must invest time and resources to train new hires, who attend and review OGE trainings, participate in monthly interagency ethics meetings, and take HHS-specific ethics training.

HHS ethics officials told us that new ethics program hires are assigned work from across the spectrum of ethics subject matter and trained one-on-one by senior staff. To address staffing shortages and prepare for potential attrition, the HHS ethics officials said they cross-train staff members and assign back-up team members to support HHS's operating and staff divisions. In addition, to track potential staff attrition or retirement, the ethics officials told us that the Ethics Division uses OPM's Federal Employee Viewpoint Survey data collected from HHS employees.[37] However, the data only give the Ethics Division a general sense of the number of personnel that are planning to leave or retire. HHS Ethics Division officials said they use survey data because there is a general sensitivity related to asking about retirement and delays in planned retirements that could affect recruiting and hiring replacements.

Interior's ethics office also reported vacancies and challenges in recruiting and hiring that contributed to the issues in the ethics program. As of November 2018, the Interior ethics office reported that out of 14 full-time positions, four were vacant (a 29 percent vacancy rate). All vacancies were ethics attorney positions.[38] Interior reported an ongoing transformation of the department's ethics program and officials said that the vacancies resulted from prioritizing the staffing at individual bureaus—such as the National Park Service and Fish and Wildlife Service—instead of the department-level ethics office, which is responsible for overseeing the bureaus' ethics programs and providing ethics services to employees at the Office of the Secretary, the Office of the Solicitor, and to all of Interior's political appointees. Interior's ethics officials said that the high

[37] The Federal Employee Viewpoint Survey measures employees' perceptions of whether, and to what extent, conditions characteristic of successful organizations are present in their agencies. The survey serves as a tool for employees to share their perceptions in many critical areas including their work experiences, their agency, and leadership. The results provide agency leaders insight into areas where improvements have been made, as well as areas where improvements are needed.

[38] Interior ethics offices submitted and received approval to restructure its ethics program in 2018. Previously, the program did not have a formal organizational chart.

vacancy rate in their ethics office affected its ability to properly collect and review financial disclosure forms—one of the main responsibilities of the federal ethics program. According to Interior's new DAEO, the office received an influx of financial disclosure reports during the presidential transition, but was unprepared to handle them. Furthermore, during 2017 one official was responsible for reviewing and certifying more than 300 public financial disclosure forms. The official was unable to balance proper and timely review of forms with other responsibilities that also included reviewing and certifying more than 800 confidential disclosure forms. In the Interior Inspector General's 2018 report on Interior's Major Management Challenges, ethics staffing was identified as a limitation, as staffing shortages could lead to delays in reviewing appointees' financial disclosure documentation.[39]

While the single Interior official was experienced in reviewing financial disclosure forms, Interior officials stated that there was not enough management support, training, or resources provided to properly review financial disclosure forms in 2017. According to the DAEO, a new supervisory ethics official for financial disclosure forms was hired in September 2018 as part of a proposed and ongoing organizational restructuring of Interior's ethics office. In addition, Interior posted a job announcement for a second ethics attorney and now has two ethics specialists for financial disclosures. The DAEO stated that the ethics program also plans to increase the number of ethics officials that review and certify financial disclosures, and has established new program goals, such as improving ethics staff competencies for technical review of financial disclosure reports.

Interior ethics officials also reported that the government-wide hiring freeze affected their ability to hire staff and address ethics program staff continuity. To build capacity within the ethics program and create a strong ethical culture at the agency and bureau levels, the Acting Deputy Secretary recommended in May 2017 that Interior develop a structure and

---

[39] Inspector General's Statement Summarizing the Major Management and Performance Challenges Facing the U.S. Department of the Interior for Fiscal Year 2018. Report No. 2018-ER-041, November 2018.

staffing plan to have a full-time ethics official for every 500 employees by fiscal year 2020. On October 26, 2018, Interior officials stated that the ethics program was implementing the Acting Deputy Secretary's staffing plan. However, OGE benchmarking guidance states that there is no "right" ratio for the number of ethics staff per employee, and that agencies should determine their ratio based on certain aspects of individual ethics programs, such as the scope of potential conflicts and the complexity of financial disclosure reports.

Interior officials could not explain how the ratio was determined nor provide a strategy for achieving the goal or evaluating whether the ratio is meeting the needs of the department in the future. We have previously identified leading practices for human capital management; these practices include that agencies should determine the workforce skills and competencies needed to achieve current and future goals and objectives as well as identify and develop strategies to address gaps. In addition, agencies should continually assess and improve human capital planning and investment, and assess the impact on accomplishing the mission. Without having a better understanding of resource needs and documenting how to properly allocate and determine needed resources, Interior may not accurately estimate its needs and may not be best positioned to assess and strengthen its ethics workforce to achieve program goals and objectives.

Moreover, staff turnover at the Interior ethics office also reduced institutional knowledge. For example, Interior's ethics office could not produce the documentation of the policies and procedures that support its ethics program—an internal control requirement—such as documenting and providing written responses to ethics queries and the tools used to ensure short and long-term continuity of operations. However, the ethics office previously provided documented evidence of some of these policies and procedures in its response to OGE's 2016 program review. Interior ethics officials stated that the OGE response was produced prior to the DAEO retiring and drafted by staff who no longer work at Interior.

Standards for Internal Control also require agencies to document key processes and procedures to retain organizational knowledge and mitigate the risk of having that knowledge limited to a few personnel, as well as a means to communicate that knowledge as needed to external parties, such as external auditors. Both HHS and SBA provided documentation of ethics program policies and procedures while Interior did not provide documentation. Since there was no formal documentation of the ethics program's policies and procedures, Interior ethics officials stated that the ethics office will document them as part of its organizational restructuring plans. As of March 2019, Interior officials had not provided this documentation. For example, the ethics program is to ensure that all ethics related advice, legal analyses, and conclusions are documented. However, without Interior completing the documentation of its policies and procedures and making them accessible to staff, institutional knowledge may be lost, and there is greater risk of not achieving the goals and objectives of the ethics program.

SBA did not report challenges to recruiting or staff continuity in part because of the small size of the ethics program. SBA's ethics program is administered by three full-time officials and during our review, the DAEO position was vacant for more than 3 months due to the retirement of the previous DAEO. However, the Alternate DAEO assumed the responsibility for managing the ethics program until a new DAEO was hired in August 2018. Ethics officials reported that the program could draw upon a pool of field attorneys previously designated to perform collateral ethics duties to temporarily address disruptions in staffing. To address continuity and succession, SBA ethics officials reported that a headquarters staff attorney was detailed to the ethics program to prepare for the possible retirement of its current Alternate DAEO.

CONCLUSION

Strong ethics programs are critical to ensuring public trust in government and the integrity of actions taken on the public's behalf. The executive branch ethics program is a shared responsibility across government. Political appointees, in particular agency heads, have a personal responsibility to exercise leadership in ethics. Some data are available on political appointees serving in the Executive Branch but the data have limitations that impede their usefulness. To facilitate independent review and analysis related to political appointees, members of the public need access to information on who is serving in political appointee positions. Otherwise, they are limited in their ability to discern whether appointees are performing their duties free of conflict. Information on the political appointees serving in the executive branch at any point in time would also facilitate congressional oversight. Both OPM and PPO are positioned to report these data, but there are some benefits and drawbacks of each agency's current capacity that will need to be considered. Ultimately, it is a policy decision as to which agency is best positioned to report comprehensive and timely data on political appointees.

Further, a robust internal control system is critical for agency ethics programs to achieve their mission of preventing conflicts of interest on the part of their employees. Without effective internal controls, agency ethics programs cannot reasonably assure that they are mitigating the risk—or the appearance of—public servants making biased decisions when carrying out the governmental responsibilities entrusted to them. During the course of our review SBA took steps to establish written procedures for initial ethics training, but still needs to complete the implementation of procedures to track and verify that all political appointees meet ethics training requirements.

As Interior continues to reorganize its ethics program, improved strategic workforce planning can help to accurately assess its needs, maintain continuity, and achieve program goals and objectives. Finally, ensuring that Interior's ethics processes and procedures are fully documented and easily accessible to staff can help mitigate the risk of reduced institutional knowledge, and can improve the ability to communicate with external parties.

MATTER FOR CONGRESSIONAL CONSIDERATION

Congress should consider legislation requiring comprehensive and timely information on political appointees serving in the executive branch to be collected and made publicly accessible. (Matter for Consideration 1).

RECOMMENDATIONS FOR EXECUTIVE ACTION

We are making a total of three recommendations, including one to SBA, and two to Interior.

The Administrator of the Small Business Administration should implement procedures to track and verify that required employees complete initial ethics training and that completion of this training is documented (Recommendation 1).

The Secretary of the Interior should direct the Departmental Ethics Office, in conjunction with the Chief Human Capital Officer, to develop, document, and implement a strategic workforce planning process that aligns with its ongoing departmental reorganization and that is tailored to the specific needs of the ethics program. As part of this process, Interior should monitor and assess the critical skills and competencies that its ethics program needs presently and is projected to need in the future (Recommendation 2).

The Secretary of the Interior should ensure that the department's ethics program policies and procedures are documented and easily accessible to program staff (Recommendation 3).

AGENCY COMMENTS AND OUR EVALUATION

We provided a draft of this chapter for comment to the Department of Justice (DOJ), the White House Counsel's Office at the Executive Office of the President (EOP), the Department of Health and Human Services

(HHS), the Department of the Interior (Interior), the Inspector General of the Department of the Interior (OIG), the Office of Government Ethics (OGE), the Office of Personnel Management (OPM), and the Small Business Administration (SBA).

Interior, SBA, and OGE provided written comments, which are reproduced in appendixes IV, V, and VI respectively. Interior officials concurred with our recommendations and described steps they are taking to begin addressing them.

In our draft report, we made two recommendations to SBA. Our first recommendation was that SBA establish written procedures for initial ethics training as required. SBA officials did not agree or disagree with this recommendation, but during their review of the draft report, they provided documentation to show that they had established written procedures in line with our draft recommendation. As such, we revised our final report to include the actions taken by SBA in February 2019 and to delete our recommendation to establish written procedures for initial ethics training.

With regard to our second draft recommendation to SBA, which remains in our final report as our first recommendation, SBA again did not agree or disagree with the recommendation. SBA officials provided documentation to support that they have taken initial steps to address our recommendation to implement procedures to track and verify completion of initial ethics training by political appointees. We plan to assess the implementation of these new procedures to confirm that, in operation, these procedures meet the intent of our recommendation.

In addition to the written comments we received, SBA, HHS, OGE, and OPM provided technical comments, which we incorporated as appropriate.

DOJ and the Interior OIG had no comments on the draft report. EOP did not respond to our request for comments.

As agreed with your offices, unless you publicly announce the contents of this chapter earlier, we plan no further distribution until 1 day from the report date.

At that time, we will send copies to the appropriate congressional committees, the Acting Attorney General of DOJ, the White House Counsel, the Secretary of HHS, the Acting Secretary of the Interior, the Acting Inspector General at the Interior, the Director of OGE, the Acting Director of OPM, the SBA Administrator, and other interested parties.

Tranchau (Kris) T. Nguyen,
Acting Director Strategic Issues

APPENDIX I: OBJECTIVES, SCOPE, AND METHODOLOGY

Our objectives were to evaluate the extent to which (1) existing data identify political appointees serving in the executive branch at any point in time, and (2) selected agencies use appropriate internal controls to reasonably ensure that their ethics programs are designed and implemented to meet statutory and regulatory requirements.

To evaluate the extent to which data identifying political appointees serving in the executive branch at any point in time exist, we first synthesized requirements for reporting and developed criteria for comprehensive and timely reporting. We reviewed relevant laws and standards, and the United States Government Policy and Supporting Positions (Plum Book).[40] We used the Office of Management and Budget's Open Government Directive (M-10-06) memorandum to develop criteria for transparency and public availability.

We interviewed officials from the Office of Personnel Management (OPM) to understand the extent to which data they collect on current political appointees are comprehensive, timely, and reportable.

[40] The Plum Book is published after each presidential election. It lists federal civil service leadership and support positions in the legislative and executive branches of the federal government that may be subject to noncompetitive appointment.

OPM provided data on the political appointees serving in the federal government between January 2017 and June 2018. We also requested and obtained information from OPM on the volume of Freedom of Information Act requests for data on political appointees to assess demand for this type of data. To further evaluate public demand for political appointee data, we interviewed two nongovernmental organizations that track political appointees in the executive branch, ProPublica, and the Partnership for Public Service. We gathered information on the public's demand for information regarding political appointees, and the use and limitations of data. Both organizations provided statistics quantifying public demand, including number of unique visitors to their website and media impressions. Media impressions are any viewing of or interaction with a piece of content. We requested information or interviews with the Office of Presidential Personnel (PPO) and several White House Liaisons to understand how they track, maintain, and use data on political appointees serving in the executive branch. A senior leader at PPO and one White House Liaison acknowledged our request for an interview but deferred to the White House Counsel's Office. As well, an ethics officer indicated they would be unable to facilitate the exchange of information with the White House Liaison Office in their agency. The White House Counsel's Office did not acknowledge requests for information or interviews. We interviewed former senior PPO officials from the two previous administrations to understand how they tracked, maintained and used data on political appointees.

To identify internal control processes and determine the extent to which selected agencies use appropriate controls to ensure their ethics programs are designed and implemented to meet statutory and regulatory requirements, we first identified four case study agencies. We selected a range of case study agencies based on the number and type of political appointees as well as the strength of their ethics programs, as determined by Office of Government Ethics (OGE) reviews.

Using data from the 2016 Plum Book, we identified the total number of political appointee positions within each agency or department across the following four categories: presidential appointees with Senate confirmation (PAS), presidential appointees, noncareer members of the Senior Executive Service, and Schedule C appointees.

We selected the Executive Office of the President (EOP) as a case study agency because EOP has the largest number of presidential appointees, and because OGE has not recently conducted a program review of EOP. According to OGE, ethics program reviews are a primary means of conducting systematic oversight of executive branch ethics programs. OGE completed a review of each agency between January 2014 and January 2018.[41] Since the White House Counsel's Office did not acknowledge receipt of our notification letter we could not review EOP's practices.

To allow for more comparability among case studies, we excluded agencies and departments that did not have at least one PAS, and one presidential appointee or noncareer member of the Senior Executive Service. From the remaining list of departments and agencies, we excluded those with nine or fewer total political appointee positions. We divided the remaining agencies into two groups: large agencies with more than 100 political appointees and small agencies with fewer than 100 political appointees. To ensure we observed a range of practices, we selected a large agency with no recommendations in its most recent OGE program review—the Department of Health and Human Services and an agency with multiple unaddressed recommendations from its most recent OGE program review—the Department of the Interior.

To select our final case study, we used human resources data from OPM's FedScope tool to determine the number of employees at each agency as of September 2017. We limited our selection to noncabinet agencies with between 2,000 and 10,000 employees. Out of the four remaining agencies, we randomly selected the Small Business Administration.

---

[41] See https://oge.gov/web/oge.nsf/Program%20Review.

To evaluate the extent to which the three reviewed agencies have and use appropriate internal controls to reasonably ensure that the objectives of their ethics programs are achieved, we reviewed selected principles from Standards for Internal Control in the Federal Government based on our review, analysis and professional judgment as to which were relevant to effectively execute an executive branch ethics program. Selected internal control principles included:

- 3.01: Management should establish an organizational structure, assign responsibility, and delegate authority to achieve the entity's objectives;
- 4.01: Management should demonstrate a commitment to recruit, develop, and retain competent individuals;
- 10.01: Management should design control activities to achieve objectives and respond to risks; and
- 14.01: Management should internally communicate the necessary quality information to achieve the entity's objectives.

Reviewed agencies confirmed that these internal control principles were relevant to effectively execute their ethics program. We provided each agency with an identical set of questions based on the selected internal control principles and components. We used agency responses to questions and supporting documentation to evaluate whether agencies' policies and processes to oversee ethics compliance for political appointees were consistent with the internal control principles.

We used a nongeneralizable random sampling method to select political appointees whose documentation we would review for compliance with certain ethics requirements. Agencies provided data detailing the political appointees within the agency at any point in time beginning January 20, 2017 and as of January 28, 2018. To assess the reliability of the data, we asked each agency's officials about how the data were obtained, where the data came from, and what steps, if any, they each took to assure the accuracy and completeness of the data.

Officials at each agency knowledgeable about their data provided responses. Based on those responses, we determined that the data were sufficiently reliable to indicate each agency's political appointees, with start and end dates, for use in selecting a sample of appointees at each agency. Within each agency, we used random sampling to identify up to three PAS appointees and up to nine non-PAS appointees, including up to three appointees that separated from the agency during the time frame above. Each case study agency completed a data collection instrument that identified the applicable ethics requirements for each selected appointee.[42] Each agency provided documentation to communicate how those requirements were met for each appointee. We reviewed the documentation to determine whether agency internal controls were sufficient to ensure that certain ethics program requirements were met. In addition, we conducted interviews with agency ethics officials, as needed, to discuss documentation provided. We also conducted several interviews with OGE officials to inform how we developed the data collection instrument and evaluate appointee compliance in alignment with OGE's principles and practices. Our review of political appointees' documentation was limited to testing the sufficiency of the agencies' ethics program processes and procedures. We did not review financial disclosure forms with the intent of identifying conflicts of interest nor did we perform a conflict of interest analysis. Also, because we used a nongeneralizable sample of political appointees, results from the sample cannot be used to make inferences about all the agencies' political appointees.

We conducted this performance audit from October 2017 to February 2019 in accordance with generally accepted government auditing standards. Those standards require that we plan and perform the audit to obtain sufficient, appropriate evidence to provide a reasonable basis for our findings and conclusions based on our audit objectives. We believe that the evidence obtained provides a reasonable basis for our findings and conclusions based on our audit objectives.

---

[42] Applicable ethics requirements included Executive Order 13370 and sections 2634.201-2638.205, 2634.601, 2634.605, 2634.801-2634.805, 2638.304-2638.305, and 2638.308-2638.309 of title 5, Code of Federal Regulations.

Appendix II: Use of Internal Controls in Reviewed Agencies' Ethics Programs

Table 2. Analysis of Internal Control Principles to Reviewed Agencies' Ethics Programs

Selected Internal Control Components and Principles	Ethics Program Evaluative Questions	Reviewed Agency Results		
Control Environment		HHS	SBA	Interior
Management should establish an organizational structure, assign responsibility, and delegate authority to achieve the entity's objectives.	Has the agency established an organizational structure for its ethics program?	●	●	◐
Management should demonstrate a commitment to recruit, develop, and retain competent individuals.	Are agency ethics program staff evaluated?	●	●	◐
	Are agency ethics program staff's expectations developed and documented?	●	●	◐
	Does the agency commit resources to the ethics program?	●	●	◐
	Does the agency recruit, develop, and train ethics program staff?	●	●	○
	Does the agency prepare alternate or contingency plans for ethics program staff attrition, succession, or other potential disruptions to staff levels?	●	●	○
Control Activities				
Management should design control activities to achieve objectives and respond to risks.	Does the agency have goals and objectives for the ethics program?	●	●	●
	Are these goals and objectives documented?	●	●	●
	Does the agency have processes and procedures in place to support the goals and objectives of the ethics program?	●	●	◐
	Does the agency have processes and procedures in place to ensure political appointees who are not Presidential Appointees with Senate Confirmation do not undertake an activity that represents an actual or apparent conflict of interest?	●	●	◐
	Does the agency have processes and procedures in place to ensure that political appointees receive required training?	●	◐	●
Information and Communication				

Selected Internal Control Components and Principles	**Ethics Program Evaluative Questions**	**Reviewed Agency Results**		
Control Environment		HHS	SBA	Interior
Management should internally communicate the necessary quality information to achieve the entity's objectives.	Does the agency communicate ethics program related information to political appointees?	●	●	●

Legend: ● = Met; ◐ = Partially Met; ○ = Not Met.

Source: GAO analysis of ethics program documentation. | GAO-19-249.

APPENDIX III: ETHICS PROVISIONS APPLICABLE TO POLITICAL APPOINTEES AND RESULTS OF POLITICAL APPOINTEE ETHICS DOCUMENTATION ANALYSIS

Table 3. Number of Sampled Political Appointees in Each Agency That Addressed Selected Ethics Requirements Number of political appointees in each agency sample that the requirement applied to, and the number that met the requirement

	Number of political appointees in each agency sample that the requirement applied to, and the number that met the requirement					
Selected Ethics Requirements	**Small Business Administration**		**Department of Health and Human Services**		**Department of the Interior**	
	REQUIRED	MET	REQUIRED	MET	REQUIRED	MET
Signed the Executive Order 13770, "Ethics Pledge	10	10	11	11	12	12
Presidential Appointee with Senate confirmation (PAS) nominee financial disclosure report filed no later than 5 days after nomination by the President	2	2	1a	1	3	3
PAS nominee signed an Ethics Agreement to address identified conflicts of interest	2	2	3	3	3	3
PAS nominee signed an Ethics Agreement to address identified conflicts of interest	8	6	10	10	9	8d

Table 3. (Continued)

Selected Ethics Requirements	Small Business Administration		Department of Health and Human Services		Department of the Interior	
	REQUIRED	MET	REQUIRED	MET	REQUIRED	MET
Completed initial ethics training within 3 months of appointment	10	10	11b	11	12	12
Received live ethics briefing within 15 days of appointment (PAS only)	2	2	1c	1	3	3
Termination financial disclosure report filed within 30 days of leaving government (if appointee departed from the agency)	1	1	3	3	1	0

Source: GAO analysis of ethics documentation for a sample of political appointees. | GAO-19-249.

Notes: We reviewed ethics documentation for a randomly selected nongeneralizable sample of 10 political appointees in positions at SBA and 12 political appointees in positions at HHS and Interior in place between January 20, 2017 and January 28, 2018. To ensure we included certain types of political appointees in our review, we grouped the political appointees from each agency into three groups: individuals in presidentially appointed, Senate confirmed (PAS) positions, individuals who left the agency during the time frame of our review, and all remaining individuals. We randomly selected three, three, and six political appointees from each target group, respectively. At SBA, the total PAS appointees and total individuals who left the agency during our review time frame was less than the target. As a result, there were fewer appointees in our SBA sample compared to the other agencies.

Because we used a nongeneralizable sample of political appointees, results from the sample cannot be used to make inferences about all of the agencies' political appointees.

[a]Two of the three PAS appointees in our HHS sample were incumbents from previous administrations. Due to records retention schedule, we were unable to evaluate the nominee reports filed by those two appointees.

[b]As noted, two PAS appointees in our HHS sample were incumbent appointees. Due to records retention schedule we were unable to review documentation and assess whether one of the incumbent appointees received the training. However, HHS provided email documentation to support that the other incumbent appointee received initial ethics training.

[c]The requirement for PAS appointees to receive an additional ethics briefing was not applicable at the time of appointment for two incumbent appointees from HHS.

[d]One appointee at Interior did not file a new entrant or a termination financial disclosure report. According to ethics officials at Interior, they mistakenly determined that the appointee was not required to file because she did not serve in her position for more than 60 days. Based on our analysis of the appointees' appointment and departure dates, the appointee served for 63 days and should have been required to file.

APPENDIX IV: COMMENTS FROM THE DEPARTMENT OF THE INTERIOR

United States Department of the Interior

OFFICE OF THE SECRETARY
Washington, DC 20240

MAR 01 2019

Ms. Tranchau (Kris) Nguyen
Acting Director, Strategic Issues
U.S. Government Accountability Office
441 G Street, NW
Washington, DC 20548

Dear Ms. Nguyen:

Thank you for giving the Department of the Interior (Department) the opportunity to review and comment on the draft Government Accountability Office (GAO) report entitled, *Federal Ethics Program: Government-wide Political Appointee Data and Ethics Oversight Procedures at Interior and SBA Could Be Improved* (GAO-19-249). We appreciate GAO's review of compliance with ethics requirements for political appointees in the executive branch.

GAO issued four recommendations including two to the Department. Below is a summary of actions planned to implement the recommendations:

Recommendation 3: The Secretary of the Interior should direct the Departmental Ethics Office in conjunction with the Chief Human Capital Officer to develop, document, and implement a strategic workforce planning process that aligns with its ongoing departmental reorganization and that is tailored to the specific needs of the ethics program. As part of this process, Interior should monitor and assess critical skills and competencies that its ethics program needs presently and is projected to need in the future.

Response: Concur. The Departmental Ethics Office (DEO) is in the process of reorganizing the Department's ethics program including its reporting structure to improve accountability and provide better ethics-related services to all Department employees in a more efficient manner. Several of the specific issues raised during the GAO review (i.e., ethics pledge executions, timely initial ethics training, and timely submission of financial disclosure reports) have already been addressed. Supervisory attorneys hired to oversee ethics training and financial disclosure have implemented new procedures in this area. The DEO will work closely with the Chief Human Capital Officer to develop and implement strategic workforce planning as the reorganization of the Department and its ethics program continue.

Recommendation 4: The Secretary of the Interior should ensure that the Department's ethics program policies and procedures are documented and easily accessible to program staff.

Response: Concur. The Department is currently in the process of developing policies and procedures relevant to the ethics program and once finalized will document and have them easily accessible to the program staff.

Sincerely,

Scott J. Cameron
Principal Deputy Assistant Secretary
for Policy, Management and Budget

Appendix V. Comments from the U.S. Small Business Administration

U.S. Small Business Administration

March 1, 2019

Ms. Tranchau (Kris) T. Nguyen, Acting Director
Strategic Issues
U.S. Government Accountability Office
Washington, D.C. 20548

Dear Ms. Nguyen:

Thank you for providing the U.S. Small Business Administration (SBA) with the opportunity to respond to the U.S. Government Accountability Office (GAO) draft report 19-249, titled *"Federal Ethics Programs: Government-wide Political Appointee Data and Ethics Oversight Procedures at Interior and SBA Could Be Improved."* According to the report, GAO's objective in conducting the audit was to examine the extent to which (1) existing data identify political appointees serving in the executive branch, and (2) the selected agencies use internal controls to reasonably ensure that their ethics programs are designed and implemented to meet statutory and regulatory requirements.

During the exit conference at SBA on October 31, 2018, GAO indicated that it found SBA did not have adequate written procedures applicable to providing, tracking, verifying, and documenting initial ethics training for political appointees. GAO did not indicate any other adverse findings related to SBA's Ethics Program's internal controls or compliance with applicable statutory and regulatory requirements. SBA promptly accepted GAO's preliminary findings and began development of new initial ethics training procedures for political appointees, which incorporated existing program processes with new documentation methods, in November 2018. Progress was necessarily halted by the lapse in appropriations from late December 2018 through late January 2019, but SBA was able to finalize and implement its written procedures for initial ethics training for political appointees in early February 2019, shortly after the shutdown ended. SBA provided GAO a copy of those written procedures, which address both the provision of initial ethics training as well as the procedures for certifying and documenting training provided to new appointees, on February 8, 2019. These procedures are currently in use to document the initial ethics training of political appointees.

In short, SBA has already addressed and implemented the two recommendations in the draft report applicable to it.[1] In light of this fact, and for the other reasons indicated herein, SBA

[1] The recommendations are: (i) *The Administrator of the Small Business Administration should establish written procedures for initial ethics training as required (Recommendation 1)*; and (ii) *The Administrator of the Small*

believes that the draft report should be revised as set forth below to more accurately reflect both the past and current state of SBA's Ethics Program.

The title of the draft report does not accurately reflect the scope of the findings as they relate to the SBA Ethics Program:

SBA believes the title of the draft report, which states that SBA's "ethics oversight procedures…could be improved," inaccurately suggests SBA's Ethics Program requires widespread and/or substantial improvement, even though the report's narrative clearly states otherwise.

During its audit, GAO reviewed SBA responses to questions based on "selected internal control principles and components" to determine whether SBA's policies and processes for overseeing ethics compliance for political appointees were consistent with those principles. Contrary to the broad scope of the report's title, GAO's findings regarding SBA's Ethics Program policies and processes clearly show SBA is substantially compliant with applicable statutory and regulatory requirements. For example, Appendix II: *Use of Internal Controls in Reviewed Agencies' Ethics Programs*, shows that SBA fully met 11 out of the 12 internal control components and principles used by GAO to determine SBA's compliance. For the one component on which the draft recommendations are based, GAO determined SBA partially met applicable requirements. Moreover, the report states that GAO's review of "SBA's informal documentation…found that political appointees completed required initial ethics training on time." The report also concludes that SBA "generally used appropriate internal controls" to ensure it "met basic ethics program requirements." SBA therefore believes the report title's broad and vague language that "ethics oversight procedures…could be improved" does not properly capture the report's findings and content as they relate to SBA's Ethics Program, particularly since SBA has in fact fully addressed the two areas of concern identified in the draft recommendations.

SBA understands the challenges in developing a succinct title to accurately describe a report covering multiple agencies. However, we believe that attempting to encapsulate different issues for different agencies by using broad or vague language is, in this particular instance, both confusing to the reader and unfair to the affected agencies, and we therefore believe it would be more appropriate to simply refrain from referring to specific agencies in the title at all.

Language in the draft report does not accurately reflect the scope of the findings or the current state of the SBA Ethics Program:

GAO Highlights Page:

- "Until SBA addresses the requirement to establish written procedures for initial ethics training and track and documents training dates, it cannot reliably hold appointees accountable for meeting the training required."

Business Administration should implement procedures to track and verify that required employees complete initial ethics training and that competition of this training is documented (Recommendation 2).

SBA believes this language should not be contained in the final report because the Agency has already established and implemented applicable written procedures. Moreover, the report states that after reviewing "SBA's informal documentation...[GAO] found that political appointees completed required initial ethics training on time."

- "HHS and Interior had procedures for providing initial ethics training as required beginning in January 2017; however, SBA did not. SBA also did not adequately document political appointees' training dates."

  SBA believes this language should be amended to reflect that the Agency established and implemented applicable written procedures in February 2019. Moreover, the report states that after reviewing "SBA's informal documentation...[GAO] found that political appointees completed required initial ethics training on time."

<u>Page 17</u>:

- "According to SBA ethics officials, SBA is developing written procedures during Fiscal Year 2019 to address the requirement that became effective in 2017."

  SBA believes this language should be amended to reflect that the Agency established and implemented applicable written procedures in February 2019.

<u>Pages 17 and 18</u>:

- "In the absence of formally documenting its procedures, SBA cannot have reasonable assurance that the procedures are implemented as intended and that all required appointees are provided initial ethics training."

  SBA believes this language should not be contained in the final report because the Agency has already established and implemented applicable written procedures. Moreover, the report states that after reviewing "SBA's informal documentation...[GAO] found that political appointees completed required initial ethics training on time."

<u>Page 18</u>:

- "SBA does not adequately document political appointee's training dates."

  SBA believes this language should be amended to reflect the Agency established and implemented applicable written procedures in February 2019.

- "SBA officials told us that the written procedures they are developing for initial ethics training will include new guidance to track training dates. As of October 2018, SBA had not provided us a draft of the new procedures."

  SBA believes this language should be amended to reflect the Agency established and implemented applicable written procedures in February 2019.

- "SBA cannot reliably hold political appointees accountable for meeting the requirement without developing these procedures, including processes to track and document initial ethics training dates."

  SBA believes this language should not be contained in the final report because the Agency has already established and implemented applicable written procedures.

Page 24:

- "In particular, until SBA addresses the requirement to establish written procedures for initial ethics training and tracks and documents training dates SBA may not have reasonable assurance that all political appointees met the ethics training requirement."

  SBA believes this language should not be contained in the final report because the Agency has already established and implemented applicable written procedures.

In conclusion, we respectfully request that GAO strongly consider these comments and concerns to ensure its final report accurately reflects the past and current state of SBA's Ethics Program and the accomplishments of its personnel.

Thank you again for affording SBA the opportunity to comment on this draft report, and for taking our comments into consideration as you prepare your final report. Please contact us if you have any questions concerning this letter.

Sincerely,

Andrew T. Krog
Designated Agency Ethics Official
Office of General Counsel
U.S. Small Business Administration

Appendix VI: Comments from the United States Office of Government Ethics

UNITED STATES OFFICE OF
GOVERNMENT ETHICS

February 21, 2019

Tranchau (Kris) Nguyen
Acting Director, Strategic Issues
U.S. Government Accountability Office
441 G Street, NW
Washington, DC 20548

RE: Draft Report GAO-19-249, "Federal Ethics Program: Government-Wide Political Appointee Data and Ethics Oversight Procedures at Interior and SBA Could Be Improved."

Dear Ms. Nguyen:

Thank you for the opportunity to comment on the U.S. Government Accountability Office's (GAO) draft report, "Federal Ethics Program: Government-Wide Political Appointee Data and Ethics Oversight Procedures at Interior and SBA Could Be Improved." The U.S. Office of Government Ethics (OGE) appreciates GAO's work in planning and conducting its review and issuing this report.

The draft report contains no recommendations for OGE; however, some of the recommendations touch on issues related to the executive branch ethics rules and the work of our office. In particular, the draft report recommends that the Small Business Administration (SBA) should establish written procedures for initial ethics training and processes to document that training was completed; that the Department of the Interior (Interior) should conduct more strategic planning for its ethics workforce and document ethics program policies and procedures; and that the Secretary of the Interior should ensure that the Department's ethics program policies and procedures are documented and easily accessible to program staff.

With regard to the recommendation for SBA, OGE concurs. OGE has long held that written procedures for all ethics-related policies and practices, in addition to the procedures for financial disclosure required by the Ethics in Government Act, help to ensure the consistent administration of the ethics program and foster more efficient transition of program responsibilities from departing ethics officials to newly appointed officials.

Regarding the recommendations for Interior, OGE notes that its most recent review of Interior's ethics program identified numerous deficiencies. In the June 2016 report on this review, OGE issued 14 recommendations for program improvement. Notably, the report indicated that ethics office officials acknowledged the need for additional staffing and stated that the previous Secretary had agreed to an action plan that included adding 13 new positions to the office. However, OGE's report goes on to note that at the time of OGE's review staffing levels had not increased due to funding constraints.

Since the issuance of the June 2016 report, OGE has conducted two follow-up reviews to assess the implementation of these recommendations and plans to meet with Interior ethics officials later this month to discuss the steps the Designated Agency Ethics Official has taken to improve the program since being appointed to the position.

Again, thank you for the opportunity to comment on this draft report. Technical comments were previously provided. Please feel free to contact Shelley Finlayson, OGE's Chief of Staff and Program Counsel, if you have any questions. We look forward to working with you in the future.

Sincerely,

Emory A. Rounds, III
Director

In: Government Reports …
Editor: Evie Boan
ISBN: 978-1-53615-928-8

Chapter 4

FEES, FINES, AND PENALTIES: BETTER REPORTING OF GOVERNMENT-WIDE DATA WOULD INCREASE TRANSPARENCY AND FACILITATE OVERSIGHT*

United States Government Accountability Office

ABBREVIATIONS

APHIS	Animal and Plant Health Inspection Service
AQI	Agricultural Quarantine Inspection
CAA	Clean Air Act
CBO	Congressional Budget Office
CFO	Chief Financial Officer

* This is an edited, reformatted and augmented version of United States Government Accountability Office; Report to the Ranking Member, Subcommittee on Government Operations, Committee on Oversight and Reform, House of Representatives. Publication No. GAO-19-221, dated March 2019.

Combined Statement	*Combined Statement of Receipts, Outlays, and Balances*
CRS	Congressional Research Service
CSV	comma separated values
CWA	Clean Water Act
DATA Act	Digital Accountability and Transparency Act of 2014
DTD	document type definition
ECHO	Enforcement and Compliance History Online
EPA	United States Environmental Protection Agency
Financial Report	Financial Report of the U.S. Government
FFATA	Federal Funding Accountability and Transparency Act of 2006
GPRAMA	GPRA Modernization Act of 2010
HTML	hypertext markup language
OMB	Office of Management and Budget
PDF	portable document format
Treasury	Department of the Treasury
USDA	U.S. Department of Agriculture

WHY GAO DID THIS STUDY

Congress has authorized federal agencies to collect hundreds of billions of dollars annually in fees, fines, and penalties. These collections can fund a variety of programs, including programs related to national security, and the protection of natural resources. Data on collections are important for congressional oversight and to provide transparency in agencies' use of federal resources.

GAO was asked to review the availability of government-wide data on fees, fines, and penalties. This chapter examines (1) the extent to which data on collections of fees, fines, and penalties are publically available and useful for the purpose of congressional oversight; and (2) the benefits and challenges to government-wide reporting of fees, fines, and penalties. GAO assessed government-wide fee, fine, and penalty data against criteria for availability and usefulness based on multiple sources, including prior GAO work and input from staff of selected congressional committees. GAO interviewed OMB staff, Treasury officials, and representatives of organizations with expertise in federal budget issues and reviewed prior GAO work to identify benefits and challenges of reporting these data.

What GAO Recommends

GAO is making four recommendations to enhance OMB reporting on fees, fines, and penalties, including making disaggregated data publically available, updating instructions to federal agencies to review accounts designated as containing fees, and disclosing limitations in data reported. OMB did not provide comments.

What GAO Found

There are no comprehensive, government-wide data at the level of detail that identifies specific fees, fines, or penalties. The Office of Management and Budget (OMB) and the Department of the Treasury (Treasury) report data that include these collections at the budget account level, which generally covers a set of agency activities or programs. OMB and Treasury also report some summary data for budgeting and financial management purposes. In the *Budget of the U.S. Government*, for example, OMB data showed government-wide fees totaled just over $335 billion in fiscal year 2017. These reports, however, are not designed to inventory or analyze fee, fine, or penalty collections and have significant limitations for that purpose.

- Although OMB collects more disaggregated data on fees, fines, and penalties, it does not make the data publicly available. OMB uses the disaggregated data in its OMB MAX database—such as the agency and account—to compile reported totals, such as the government-wide fees total in the *Budget of the U.S. Government*. Until OMB makes more disaggregated data publicly available, Congress has limited information on collections by agency to inform oversight and decision-making.
- OMB's government-wide total of fees includes collections that are not fees and excludes some fee collections. The total includes all collections for accounts in which fees make up at least half of the account's collections and excludes all others. OMB does not direct agencies to regularly review and update the accounts included in the total. Therefore, if accounts' makeups change such that fee collections drop below, or rise above, the 50 percent threshold, accounts may have incorrect fee designations and the total may be inaccurate.
- Further, OMB does not disclose the limitation that the total may exclude some fees and include other collections that are not fees. As a result, some users of the data are likely unaware of the potential for the total fees to be overestimated or underestimated.

Further, no source of government-wide data consistently reports data elements on fees, fines, and penalties that could help inform congressional oversight. Generally, congressional staff told us that additional data, such as amounts of specific penalties, would increase transparency and facilitate oversight. These data could help Congress identify trends in collections and significant changes that could be an indication of an agency's performance. While reporting government-wide fee, fine, and penalty data provides benefits, there are tradeoffs in terms of the time and federal resources it would take to develop and implement a process for agencies to report these data. The level of federal investment would vary depending on factors, such as the number of data elements included and the level of detail reported. Developing a comprehensive and accessible data source would provide greater benefits, but would likely be resource intensive. Alternatively, incorporating a small number of data elements that Congress identifies as most useful for oversight into ongoing government-wide reporting efforts could incrementally improve transparency and information for oversight and decision-making, with fewer resources.

March 7, 2019

The Honorable Mark Meadows
Ranking Member
Subcommittee on Government Operations
Committee on Oversight and Reform
House of Representatives

Dear Mr. Meadows:

Congress has authorized federal agencies to collect hundreds of billions of dollars annually in fees, fines, and penalties. These collections can fund a wide variety of programs, including programs integral to our nation's security, to the security of our financial system, and to the protection of our natural resources. Agencies are authorized to charge more than 3,600 different user fees, such as for visiting national parks, patent applications, and customs inspections.[1] Agency authority to assess and collect fines and penalties is a critical method for enforcing policies and deterring violations of laws and regulations. For example, the Office of Management and Budget (OMB) has identified more than 50 different agencies as having civil monetary penalty authority.[2] In fiscal year 2017,

---

[1] GAO, 2012 *Annual Report: Opportunities to Reduce Duplication, Overlap and Fragmentation, Achieve Savings, and Enhance Revenue*, GAO-12-342SP (Washington, D.C.: Feb. 28, 2012). In 2011, we surveyed the 24 agencies covered by the Chief Financial Officers Act about their fees; 21 of the 23 agencies that responded reported charging more than 3,600 fees at that time. We noted significant limitations in the counts of fees agencies reported collecting.

[2] For more information, see GAO, *Civil Penalties: Certain Federal Agencies Need to Improve Inflation Adjustment Reporting*, GAO-18-519 (Washington, D.C.: Jul. 18, 2018); and *Civil Penalties: Certain Federal Agencies Need to Improve Efforts to Comply with Inflation Adjustment Requirements*, GAO-17-634 (Washington, D.C.: Aug. 31, 2017)

these federal agencies assessed millions of dollars in civil monetary penalties for violations of statutory requirements, such as phone calls that violated federal telemarketing law.

Given the nation's fiscal condition, it is critical Congress has full visibility over all federal resources. Federal collections of fees, fines, and penalties vary in the extent to which revenue collected is dedicated to the related program or agency and the extent to which the agency has authority to obligate and expend collections. Congress retains oversight over fees, fines, and penalties, regardless of agencies' authority to use these collections. As such, data that provide visibility on collections and how they are used are important for Congress to oversee agencies and programs, and provide transparency in agencies' use of federal resources.

OMB reports high-level, government-wide summary data on fee, fine, and penalty collections in the *Budget of the U.S. Government's Analytical Perspectives* and the Department of the Treasury (Treasury) reports data on agency receipts in the *Combined Statement of Receipts, Outlays, and Balances (Combined Statement).*[3] These reports are designed to serve specific purposes and audiences, and provide information targeted to meet those needs.

You asked us to review issues related to the availability of government-wide data on fees, fines, and penalties. This chapter examines: (1) the extent to which government-wide data on collections of fees, fines, and penalties are publicly available and useful for the purpose of congressional oversight; and (2) the benefits and challenges to government-wide reporting of specific fees, fines, and penalties including data elements that facilitate congressional oversight.

To address these objectives, we developed criteria for the availability and usefulness of data on collections of fees, fines, and penalties for the purpose of congressional oversight based on:

---

[3] For the purpose of this chapter, we use the term "collections" to refer to revenues that federal agencies collect from user fees, fines, and penalties regardless of the agency's authority to use the funds.

- our Standards for Internal Control,
- requirements found in the Digital Accountability and Transparency Act of 2014 (DATA Act),
- government-wide instructions from OMB on public access to data and open government,
- our prior work on user fees, fines, and penalties, and
- input from staff of congressional committees on appropriations, budget, and oversight (see Table 1).[4]

We shared the criteria with OMB staff and Treasury officials, and they agreed the criteria are relevant and reasonable. See appendix I for more information on the data elements that are useful for congressional oversight.

To determine the extent and usefulness of publicly available data for our first objective, we first identified government-wide sources containing data on fees, fines, and penalties to include in our review. We reviewed our prior work, conducted background research, including reviewing Congressional Budget Office and Congressional Research Service reports, and interviewed Treasury officials and OMB staff. As a result, we identified the *Budget of the U.S. Government*—including *Analytical Perspectives*, the *Budget Appendix*, and the Public Budget Database— produced by OMB, and the *Combined Statement* produced by Treasury. We assessed these sources and related documents and processes using the applicable criteria we developed on availability and usefulness of data on fees, fines, and

---

[4] The DATA Act amended the Federal Funding Accountability and Transparency Act of 2006. Pub. L. No. 109-282, 120 Stat. 1186 (Sept. 26, 2006)—amended by Pub. L. No. 113-101, 128 Stat. 1146 (May 9, 2014)—codified at 31 U.S.C. § 6101 note. Sources of government-wide instructions are: OMB Memorandum on Improving Public Access to and Dissemination of Government Information and Using the Federal Enterprise Architecture Data Reference Model (M-06-02), and on Open Government (M-10-06). For more information on our prior work used to develop criteria, see *GAO, Permanent Funding Authorities: Some Selected Entities Should Review Financial Management, Oversight, and Transparency Policies*, GAO-17-59 (Washington, D.C.: Dec. 9, 2016); *Federal User Fees: Fee Design Options and Implications for Managing Revenue Instability*, GAO-13-820 (Washington, D.C.: Sept. 30, 2013); and *Federal User Fees: A Design Guide*, GAO-08-386SP (Washington, D.C.: May 29, 2008).

penalties for the purpose of congressional oversight and *Standards for Internal Control in the Federal Government*. [5]

Table 1. GAO Criteria for the Availability and Usefulness of Data on Fees, Fines, and Penalties for the Purpose of Congressional Oversight

Criteria	Description
Clear and Accessible Presentation	• User is able to aggregate or disaggregate reported data. • Data are provided in machine-readable and open formats and can be downloaded in bulk, to the extent practicable for automated processing. • Data are comparable across agencies. • Data are clearly described and presented with known limitations.
Accurate	• Data reported as collections of fees, fines, and penalties are correctly labeled and do not include other sources of funding.
Complete	• Source reports all collections of fees, fines, and penalties.
Useful for the Purpose of Congressional Oversight	Data elements capturing the characteristics of fee, fine, or penalty collections that our prior work and cognizant committee staff identify as facilitating oversight: • Descriptive title • Agency administering • Agency collecting • Annual dollar amount collected (for multiple years) • Account balance • Authorities to collect and obligate funds • Limitations on obligations • Categories of collections (i.e., budgetary collection type, budget function) • Specific review requirement • Specific reporting requirement • Fund type receiving collections (e.g., special fund, trust fund, etc.)

Source: GAO analysis of GAO's Standards for Internal Control, requirements found in the DATA Act, OMB instructions, prior GAO work on user fees and permanent funding authorities, and input from staff of congressional committees on appropriations, budget, and oversight.

We also analyzed OMB and Treasury data to identify and report government-wide totals for fees, fines, and penalties to the extent that they were reported. To assess the reliability of OMB's MAX database data related to the collections of fees, fines, and penalties, we reviewed related documentation, interviewed knowledgeable OMB staff, and conducted

[5] See Principle 13 – Use Quality Information. *For more information, see GAO, Standards for Internal Control in the Federal Government*, GAO-14-704G (Washington, D.C.: September 2014).

electronic data testing. To assess Treasury's Bureau of the Fiscal Service data related to the collections of fees, fines, and penalties, we reviewed related documentation and interviewed knowledgeable Treasury officials. In both cases, we found the data to be reliable for our purposes. We did not examine whether agencies accurately report collections as fees, fines, and penalties to OMB and Treasury.

To determine the benefits and challenges of government-wide reporting of fees, fines, and penalties for our second objective, we interviewed staff of congressional committees on appropriations, budget, and oversight, OMB staff and Treasury officials, and external organizations on the potential benefits and challenges of government-wide reporting of fees, fines, and penalties. In addition, we reviewed our prior reports on the DATA Act, federal program inventories, and federal fees to identify and assess issues to consider in government-wide reporting. See appendix I for additional details on our scope and methodology.

We conducted this performance audit from November 2017 to March 2019 in accordance with generally accepted government auditing standards. Those standards require that we plan and perform the audit to obtain sufficient, appropriate evidence to provide a reasonable basis for our findings and conclusions based on our audit objectives. We believe that the evidence obtained provides a reasonable basis for our findings and conclusions based on our audit objectives.

BACKGROUND

The federal government receives funds from numerous sources in addition to tax revenues, including collections of user fees, fines, and penalties. According to the *Budget of the U.S. Government*, in fiscal year 2017, the U.S. government's total receipts were $3.3 trillion and collections of fees, fines, penalties, and forfeitures were more than $350 billion.[6]

[6] Forfeitures are confiscations of money, assets, or property resulting from enforcement actions. OMB and Treasury data categorize fines, penalties, and forfeitures together, and cannot be

- User fees (fees): Fees are charges assessed to users for goods or services provided by the federal government, such as fees to enter a national park, and charges assessed for regulatory services, such as fees charged by the Food and Drug Administration for prescription drug applications. Fees are an approach to financing federal programs or activities that, in general, are related to some voluntary transaction or request for government services above and beyond what is normally available to the public. By requiring identifiable beneficiaries to pay all or part of the cost of a good or service, fees can promote both equity and economic efficiency.[7] Regularly reviewing fees help ensure that agencies, Congress, and stakeholders have complete information.[8]
- Fines and penalties: Criminal fines and penalty payments are imposed by courts as punishment for criminal violations. Civil monetary penalties are not a result of criminal proceedings but are employed by courts and federal agencies to enforce federal laws and regulations.[9] For example, civil monetary penalty payments are collected from financial institutions by certain financial regulators, such as the Federal Deposit Insurance Corporation, from enforcement actions assessed against financial institutions for violations related to anti-money laundering requirements. Reviews and, as needed, adjustments to fines and penalties could help ensure they provide a meaningful incentive for compliance.[10]

---

disaggregated to fines and penalties only. The more than $350 billion in collections of fees, fines, penalties, and forfeitures is not a subset of the $3.3 trillion in receipts because some collections are offsets to spending, as defined by their statutory authority.

[7] GAO-08-386SP.

[8] The CFO Act requires an agency's CFO to biennially review the fees, royalties, rents, and other charges imposed by the agency for services and things of value it provides and make recommendations on revising those charges to reflect costs incurred by the agency in providing those services and things of value. 31 U.S.C. § 902(a)(8). OMB Circular No. A-25 on user fees directs agencies to set fees to recover all direct and indirect costs to the federal government of a good or service, to review their fees biennially, and to recommend fee adjustments as appropriate. For more information, see GAO-08-386SP.

[9] GAO, *Federal Fees, Fines, and Penalties: Observations on Agency Spending Authorities*, GAO-17-268T (Washington, D.C.: Dec. 1, 2016).

[10] We previously reported that civil monetary penalties prescribed by statute that are timely adjusted for inflation allow agencies to punish violators appropriately and serve as a deterrent to future violations. In addition, without timely and complete reporting of their

The design and structure of statutory authorities for fees, fines, and penalties can vary widely. In prior work, we have identified key design decisions related to how fee, fine, and penalty collections are used that help Congress balance agency flexibility with congressional control and oversight.[11] Congress determines the availability of collections by defining the extent to which an agency may obligate and expend them, including the availability of the funds, the period of time the collections are available for obligation, the purposes for which they may be obligated, and the amount of the collections that are available to the agency. Fees, fines, and penalties may be categorized as one of three types of collections based on the structure of their statutory authority: offsetting collections, offsetting receipts, or governmental receipts (see Figure 1).[12]

Offsetting collections can provide agencies with more flexibility because they are generally available for agency obligation without an additional annual appropriation. In contrast, offsetting receipts and governmental receipts involve greater congressional opportunities for control and oversight because, generally, additional congressional action is needed before the collections are available for agency obligation. For example, Congress must appropriate collections from offsetting receipts before agencies are authorized to obligate these funds.[13]

The type of collection also determines how OMB and Treasury report the collections. Offsetting collections and offsetting receipts result from businesslike transactions and are recorded as offsets to spending. Offsetting collections are authorized by law to be credited to appropriation or fund expenditure accounts, while offsetting receipts are deposited in

---

civil monetary penalties in agency financial reports, decision makers may not have the information needed to help ensure the effectiveness of civil monetary penalties in enforcing statutes and preventing violations. For more information, see GAO-17-634.

[11] GAO-17-268T; *Department of Justice: Alternative Sources of Funding Are a Key Source of Budgetary Resources and Could Be Better Managed*, GAO-15-48 (Washington, D.C.: Feb. 19, 2015); and GAO-13-820.

[12] The Budget Enforcement Act of 1990 defines offsetting collections and receipts as negative budget authority and the reductions to it as positive authority. Pub. L. No. 101- 508. Title XIII, § 13211, 104 Stat. 1388-573, 1388-620 codified at 2 U.S.C. § 622. According to OMB staff, OMB assigns a collection type based on its analysis of the statutory authority, in consultation with Treasury.

[13] Receipts of select trust funds are permanently appropriated in statute and, therefore, can be used without subsequent annual appropriation legislation. 31 U.S.C. § 1321.

receipt accounts. Because offsetting collections are offsets to spending, an account will generally show the net amount that was collected and spent at any point in time.

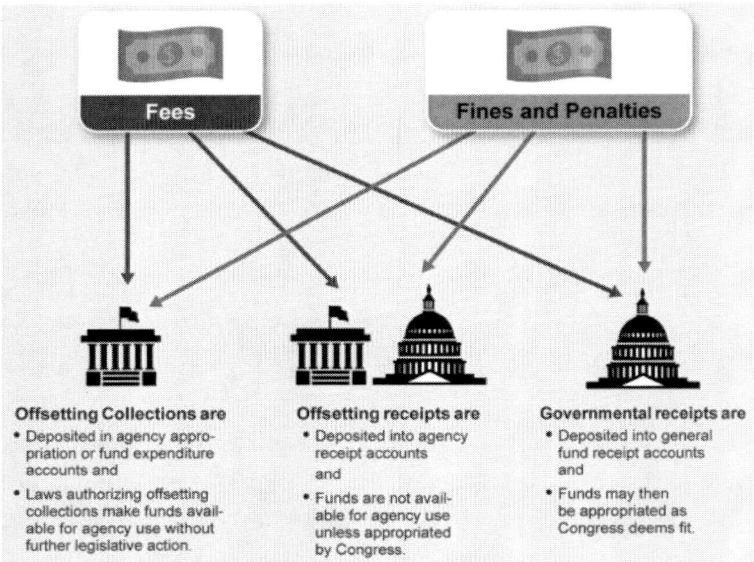

Source: GAO's Budget Glossary (GAO-05-734SP). | GAO-19-221.

Note: Fees, fines, and penalties can be any of the three types of collections or a combination of types. For examples of each, see GAO, *Federal Fees, Fines, and Penalties: Observations on Agency Spending Authorities*, GAO-17-268T (Washington, D.C.: Dec. 1, 2016).

Figure 1. Fees, Fines, and Penalties Can Be Any of Three Types of Collections.

Congressional Actions to Make Government-wide Data Publicly Available

While there is no statutory requirement for government-wide reporting of data of specific fees, fines and penalties, Congress has enacted legislation to make other data on federal spending and federal programs publicly available:

- The Digital Accountability and Transparency Act of 2014 (DATA Act). The DATA Act built on previous transparency legislation by expanding what federal agencies are required to report regarding their spending.[14] The act significantly increased the types of data that must be reported, and required the use of government-wide data standards and regular reviews of data quality to help improve the transparency and accountability of federal spending data. These data are reported on the USAspending.gov website.[15]
- The GPRA Modernization Act of 2010 (GPRAMA). GPRAMA, in part, requires OMB to present a coherent picture of all federal programs by making information available about each federal program on a website, including related budget and performance information.[16] Programs have been defined as an organized set of activities directed toward a common purpose or goal that an agency undertakes or proposes to carry out its responsibilities.[17] A federal program inventory would consist of the individual programs identified by the agencies and OMB and information collected about each of them. OMB and agencies implemented the inventory once, in May 2013. In October 2014, we found several issues limited the usefulness of that inventory and made several recommendations to OMB to ensure the effective implementation of federal program inventory requirements and to make the inventories more useful.[18] Further, in September 2017, we found

---

[14] Pub. L. No. 113-101, 128 Stat. 1146 (May 9, 2014). The DATA Act amended the Federal Funding Accountability and Transparency Act of 2006 (FFATA). Pub. L. No. 109- 282, 120 Stat. 1186 (Sept. 26, 2006), codified at 31 U.S.C. § 6101 note.

[15] FFATA required OMB to establish a website to provide information on grant and contract awards, and subawards.

[16] Pub. L. No. 111-352, § 7, 124 Stat. 3866, 3876 (Jan. 4, 2011), codified at 31 U.S.C. §1122(a). GPRAMA updated the Government Performance and Results Act of 1993. Pub. L. No. 103-62, 107 Stat. 285 (Aug. 3, 1993).

[17] This definition acknowledges that because the term program has many uses in practice, it does not have a well-defined, standard meaning in the legislative process. It is used to describe an agency's mission, functions, activities, services, projects, and processes. See GAO, *A Glossary of Terms Used in the Federal Budget Process*, GAO-05-734SP (Washington, D.C.: September 2005).

[18] OMB agreed with five of the recommendations and neither agreed nor disagreed with three of the recommendations. As of November 2018, OMB had not implemented these recommendations. For more information, see GAO, *Government Efficiency and*

that OMB continued to delay implementation of the program inventory. We recommended that OMB consider a systematic approach to developing the program inventory and issue instructions to provide time frames and milestones for its implementation.[19] Although OMB updated its instruction in June 2018, it did not provide any time frames or milestones for implementing the inventory. OMB has yet to develop a systematic approach for resuming implementation of the inventory or specific time frames for doing so.

OMB, Treasury, and Agencies Publicly Report Some Data on Fees, Fines, and Penalties, but the Data Have Significant Limitations

OMB, Treasury, and Agencies Report Broad Financial Information, but Not All Collections from Specific Fees, Fines, and Penalties

There is no source of data that lists all collections of specific fees, fines, and penalties at a government-wide or agency level. Both OMB and Treasury report government-wide budgetary and financial data, including some information on collections of fees, fines, and penalties; however, none of the reports identifies all specific fees, fines, and penalties, and their associated collection amounts at a government-wide level. OMB reports budgetary and financial data in various parts of the *Budget of the U.S. Government*, including *Analytical Perspectives*, the *Budget Appendix*, and the Public Budget Database.[20] Treasury reports financial data in the

---

Effectiveness: Inconsistent Definitions and Information Limit the Usefulness of Federal Program Inventories, GAO-15-83 (Washington, D.C.: Oct. 31, 2014).

[19] GAO, *Managing for Results: Further Progress Made in Implementing the GPRA Modernization Act, but Additional Actions Needed to Address Pressing Governance Challenges*, GAO-17-775 (Washington, D.C.: Sept. 29, 2017).

[20] To access the Public Budget Database, see: https://www.govinfo.gov/app/details/BUDGET-2019-DB/summary.

Combined Statement. Each source provides information for a broader purpose than reporting on collections of fees, fines, and penalties. OMB and Treasury provide specific instructions for agency submission of the underlying data, as described in Table 2.

OMB's reports include budgetary and financial information on federal collections at different levels of detail—from aggregated government-wide data to agency account-level data—depending on the source and its purpose.[21] *Analytical Perspectives* identifies collections as fees and as fines, penalties, and forfeitures and reports government-wide summary information on these collections. For example, in a table summarizing government-wide governmental receipts in *Analytical Perspectives*, OMB reported fines, penalties, and forfeitures in federal funds as $20.98 billion and in trust funds as $1.17 billion for fiscal year 2017.[22] These summary data do not provide a government-wide total of all federal collections from fines, penalties, and forfeitures because they do not include those that are categorized as offsetting collections or offsetting receipts, according to OMB staff. OMB staff said that OMB does not publish a government-wide total of fines, penalties, and forfeitures. OMB data on governmental receipts include source codes—including a code that identifies fines, penalties, and forfeitures—but data on offsetting collections and offsetting receipts do not include a comparable source code. In the *Budget Appendix* and the Public Budget Database, OMB reports account-level information by agency, identified by types of collections, such as offsetting collections, offsetting receipts, and governmental receipts. The *Budget Appendix* and the Public Budget Database do not label collections as fees, fines, or penalties and therefore, cannot be used to calculate government-wide totals for fees, fines, or penalties. To assemble *Analytical Perspectives,* the *Budget Appendix*, and the Public Budget Database, OMB compiles data from federal agencies into OMB MAX.[23]

---

[21] A budget account generally covers an organized set of activities, programs, or services directed toward a common purpose or goal for which Congress has provided budget authority.

[22] Federal fund accounts are budgetary accounts composed of moneys collected and spent by the federal government other than those designated as trust funds.

[23] OMB instructs agencies on how to report data for OMB MAX in OMB Circular No. A-11, *Preparation, Submission, and Execution of the Budget*.

Table 2. Purpose of Government-wide Sources of Data on Fees, Fines, and Penalties

Source	Agency Responsible	Instructions for Agency Data Submissions	Report Format	Purpose
Analytical Perspectives	Office of Management and Budget (OMB)	OMB Circular No. A-11, *Preparation, Submission, and Execution of the Budget*	Available for download as portable document format (PDF) document and some supplemental tables available as Excel spreadsheets	Annual presentation of budget data, including analyses that place the *Budget of the U.S. Government* in context, focusing on analyses of government-wide collections and spending, among others.
Budget Appendix	OMB	OMB Circular No. A-11, Preparation, Submission, and Execution of the Budget	Available for download as PDF document and document type definition (DTD), and hypertext markup language (HTML) files.	Annual presentation of budget schedules for each appropriation account and other detailed information on various appropriations and funds that constitute the budget, focusing on more detailed budgetary information for individual programs and accounts than other budget documents, such as objectives of the program.
Public Budget Database	OMB	OMB Circular No. A-11, Preparation, Submission, and Execution of the Budget	Available as download as Excel and comma separated values (.CSV) spreadsheets.	Annual presentation of an extract of the OMB's budget database focusing on receipts, budget authority, and outlays by account, that may be used to reproduce many of the totals published in the Budget of the U.S. Government.
Combined Statement of Receipts, Outlays and Balances	Department of the Treasury (Treasury)	Treasury Financial Manual	Available for download as PDF document or Excel spreadsheet.	Annual presentation of budgetary results based on reporting of Treasury account balances of the Federal Reserve banks, focusing on consolidated financial data by account.

Source: GAO analysis of OMB and Treasury reports. | GAO-19-221.

OMB MAX, which is not publicly available, contains government-wide data at the account level and captures information such as the type of collection and the type of fund to which collections are deposited. While the data in OMB MAX help drive reporting in the Budget, not all data compiled in OMB MAX appear in the Budget. For example, OMB MAX includes an indicator for accounts that contain fees, but that information is not made available in the *Budget of the U.S. Government*. According to congressional staff we spoke with, they do not have open access to OMB MAX, but OMB provides excerpts of OMB MAX data to staff upon request.

Treasury's *Combined Statement* reports both government-wide totals and agency account-level data for collections classified as receipts, by various source categories—such as proprietary receipts from the public, miscellaneous receipts, and fines, penalties, and forfeitures.[24]

- Fees. Fees may fall within several source categories. Therefore, Treasury does not have a single government-wide total for fees. It does present government-wide totals for various source categories, including, Sale of Products and Fees for Permits and Regulatory and Judicial Services, for example. Treasury also reports some fees under non-fee categories, such as Miscellaneous Taxes and Excise Taxes.
- Fines, Penalties, and Forfeitures. Treasury reports a government-wide total of receipts of fines, penalties, and forfeitures, which in fiscal year 2017 was $22.2 billion. Treasury's *Combined Statement* presents these data, disaggregated by account, in the tables Receipts by Source Categories and Receipts by Department. For example, it identifies total Internal Revenue Service receipts in the category Fines, Penalties, and Forfeitures of about $6.8 million in fiscal year 2017. Treasury also reports some fines, penalties, and forfeitures receipts under other categories; these receipts are not included in its total of fines, penalties, and forfeitures. For example, Department of Homeland Security breached bond penalties are reported in two categories labeled as fees: Miscellaneous Receipts – Fees for Permits and

---

[24] The *Combined Statement* does not identify offsetting collections, including offsetting collections of fees, fines, and penalties.

Regulatory and Judicial Services and Offsetting Governmental Receipts – Regulatory Fees (see Figure 2).

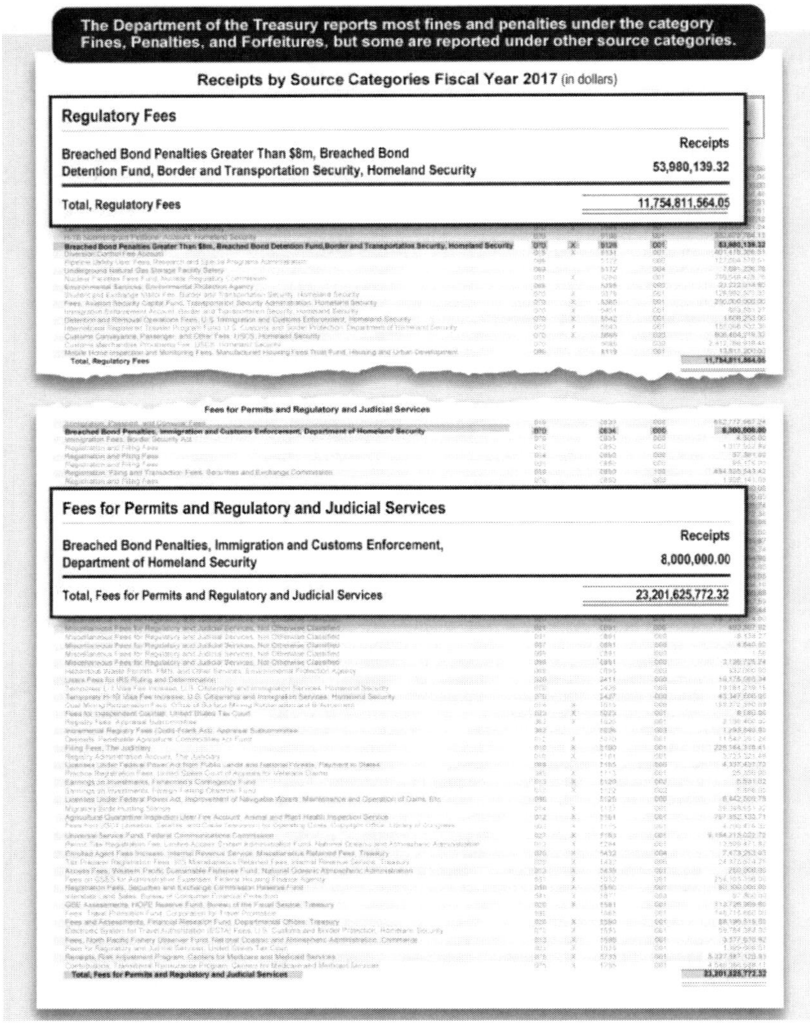

Source: GAO analysis of Department of the Treasury's Combined Statement of Receipts, Outlays and Balances. | GAO-19-221.

Figure 2. Examples of Penalties Not Categorized as Fines, Penalties, and Forfeitures in the Department of the Treasury's *Combined Statement of Receipts, Outlays, and Balances.*

In addition to the government-wide data sources, agencies report some data on their collections of specific fees, fines, and penalties in their annual financial reports, congressional budget justifications, and on agency websites. These data are dispersed by agency, are not comprehensive, and cannot be aggregated to create government-wide data because they vary in format and in the level of detail presented. For example:

- The Environmental Protection Agency (EPA) has an online, searchable database of enforcement and compliance information that includes data on individual fine and penalty assessments for violations of certain, but not all, statutes.[25]
- The Department of Labor also makes selected enforcement data accessible in an online database collected by the Employee Benefits Security Administration, the Mine Safety and Health Administration, the Occupational Safety and Health Administration, and the Wage and Hour Division without Department of Labor-wide data standards on individual fine and penalty assessments.[26]
- USDA's Animal and Plant Health Inspection Service's 2019 Congressional Budget Justification, on the other hand, is a PDF document that provides annual collection totals for Agriculture Quarantine Inspection Fees, Import-Export User Fees, Phytosanitary Certificate User Fees, Veterinary Diagnostics User Fees, and Other User Fees, rather than disaggregated to individual fee assessments.

---

[25] According to EPA, its Enforcement and Compliance History Online (ECHO) website contains enforcement actions from violations of specific statutes at: (1) Clean Air Act (CAA) stationary source facilities, (2) Clean Water Act (CWA) major direct discharge facilities, (3) Resource Conservation and Recovery Act hazardous waste handlers, and (4) systems violations of the Safe Drinking Water Act. EPA regulates facilities under many other programs and statutes that are not shown in the ECHO site. Data not generally available within ECHO include: (1) most violations at CWA minor direct discharge facilities, (2) CAA mobile source and asbestos violations, and (3) Superfund violations. See EPA's ECHO website for more information: https://echo.epa.gov/.

[26] For more information, see: https://enforcedata.dol.gov.

OMB Reports Government-wide Totals that Cannot Be Disaggregated and Does Not Disclose Limitations or Regularly Review Its Designation of Fees

OMB Reports Government-wide Data That Cannot Be Disaggregated

The government-wide totals for fees that OMB reports in *Analytical Perspectives* are not presented at a more disaggregated level, such as by agency or program, except for some major fee collections identified by OMB.[27] For example, in *Analytical Perspectives* for fiscal year 2017, OMB reported $335.4 billion as a government-wide total of fee collections.[28] OMB also reported some disaggregated data for the subset of fees that were offsetting collections and offsetting receipts. Specifically, it listed 11 fees totaling $258.4 billion collected by specific agencies and listed the remaining $72.3 billion as "all other user charges" without identifying the agency or program. As described in Table 1 above, clear and accessible data can be aggregated or disaggregated by the user. OMB has more detailed data on collections in OMB MAX, including the agency, account, type of collection, and fund type, which it uses to compile reported totals of fees as well as fines, penalties, and forfeitures.

OMB does not publicly report these data disaggregated below the government-wide level, such as at the agency level. OMB staff said that they do not report the disaggregated data because the purpose of *Analytical Perspectives* is to develop or support the President's policies and more detailed tables may not be included if they are not considered necessary for that purpose. However, *Analytical Perspectives* also serves to provide other significant data that place the President's Budget in context and assist the public and policymakers in better understanding the budget proposals. For example, *Analytical Perspectives* includes a chapter on aid to state and local governments that presents the President's budget proposals for grant

---

[27] Major collections include, for example, proceeds from Postal Service sales, electrical power sales, proceeds from military assistance program sales, and rents and royalties from Outer Continental Shelf oil extraction.

[28] OMB uses the term user charges for user fees in its annual budget documents. We define these terms interchangeably (see GAO-05-734SP) and use the term fee for the purposes of this chapter.

programs along with crosscutting information on federal grants to state and local governments, including government-wide grant spending, by agency and program. *Analytical Perspectives* also presents a summary of fee proposals but does not provide comparable crosscutting information about current fees. For fines and penalties, neither proposals nor crosscutting information is presented by agency. Until OMB makes more disaggregated data on fees, fines, and penalties maintained in its OMB MAX database—such as collections by agency—publicly available, Congress has limited information on such collections to inform oversight and decision-making.

OMB Does Not Disclose Limitations or Regularly Review Its Designation of Fees

Analytical Perspectives' government-wide totals of fees may include inaccurately labeled collections—other collections that are not fees—and may exclude some fee collections. Data that are clear and accessible are presented with known limitations, as shown in Table 1. OMB Circular No. A-11 states that all accounts in which more than half of collections are from fees will be designated as containing fees. OMB staff said that the entire account is designated as containing fees because account-level data are the most disaggregated data OMB collects from agencies. OMB calculates its government-wide total for fees by adding collections in all accounts designated in OMB MAX as containing user fees. However, agency accounts can include multiple sources of budget authority. For example, Treasury's U.S. Mint's account "United States Mint Public Enterprise Fund" includes offsetting collections from Mint operations and programs; these include the production and sale of commemorative coins and medals, the production and sale of circulating coinage, the protection of government assets, as well as gifts and bequests of property.[29] The United States Mint Public Enterprise Fund is designated as containing fees in OMB MAX. Therefore, budget authority that is not derived from the collection of fees but is still included in this account will be designated as fees as well when calculating a government-wide total.

---

[29] Our 2013 review of fee-funded agencies examined unobligated balances in the U.S. Mint account.GAO-13-820.

Conversely, accounts in which fees contribute to less than half of collections are not designated as containing fees amounts, and those fees will not be included in the government-wide total OMB calculates. OMB Circular No. A-11 describes the designation of fee accounts, but the data presented in *Analytical Perspectives* as totals for fees do not disclose OMB's designation criteria, including the limitations to the accuracy of the data. OMB staff said they do not report this limitation because they consider OMB Circular No. A-11 a more appropriate document for providing technical information like the designation of accounts containing user fees. However, the section on fees in *Analytical Perspectives* does not direct the reader to OMB Circular No. A-11 for key information related to the data presented on fees. For other topics, including lease-purchase agreements, *Analytical Perspectives* directs the reader to OMB Circular No. A-11 for further details. Furthermore, for other topics, OMB provided explanatory information along with the data in *Analytical Perspectives*. For example, OMB explained a recent change to definitions in the research and development section of *Analytical Perspectives* and the effect of the change on budget authority. Until OMB provides a description of data limitations regarding the criteria used to identify accounts with fees for compiling government-wide totals in *Analytical Perspectives*, or directs users to the relevant section of OMB Circular No. A-11, some users are likely to be unaware of the potential for the total user fees to be overestimated or underestimated.

In addition, OMB does not regularly review and update implementation of its criteria for designating fees. *Standards for Internal Control in the Federal Government* state that agency management should use quality information to achieve the objectives, such as processing data into quality information that is current and accurate.[30] OMB Circular No. A-11 states that the fee designation is applied at the time the account is established. OMB staff told us that when establishing a new account, OMB collaborates with Treasury to determine the legal attributes of the account, including any fee authorities, and whether to designate the account as

---

[30] GAO-14-704G.

containing fees. OMB staff further explained they review the designation when new legislation is enacted that would change the attributes of the account, or if an agency informs OMB that the makeup of an account has changed because of programmatic changes. However, OMB Circular No. A-11 does not instruct agencies to regularly review or update this designation and report changes to OMB. Therefore, if the makeup of collections in an account changes so that fees go from being more than half of the collections to less than half, or vice versa, the account's fee designation may not be updated accordingly. Until OMB instructs agencies to regularly review the fee designation in OMB MAX and update the designation, as needed, OMB cannot provide reasonable assurance that accounts are designated correctly, and that the government-wide totals of fees reported in *Analytical Perspectives* are accurate.

OMB and Treasury Sources Do Not Completely Identify Fees, Fines, and Penalties

Users Cannot Disaggregate the Agency Account-Level Data to Specific Fee, Fine, and Penalty Collections

While *Analytical Perspectives* reports government-wide data labeled as fees, fines, and penalties, the other three sources we reviewed—the *Budget Appendix*, the Public Budget Database, and the *Combined Statement*—report account-level information by agency. Users cannot further disaggregate the data presented to specific fee, fine, and penalty collections. For example, USDA's Animal and Plant Health Inspection Service (APHIS) is funded in part by six fees: (1) Agricultural Quarantine Inspection (AQI) fee, (2) Phytosanitary Export Certification fee, (3) Veterinary Services Import Export fee, (4) Veterinary Diagnostics fee, (5) Reimbursable Overtime, and (6) Trust Funds and Reimbursable Funds.[31] However, a user cannot identify collections from each of these APHIS fees in the *Budget Appendix*. The *Budget Appendix* specifically identifies AQI

[31] We reported on the APHIS fees in our 2016 report on permanent funding authorities. See GAO-17-59.

fee collections—$768 million in fiscal year 2017—because they are receipts deposited to a trust fund. The other five fees are combined within the total for offsetting collections—$152 million (see Figure 3).

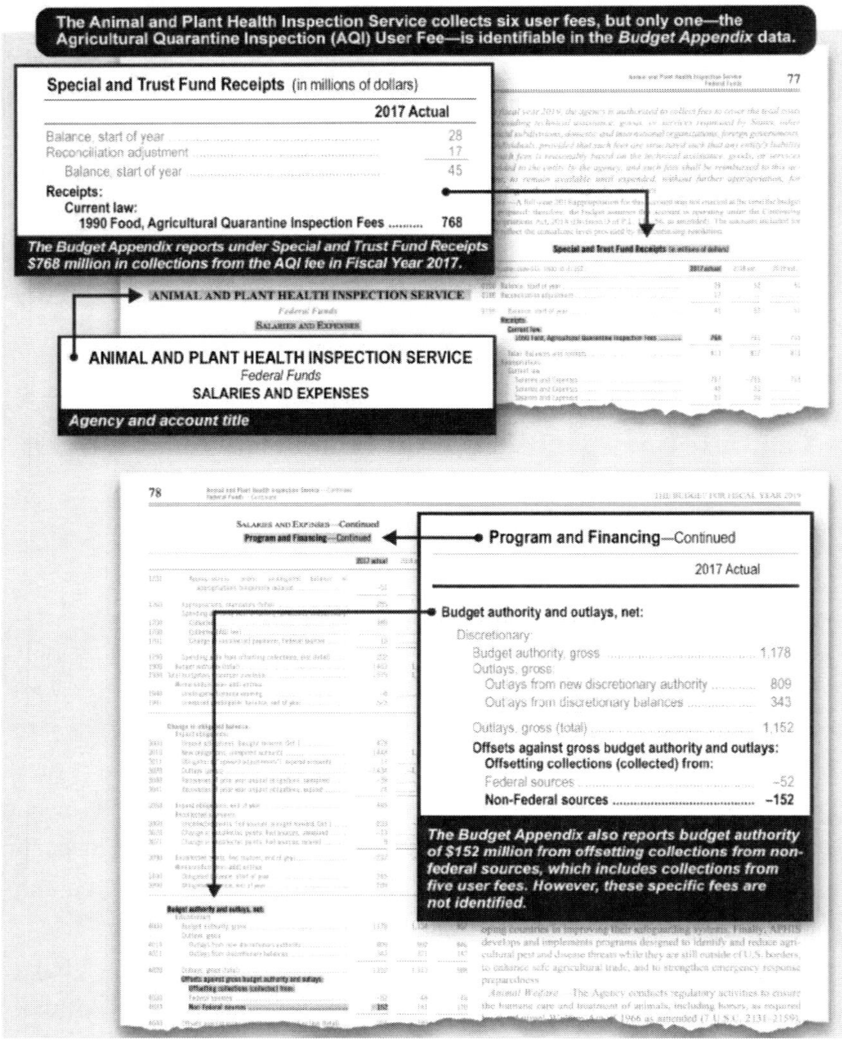

Source: GAO analysis of the Budget Appendix.

Figure 3. The *Budget Appendix* Reporting of Fee Collections by the Animal and Plant Health Inspection Service.

The *Budget Appendix*, the Public Budget Database, and the *Combined Statement* report data at the account level because the purposes of these reports are broader than fees, fines, and penalties, and OMB and Treasury instruct agencies to report data at that level. Treasury's Financial Manual states that agencies post appropriations and spending authorizations by Congress to accounts established by Treasury. OMB's Circular No. A-11 instructs agencies to report data at the budget account level in OMB MAX, which supports the data in the *Budget Appendix* and the Public Budget Database. Because OMB and Treasury do not collect data that can be disaggregated to the level of fee, fine, or penalty, the collections for specific fees, fines, and penalties within accounts are not identifiable within account totals.

OMB Data Sources Label Data More Broadly than Fees, Fines, and Penalties

Both the *Budget Appendix* and Public Budget Database label and present data within each account by collection type: offsetting collections, offsetting receipts, and governmental receipts. These collection types include fees, fines, and penalties, as well as other sources of collections, as shown in the text box below.

Budgetary Collections as Labeled by the *Budget of the U.S. Government* Include More than Fees, Fines, and Penalties

- Offsetting Collections and Offsetting Receipts include user fees as well as reimbursements for damages, intragovernmental transactions, and voluntary gifts and donations to the government.
- Governmental Receipts include collections that result from the government's exercise of its sovereign power to tax or otherwise compel payment, and include taxes, compulsory user fees, regulatory fees, customs duties, court fines, certain license fees, and deposits of earnings by the Federal Reserve System.

Source: Fiscal Year 2019 *Analytical Perspectives.* | GAO-19-221

As a result, the user cannot separate fees, fines, and penalties from other collections. For example, offsetting collections may include fees, reimbursements for damages, gifts or donations of money to the government, and intragovernmental transactions with other government accounts.[32]

Analytical Perspectives explains that amounts collected by government agencies are recorded in two ways that broadly affect the formulation of the government-wide budget, but may not provide detail on specific agency collections: (1) governmental receipts, which are compared to total outlays in calculating the surplus or deficit; and (2) offsetting collections or offsetting receipts, which are deducted from gross outlays to calculate net outlay figures. These collections are presented together for budgeting purposes, but cannot be separated to specific fees, fines, or penalties. Therefore, it is not clear what percentage of the reported collections are fees, fines, and penalties as opposed to other collections.

OMB Does Not Clearly Describe How the Public Budget Database Reports Certain Fee, Fine, and Penalty Collections

Treasury's *Combined Statement* and OMB's Public Budget Database do not identify offsetting collections, including collections of fees, fines, and penalties. Instead, the *Combined Statement* reports net outlays, which include any offsetting collections as deductions from outlays. Similarly, the Public Budget Database reports budget authority net of any offsetting collections. Treasury clearly describes this presentation of the data in the *Combined Statement*, but OMB does not in the Public Budget Database. In the "Explanation of Transactions and Basis of Figures" section of the *Combined Statement*, Treasury describes that outlays are stated net of collections representing reimbursements as authorized by law, which include offsetting collections. With the description provided in the *Combined Statement*, the user can understand that fees, fines, and penalties that are offsetting collections are not identifiable in the data.

---

[32] We have reported on budget authority that Congress has either provided in laws other than annual appropriations acts, or through permanent appropriations that permit the agency to obligate budget authority without further congressional action. This chapter includes fees, fines, and penalties that have offsetting collections authority. See GAO, *Federal Budget: Government-Wide Inventory of Accounts with Spending Authority and Permanent Appropriations, 1995 to 2015*, GAO-19-36 (Washington, D.C.: Nov. 29, 2018).

Offsetting Collections are Offsets to Spending in the Budget

According to Fiscal Year 2019, *Analytical Perspectives*, offsetting collections are recorded as offsets to spending so that the budget totals for receipts and (net) outlays reflect the amount of resources allocated by the government through collective political choice, rather than through the marketplace. Fees, fines, or penalties can be offsetting collections.

Source: Fiscal Year 2019 *Analytical Perspectives*. | GAO-19-221

OMB reports receipts and budget authority—which include collections from fees, fines, and penalties—in separate spreadsheets of the Public Budget Database. Similar to outlays reported in Treasury's *Combined Statement*, the Budget Authority spreadsheet reports the net budget authority of accounts after agencies have credited offsetting collections from fees, fines, penalties, or other collections. For example, the National Park Service reported net budget authority of $2.425 billion for the Operation of the National Park System account in fiscal year 2017 in both the *Budget Appendix* and the Public Budget Database, both of which present data compiled in OMB MAX. The *Budget Appendix* presents additional information, reporting offsetting collections that are at least partially derived from fees of $35 million, and gross budget authority of $2.46 billion, as shown in Figure 4. The Public Budget Database, on the other hand, does not identify the amount of offsetting collections in the account or gross budget authority.

OMB does not describe this presentation of the data in the Public Budget Database User's Guide. As shown in Table 1, data that are clear and accessible are presented with descriptions of the data. The User's Guide directs users who may not be familiar with federal budget concepts to *Analytical Perspectives* and OMB Circular No. A-11. However, OMB does not describe, either in the User's Guide or in the Budget Authority spreadsheet of the Public Budget Database, that this source reports budget authority net of offsetting collections, such as collections of fees, fines, and penalties. OMB staff said they do not describe the presentation because it is explained in *Analytical Perspectives*. However, the Public Budget

Database is available for download separate from *Analytical Perspectives*, and the User's Guide specific to the Public Budget Database includes other information describing the data in the spreadsheets.[33] Describing the presentation of the data in the User's Guide would help ensure that users of the Public Budget Database can correctly interpret the information and not underestimate agencies' fee, fine, or penalty collections.

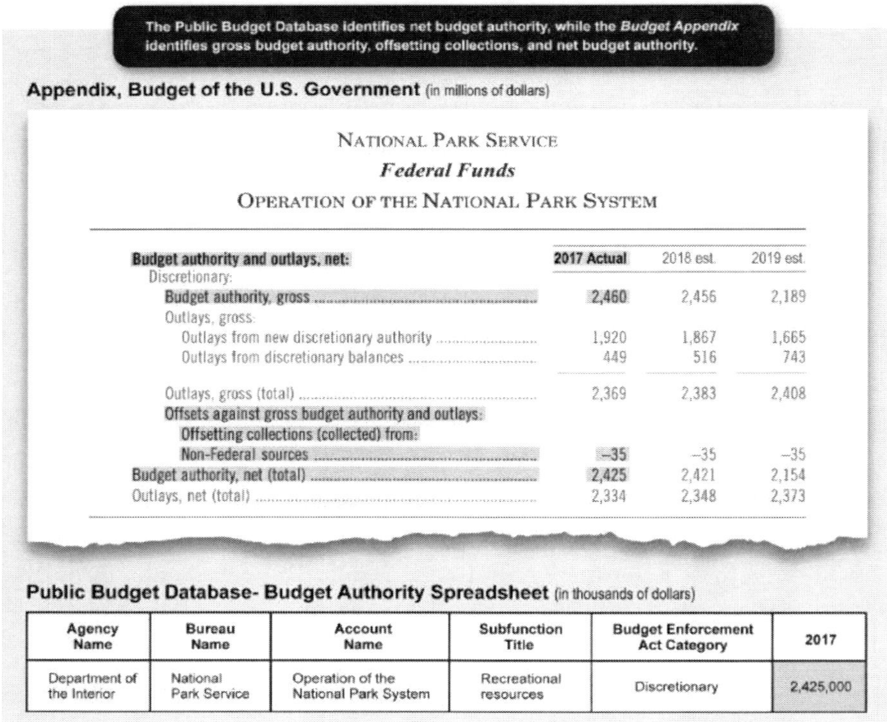

The Public Budget Database identifies net budget authority, while the *Budget Appendix* identifies gross budget authority, offsetting collections, and net budget authority.

Appendix, Budget of the U.S. Government (in millions of dollars)

NATIONAL PARK SERVICE

Federal Funds

OPERATION OF THE NATIONAL PARK SYSTEM

Budget authority and outlays, net:	2017 Actual	2018 est.	2019 est.
Discretionary:			
Budget authority, gross	2,460	2,456	2,189
Outlays, gross:			
Outlays from new discretionary authority	1,920	1,867	1,665
Outlays from discretionary balances	449	516	743
Outlays, gross (total)	2,369	2,383	2,408
Offsets against gross budget authority and outlays:			
Offsetting collections (collected) from:			
Non-Federal sources	–35	–35	–35
Budget authority, net (total)	2,425	2,421	2,154
Outlays, net (total)	2,334	2,348	2,373

Public Budget Database- Budget Authority Spreadsheet (in thousands of dollars)

Agency Name	Bureau Name	Account Name	Subfunction Title	Budget Enforcement Act Category	2017
Department of the Interior	National Park Service	Operation of the National Park System	Recreational resources	Discretionary	2,425,000

Source: GAO analysis of the Budget Appendix and the Public Budget Database. | GAO-19-221.

Figure 4. Offsetting Collections Are Not Identifiable in the Public Budget Database.

---

[33] The Public Budget Database User's Guide describes the spreadsheets that make up the Public Budget Database, including information on data sources and limitations. This information includes details such as the unit of measure used in the spreadsheets; the inclusion of budget estimates with historical data; information not included, such as object classes, which are categories that present obligations by the items or services purchased by the federal government; and, instances in which the data do not present account-level data.

Government-wide Sources Do Not Consistently Report Data that Would Facilitate Oversight

	Budget Appendix	Public Budget Database	Combined Statement of Receipts, Outlays, and Balances
Descriptive title	⚠	⚠	⚠
Agency administering	⚠	⚠	⚠
Agency collecting	⚠	X	X
Annual dollar amount collected for multiple years	X	⚠	X
Account balance	⚠	X	⚠
Authorities to collect and obligate funds	⚠	X	X
Limitations on obligations	⚠	X	X
Categories of collections (i.e. budget collection type, budget function)	⚠	⚠	⚠
Review requirement	X	X	X
Reporting requirement	X	X	X
Fund type receiving collection	⚠	⚠	⚠

✓ Data element included

⚠ Data element included to a limited extent (i.e., element included for some, but not all, fees, fines, and penalties)

X Data element not included

Source: GAO analysis of Office of Management and Budget and Department of the Treasury reports. | GAO-19-221.

Note: We identified data elements useful for congressional oversight based on our prior work on fees, fines, and penalties as well as input from staff of congressional committees on appropriations, budget, and oversight.

Figure 5. Extent to Which Government-wide Reports Include Data Elements Useful for the Purpose of Congressional Oversight of Fees, Fines, and Penalties.

No source of government-wide data consistently reports data elements related to fees, fines, and penalties that could help inform congressional oversight of agencies and programs, such as the amount collected annually, account balances, and whether the collection is a fee, fine, or penalty. See Figure 5 for the extent to which data elements are included in the *Budget Appendix*, Public Budget Database, and *Combined Statement*.[34] See

[34] We reviewed *Analytical Perspectives* but did not include it in our analysis for useful for congressional oversight because the data it reports on fees, fines, and penalties are presented

appendix I for more detailed information on the data elements that are useful for congressional oversight.

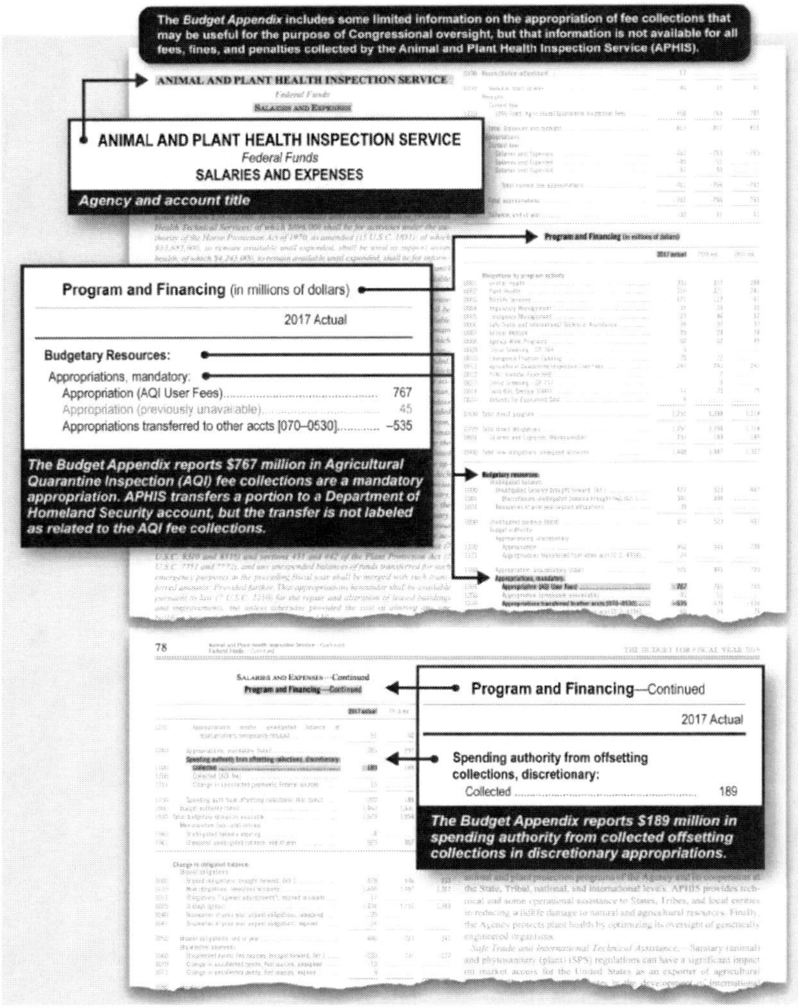

Source: GAO analysis of the Budget Appendix. | GAO-19-221.

Figure 6. The *Budget Appendix* Reports Some Information on Fee Collections that is Useful for Congressional Oversight.

---

in aggregate government-wide totals, and are not designed to report account-level or more detailed information.

To a limited extent there are some cases where government-wide reports included data elements useful for the purpose of congressional oversight of fees, fines, and penalties. In some cases the *Budget Appendix* includes information on the fund type receiving collections and the extent to which the collections from fees may be appropriated to the agency collecting the fee. The *Budget Appendix*, for example, reports that collections for the Agricultural Quarantine Inspection (AQI) fee are recorded under "Special and Trust Fund Receipts," as shown previously in Figure 3. The user can also identify the appropriation of collections from the AQI fee under "Program and Financing, Budgetary resources," as shown below in Figure 6. As discussed previously, the other five fees the Animal and Plant Health Inspection Service (APHIS) collects are not individually identifiable in the *Budget Appendix*, but fall under offsetting collections.

OMB and Treasury reports, and the systems that support them, are designed for budget and financial information and not for an inventory of fees, fines, and penalties that includes the data elements that Congress may use in oversight. OMB staff said the agency does not have a requirement to prioritize reporting fee, fine, and penalty data over more detailed information on other types of funds. OMB staff said while they generally agree that additional data elements would be useful for oversight, there are trade-offs between transparency and the burden of collecting and reporting additional information.

Better Reporting of Government-wide Data on Fees, Fines, and Penalties Would Increase Transparency and Data Available for Oversight, but Would Require an Investment of Federal Resources

Benefits Include Increased Transparency and Better Information for Oversight and Decision-Making

According to OMB staff and officials from Treasury, the Congressional Research Service, and external organizations with expertise in federal budget issues and data transparency, there are two primary benefits to government-wide reporting of fee, fine, and penalty data: increased transparency and better information for congressional oversight and decision-making. Generally, all congressional staff we spoke with said making additional government-wide data on fees, fines, and penalties, such as those data elements described previously, without additional outreach to agencies, would be useful and increase transparency. While some congressional staff said such data elements are available through direct outreach to agencies, other congressional staff told us they could not always obtain the information they wanted. For example, staff from a congressional committee said that one of the most critical data elements for the purpose of congressional oversight is information on agency reporting of obligations and expenditures because, in their view, currently many agencies do not adequately report this information and some agencies do not report this information at all. These data would provide Congress a more complete picture of individual agencies' activities and any potential overlap or duplication in multiple agencies' activities. Congressional staff also said having government-wide data on collections of fees could inform efforts that are crosscutting in nature. For example, APHIS and Customs and Border Protection jointly implement the AQI program to help prevent the introduction of harmful agricultural pests and diseases into the United States, and AQI fee collections are divided between the two agencies.

Publicly available data on government-wide collections of fines and penalties could inform the public on agency enforcement activities and compliance of regulated parties, such as those related to health or safety. Some officials from external organizations and congressional staff said that it would be useful to have government-wide data on individual fines and penalties levied by agencies. For example, the Environmental Protection Agency publishes an online database on its compliance and enforcement actions, *Enforcement and Compliance History Online* (ECHO).[35] According to the website, the data available on ECHO allows the public to monitor environmental compliance in communities, corporations to

[35] For more information on ECHO, see: https://echo.epa.gov/.

monitor compliance across facilities they own, and investors to more easily factor environmental performance into decisions. Further, an official from an external organization with expertise in data transparency stated that, ideally, a user would be able to link fine and penalty data to spending data on USAspending.gov to increase transparency in instances where an organization receiving a federal grant or contract has also had a fine or penalty levied against it.

Last, publicly available government-wide data on collections could inform the public, specifically payers of fees, fines, and penalties, and facilitate their participation in public comment opportunities. For example, OMB staff said government-wide data could provide the public with clear, transparent information across agencies on fee collections and allow the public to analyze differences in fee programs among agencies. Payers of fees may be able to make more informed comments on proposed changes to a fee program if they had information on how it relates to other fee programs across the federal government.

Government-wide fee, fine, and penalty data would provide more information to facilitate congressional oversight. These data could help Congress identify trends in collections and significant changes that could be an indication of an agency's performance. For example, staff of a Congressional committee stated that fine and penalty data can be used to examine enforcement actions on a particular issue or to identify potential trends over time as an indicator of stronger or weaker enforcement actions by an agency. Congress could also use these data to identify variations in enforcement action among geographic regions or as an indicator of the frequency of violations.

Additionally, data on review and reporting requirements can inform congressional oversight of fees, fines, and penalties. We previously reported that regular comprehensive reviews of fees provide opportunities for agencies and Congress to make improvements to a fee's design which, if left unaddressed, could contribute to inefficient use of government resources.[36] For example, fee reviews could help ensure that

[36] GAO-12-342SP.

fees are properly set to cover the total costs of those activities which are intended to be fully fee-funded. Fee reviews may also allow agencies and Congress to identify where similar activities are funded differently; for example, one by fees and one by appropriations. One such example is the export control system, in which the State Department charges fees for the export of items on the U.S. Munitions List, while the Commerce Department does not charge fees for those items exported under its jurisdiction.

Government-wide reporting of fee, fine, and penalty data could also inform Congress's funding decisions by providing a clearer picture of agencies' total resources. Congressional staff stated that knowing the statutory authority to collect and obligate funding from fees, fines, and penalties—along with any appropriation an agency may have received from an annual appropriation act, which are currently available to congressional staff—would provide a more complete picture of an agency's total annual funding, including the portion attributed to the taxpayer and the portion attributed to payers of specific fees, fines, and penalties. For example, staff from congressional committees we spoke with said it would be useful to have data to show programs that receive appropriations from both offsetting collections and appropriations not derived from offsetting collections to inform decisions on how the program is funded. Congressional staff also said this would provide more opportunities to track the flow of money in and out of the government. Overall funding decisions may be affected if an agency has an increase in fee collections, for example. Congressional committee staff also said it would be useful to have government-wide data on specific fees, fines, and penalties that are offsetting collections because these collections are available for obligation without going through the annual appropriations process. Our prior work has shown that it is important to consider how the agencies and entities with this authority facilitate oversight to ensure effective management, transparency, and public accountability.[37] Some committee staff said they can request data directly from agencies when

[37] GAO-17-59.

they need more disaggregated information on fees, fines, and penalties, and reported different levels of responsiveness from agencies. Publicly available data could reduce potentially overlapping or duplicative requests from staff to agencies.

Potential Challenges Exist for Standardizing Definitions of Fees, Fines, and Penalties

According to officials from agencies and external organizations, there are potential challenges to defining the government-wide data standard or definition of fee, fine, and penalty programs by which agencies could report. Because there is no statutory requirement for government-wide reporting of fee, fine, and penalty data, agencies collect and use these data for their own purposes, and are not using government-wide data elements and standards that are consistent and comparable between agencies. First, an agency may define a fee program as a single fee or a set of related fees. For example, the U.S. Citizenship and Immigration Services charges more than 40 immigration and naturalization fees to applicants and petitioners that could be grouped together as related fees or split into up to 40 different fee programs. Second, officials from external organizations said there are also challenges in defining data standards the level of detail to report.[38] For example, an official from an external organization said, for large financial penalties, it may be useful for oversight for the data to identify each instance of the penalty, including the fined party. However, that level of detail could raise privacy sensitivities. For example, reporting every individual that paid an entrance fee at a national park could present privacy concerns. Finally, for elements that are useful for congressional oversight, one challenge could be the timing of when funds are collected compared to when they are available for obligation. The amount of funds collected in a year does not necessarily equal the amount available to the agency that

---

[38] In December 2018, we found that, while providing users with detailed and disaggregated data is a key action for transparently reporting open government data, in some cases, aggregation may be necessary to protect sensitive information so that the dataset can be released to the public. See GAO, *Open Data: Treasury Could Better Align USAspending.gov with Key Practices and Legal Requirements,* GAO-19-72 (Washington, D.C.: Dec. 13, 2018).

year. For example, collections of Harbor Maintenance Fees are deposited to the Harbor Maintenance Trust Fund and are not available for obligation without appropriation. Funds collected in one year may not be necessarily appropriated and obligated until a subsequent year.

Our prior work on the Digital Accountability and Transparency Act of 2014 (DATA Act) implementation underscores the importance of standardized and clearly defined data elements. We found inconsistent and potentially confusing instructions from OMB regarding the *Primary Place of Performance* data elements that resulted in inconsistent reporting among agencies.[39] The standard established by OMB and Treasury defines *Primary Place of Performance* as "where the predominant performance of the award will be accomplished" while other instructions define it as "the location of the principal plant or place of business where the items will be produced, supplied from stock, or where the service will be performed."[40] We found some agencies used the first definition and some used the second. In one case, the Departments of Labor and Health and Human Services issued contracts to the same company for similar office printers, but one reported the primary place of performance as California, the location of the office where the printers were delivered and used. The other agency reported the primary place of performance as New Jersey, the location of the company that supplied the printers. As a result, the data were not comparable between agencies or across the federal government, limiting the usefulness for congressional oversight. We previously recommended that OMB and Treasury provide additional instruction to agencies on how to report Primary Place of Performance to ensure the definitions are clear and the data standards are implemented consistently by agencies.[41]

---

[39] GAO, *DATA Act: OMB, Treasury, and Agencies Need to Improve Completeness and Accuracy of Spending Data and Disclose Limitations*, GAO-18-138 (Washington, D.C.: Nov. 8, 2017).

[40] The four Primary Place of Performance data elements standardized by OMB and Treasury in 2015 are: (1) Primary Place of Performance Address; (2) Primary Place of Performance Congressional District; (3) Primary Place of Performance Country Code; and (4) Primary Place of Performance Country Name.

[41] See GAO, *DATA Act: Data Standards Established, but More Complete and Timely Guidance Is Needed to Ensure Effective Implementation*. GAO-16-261 (Washington,

Staff from one congressional committee cautioned that attempts to present information on budget authorities for fees, fines, and penalties in a simple and accessible database create an unacceptable risk of confusion and legislative error. The staff said an accurate description of the nature of the spending–-including whether there is authority to obligate without further appropriation–-would be labor intensive and require significant legal analysis and research.

Government-wide Reporting Would Require an Investment of Federal Resources

Government-wide reporting of fees, fines, and penalties could increase transparency and facilitate oversight and decision-making, but would require time and resources to develop given that there is currently no government-wide system or requirements for agencies to collect and report detailed fee, fine, and penalty data. The level of federal investment would vary depending on factors, such as the number of data elements included and the level of detail reported. Developing a comprehensive and accessible data source would provide greater benefits, but would likely be resource intensive. We have reported on other federal transparency efforts that could provide strategies for reporting government-wide fee, fine, and penalty data. For example, to create a clear and accessible government-wide data source that includes the data elements we identified that would be useful for congressional oversight, Treasury officials said the process would be similar to the implementation of the DATA Act for spending data. To implement the DATA Act, OMB and Treasury led an intensive effort starting in May 2014 through May 2017 when the first government-wide data were reported under the DATA Act's new standards.

- Data Standards: OMB, in coordination with Treasury, established 57 standardized data element definitions and approximately 400 associated sub-elements for reporting federal spending

---

D.C.: Jan. 29, 2016). While OMB generally concurred with our recommendation, as of November 2018, OMB had not implemented our recommendation on Primary Place of Performance.

information. OMB and Treasury created opportunities for non-federal stakeholders to provide input into the development of data standards, including publishing a *Federal Register* notice seeking public comment on the establishment of financial data standards; presenting periodic updates on the status of DATA Act implementation to federal and non-federal stakeholders at meetings and conferences; soliciting public comment on data standards using an online collaboration space; and collaborating with federal agencies on the development of data standards and the technical schema through MAX.gov, an OMB-supported website.

- Technical Process for Reporting: Treasury developed the initial DATA Act Information Model Schema, which provided information on how to standardize the way financial assistance awards, contracts, and other financial and nonfinancial data would be collected and reported under the DATA Act.
- System to Collect and Validate Data: Treasury developed a system that collects and validates agency data (the DATA Act Broker), which operationalizes the reporting framework laid out in the schema. In addition, Treasury employed online software development tools to provide responses to stakeholder questions and comments related to the development and revision of the broker.
- Public Reporting: Treasury created and updated the new USAspending.gov website to display certified agency data submitted under the DATA Act.[42]

Agencies also took steps to prepare to report spending data. They reviewed data elements OMB identified, participated in standardizing the definitions, performed an inventory of their existing data and associated business processes, and updated their systems and processes to report data

[42] While USAspending.gov was first released in 2007, Treasury recently developed a new version of the website to report information submitted under the DATA Act. For more information on the new USAspending.gov, see GAO-19-72.

to Treasury.[43] OMB and Treasury issued policy directions to help agencies meet their reporting requirements under the act. They also conducted a series of meetings with participating agencies to obtain information on any challenges that could impede effective implementation and assess agencies' readiness to report required spending data.

Although the steps to developing comprehensive, detailed reporting on government-wide collections of fees, fines, and penalties might be similar to the DATA Act efforts, the dollar amounts of collections would be smaller than those of federal spending. In fiscal year 2017, federal spending was $3.98 trillion compared to about $350 billion in collections of fees, fines, penalties, and forfeitures reported by OMB.[44] On the other hand, defining data elements and standards for fee, fine, and penalty data could be more resource intensive than developing data standards for DATA Act implementation because the DATA Act built on earlier reporting requirements. The DATA Act amended the Federal Funding Accountability and Transparency Act of 2006 (FFATA), which required OMB to establish the website USAspending.gov to report data on federal awards, including contracts, grants, and loans. The DATA Act required OMB and Treasury to standardize data required to be reported by FFATA. For fee, fine, and penalty data, OMB and Treasury would be starting without the benefit of some data elements already defined. Further, we have previously reported that effective implementation of provisions to make federal data publicly available, including the DATA Act and GPRAMA's program inventory, especially the ability to crosswalk spending data to individual programs, could provide vital information to

---

[43] Consistent with our mandate under the DATA Act, we reviewed the quality of the data collected under the act that agencies reported beginning in May 2017 and made available through Beta.USAspending.gov. We found that a total of 78 federal agencies, including all 24 CFO Act agencies, submitted data by May 2017, as required by the act. However, we identified issues and challenges with the completeness and accuracy of the data submitted, use of data elements, and presentation of the data on Beta.USAspending.gov. We made two recommendations to OMB regarding technical assistance and clarifying directions to help ensure agencies fully comply with DATA Act requirements and report data completely and accurately; and four recommendations to Treasury, including disclosing known data quality issues on its website. While OMB and Treasury generally agreed with our recommendations as of November 2018, five of these recommendations remained open. For more information, see GAO-18-138.

[44] As previously discussed, OMB's figure could be overstated or understated.

assist federal decision makers in addressing significant challenges the government faces.[45]

Incorporating a small number of data elements that Congress identifies as most useful for oversight into ongoing government-wide agency reporting efforts could incrementally improve transparency and information for oversight and decision-making, with fewer resources. For example, Congress required agencies to add selected data elements to their annual financial reports on civil monetary penalties. Specifically, the Federal Civil Penalties Adjustment Act Improvements Act of 2015 requires agencies to include information about the civil monetary penalties within the agencies' jurisdiction, including catch-up inflation adjustment of the civil monetary penalty amounts, in annual agency financial reports or performance and accountability reports.[46] As shown in Figure 7, to facilitate agencies' reporting, OMB provided a table to define the data elements required in the act in its annual instructions, OMB Circular No. A-136, *Financial Reporting Requirements*.[47]

Agencies started reporting these data in their agency financial reports in fiscal year 2016. In July 2018, we reported that 40 of 45 required agencies reported in their fiscal year 2017 agency financial report information on civil monetary penalties as directed by the OMB instructions.[48] Similarly, if Congress sought additional fine and penalty data elements, such as amounts collected and authority to spend collections, OMB could expand this table in Circular No. A-136 to include those data elements. Circular No. A-136 also outlines that agencies may include the results of biennial reviews of fees and other collections in their agency financial reports. OMB could also update this portion of the circular to require agencies to report specific data elements that are useful for oversight, such as review and reporting requirements. While this information reported in agency financial reports would be disaggregated in

---

[45] GAO, *DATA Act: Progress Made in Initial Implementation but Challenges Must be Addressed as Efforts Proceed*, GAO-15-752T (Washington, D.C.: July 29, 2015).

[46] Pub. L. No. 114-74, title VII, § 701, 129 Stat. 584, 599-601 (Nov. 2, 2015), codified at 28 U.S.C. § 2461 note.

[47] For information on agencies' compliance with the act, see GAO-17-634.

[48] GAO-18-519.

portable document format, or PDF, documents, it would provide some transparency on agencies' activities that Congress could use to prioritize its oversight efforts.

OMB Circular No. A-136: *Financial Reporting Requirements*

II.4.9. Civil Monetary Penalty Adjustment for Inflation

Under the Federal Civil Penalties Inflation Adjustment Act Improvements Act of 2015, agencies must make annual inflation adjustments to civil monetary penalties and report on the adjustments in their AFR or PAR.

Agencies must include, as OI, information about civil monetary penalties within their jurisdiction and the adjustments made under the Act and are encouraged to include a table providing this information. The following is an illustrative example from the Department of Labor's FY 2017 Financial Report.

Statutory Authority	Penalty Name & Description	Year Enacted	Latest year of adjustment (via statute or regulation)	Current Penalty (Dollar Amount or Range)	Bureau Name	Location for Penalty Update Details
29 U.S.C. 211 (d); 29 CFR 530.302 (a), (b)	Fair Labor Standards Act (FLSA) Homeworker: Violation of recordkeeping, monetary, certificate or other statutes, regulations or employer assurances.	1938	2017	Minimum: $20, Maximum: $1,005.	WHD	https://www/ecfr.gov/ 82 FR 5386 (January 18, 2017)

Source: Office of Management and Budget. | GAO-19-221.

Note: In the figure above, AFR refers to agency financial report and PAR refers to performance and accountability report. OI refers to other information.

Figure 7. Office of Management and Budget (OMB) Instructions to Agencies on Reporting Data on Civil Monetary Penalties.

In another example, if OMB implements the federal program inventory as required by GPRAMA, it could include a data element on whether a program has a fee, fine, or penalty. We previously reported that the principles and practices of information architecture—a discipline focused on organizing and structuring information—offer an approach for developing such an inventory to support a variety of uses, including increased transparency for federal programs.[49] A program inventory creates the potential to aggregate, disaggregate, sort, and filter information across multiple program facets. For example, from a user's perspective, a

[49] GAO, *Federal Programs: Information Architecture Offers a Potential Approach for Development of an Inventory*, GAO-17-739 (Washington, D.C.: Sept. 28, 2017).

program could be tagged to highlight whether it includes activities to collect fees, fines, or penalties. Then, a user interested in this data facet could select a tag (e.g., fees) that could generate a list of programs that also have fees, fines, or penalties. While the program inventory is broader than agency collections of fees, fines, and penalties and would include programmatic descriptions, it would increase transparency by enabling Congress and the public to identify and isolate all programs that include, as a source of funding or a key data element, a fee, fine, or penalty to inform oversight and target additional requests for information to agencies.

Conclusion

Federal agencies are authorized to collect hundreds of billions of dollars from fees, fines, and penalties each year that fund a wide variety of programs, but Congress and the American public do not have government-wide data on these collections that would provide increased transparency and facilitate oversight. OMB's MAX database contains some disaggregated data labeled as fees, fines, and penalties, but OMB does not make these data publicly available. Without more disaggregated, government-wide, accessible data on collections of fees, fines, and penalties, such as by agency, Congress and the public do not have a complete and accurate picture of federal finances, the sources of federal funds, and the resources available to fund federal programs.

In addition, improving the data OMB currently reports related to fees, fines, and penalties could help the user better understand the data and the potential limitations. First, until OMB describes how it identifies accounts with fees including that the government-wide totals of fees it reports in *Analytical Perspectives* may include collections that are not fees and exclude some fee collections, some users will likely be unaware that reported totals could be over- or under-estimates. Second, without OMB instruction to agencies to regularly review and update implementation of the criteria for designating accounts that contain fees, accounts could be designated incorrectly if the makeup of the collections changes.

Therefore, OMB cannot provide reasonable assurance that the total amount of fees it reports is accurate. Third, until OMB describes in the User's Guide that its Public Budget Database reports budget authority net of offsetting collections, including collections of fees, fines, and penalties, users could misinterpret the information and underestimate collections in some cases.

OMB and Treasury do not collect many of the data elements on fees, fines, and penalties that would be useful for congressional oversight, such as review and reporting requirements. There are trade-offs between the potential costs and the potential benefits. While reporting government-wide data on specific fees, fines, and penalties would improve transparency and information for decision-making, more data elements would require greater investment of resources from OMB, Treasury, and agencies. Any new reporting of fee, fine, and penalty data would be most useful if it is designed to be compatible with other transparency efforts— the DATA Act reporting and the federal program inventory. Regardless of the approach taken, linkage of data on fees, fines, and penalties with other government-wide data reporting, such as USASpending.gov, would enhance transparency and facilitate congressional oversight.

Recommendations for Executive Action

We are making the following four recommendations to OMB:

The Director of OMB should make available more disaggregated data on fees, fines, and penalties that it maintains in its OMB MAX database. For example, OMB could report data on fee collections by agency in *Analytical Perspectives*. (Recommendation 1)

The Director of OMB should present, in *Analytical Perspectives*, the data limitations related to the government-wide fee totals by describing the 50-percent criteria OMB uses to identify accounts with fees or by directing users to the relevant sections of OMB Circular No. A-11. (Recommendation 2)

The Director of OMB should instruct agencies to regularly review the application of the user fee designation in the OMB MAX data and update the designation, as needed, to meet the criteria in OMB Circular No. A-11. (Recommendation 3)

The Director of OMB should describe in the Public Budget Database User's Guide that budget authority is reported net of any offsetting collections, such as collections of fees, fines, and penalties. (Recommendation 4)

AGENCY COMMENTS

We provided a draft of this chapter to Treasury and OMB for review and comment on December 10, 2018. Treasury informed us that they had no comments. As of March 4, 2019, OMB did not provide comments.

Sincerely yours,

Tranchau (Kris) T. Nguyen,
Acting Director Strategic Issues

APPENDIX I: OBJECTIVES, SCOPE AND METHODOLOGY

This chapter examines: (1) the extent to which government-wide data on collections of fees, fines, and penalties are publicly available and useful for the purpose of congressional oversight, and (2) the benefits and challenges to government-wide reporting of specific fees, fines, and penalties including data elements that facilitate congressional oversight.

To assess the extent and usefulness of publicly available data, we developed criteria for the availability and usefulness for the purpose of congressional oversight of data on collections of fees, fines, and penalties reported in government-wide sources (see Table 3).

Table 3. GAO Criteria for the Availability and Usefulness of Data on Fees, Fines, and Penalties for the Purpose of Congressional Oversight

Category	Category details
Clear and Accessible Presentation	• User is able to aggregate or disaggregate reported data. • Data are provided in machine-readable and open formats and can be downloaded in bulk, to the extent practicable for automated processing. • Data are comparable across agencies. • Data are clearly described and presented with known limitations.
Accurate	• Data reported as collections of fees, fines, and penalties are correctly labeled and do not include other sources of funding.
Complete	• Source reports all collections of fees, fines, and penalties.
Useful for the Purpose of Congressional Oversight	• Data elements capturing the characteristics of fee, fine, or penalty collections that our prior work and cognizant committee staff identify as facilitating oversight: • **Descriptive title:** A title for the fee, fine, or penalty that conveys information about the activity or program to which it is related. • **Agency administering**: Agency authorized to administer the collection. Administrative activities include setting rates, promulgating regulations, reviewing, and reporting. • **Agency collecting:** Agency that collects the funds. In some cases, the collecting agency differs from the administering agency. • **Annual dollar amount collected (for multiple years):** Total dollar amount collected, by fiscal year. • **Account balance**: For collections dedicated by law to a specific purpose or program, the fiscal year-end balance of the budgetary account to which the collection is credited. • **Authorities to collect and obligate funds**: Citation of the law(s) providing agency authority to collect the fee, fine, or penalty and, as applicable, authority to obligate the collections. • **Limitations on obligations:** Statutory limitations on the purpose, time, or amounts available for obligation.
Categories of collections (i.e., budgetary collection type, budget function):	• Budgetary collection types describe the availability of collections set in statute as offsetting collections, offsetting receipts, and governmental receipts. Offsetting collections are deposited in agency appropriation or fund expenditure accounts and are available for agency use for the specified purpose without further legislative action. Offsetting receipts are deposited into agency receipt accounts and are not available for agency use unless appropriated by Congress. Governmental receipts are deposited into general fund receipt accounts and may then be appropriated as Congress deems fit. Budget function is a system of classifying budget authority, outlays, receipts, and tax expenditures according to the national needs being addressed. Budget functions include national defense and health, for example.

Table 3. (Continued)

Category	Category details
Categories of collections (i.e., budgetary collection type, budget function):	• **Specific review requirement:** Any review requirement specific to the collection. For example, for fees, this would include any review requirement other than the general requirement for a biennial fee review established by Chief Financial Officers Act of 1990. • **Specific reporting requirement:** Any reporting requirement specific to the collection. For example, for fees, this would include any reporting requirement other than the general requirement in OMB Circular No. A-25 for reporting the results of the biennial fee review. • **Fund type receiving collections (e.g., special fund, trust fund, etc.):** Special funds are federal fund accounts earmarked by law for a specific purpose. Trust funds are accounts designated as "trust funds" by law, regardless of any other meaning of the term "trust fund."

Source: GAO analysis of GAO's Standards for Internal Control, requirements found in the DATA Act, Office of Management and Budget instructions, prior GAO work on user fees, and permanent funding authorities, and input from staff of congressional committees on appropriations, budget, and oversight. | GAO-19-221.

The first three criteria—clear and accessible presentation, complete, and accurate—address the availability of the data and the final criterion, useful for the purpose of congressional oversight, addresses content of the data specific to congressional oversight needs. These criteria are based on:

- Standards for Internal Control in the Federal Government related to data quality,[50]
- Digital Accountability and Transparency Act of 2014 (DATA Act) requirements,
- government-wide instruction from the Office of Management and Budget (OMB) on public access to data and open government,[51]
- our prior work on user fees, fines, and penalties,[52] and

---

[50] GAO-14-704G

[51] Sources of government-wide instructions are: OMB, Memorandum on Improving Public Access to and Dissemination of Government Information and Using the Federal Enterprise Architecture Data Reference Model (M-06-02), and on Open Government (M-10-06).

[52] For more information, see GAO, *Permanent Funding Authorities: Some Selected Entities Should Review Financial Management, Oversight, and Transparency Policies*, GAO-17-59 (Washington, D.C.: Dec. 9, 2016); and *Federal User Fees: A Design Guide*, GAO-08-

- input from staff of congressional committees on appropriations, budget, and oversight.

Using a standard list of semistructured interview questions, we interviewed congressional staff that were available to meet with us on or before November 1, 2018. We shared the criteria with OMB staff and Department of the Treasury (Treasury) officials, and they agreed the criteria are relevant and reasonable.

To identify publicly available government-wide sources of data with information on collections of fees, fines, and penalties, we reviewed our prior work on user fees, fines, penalties, and permanent funding authorities, conducted general background research including reviewing Congressional Budget Office (CBO) and Congressional Research Service (CRS) reports, and interviewed staff from OMB, and officials from Treasury, CBO, and CRS. We identified the *Budget of the U.S. Government*—including *Analytical Perspectives*, the *Budget Appendix*, and the Public Budget Database—produced annually by OMB; the *Financial Report of the U.S. Government (Financial Report)*, the *Daily Treasury Statement, the Monthly Treasury Statement*, the *Combined Statement of Receipts, Outlays, and Balances*, and USAspending.gov produced by Treasury; and CBO products, such as its budget projections and historical budget tables as containing government-wide federal budget or financial data.

Of the sources we identified, we included *Analytical Perspectives*, the *Budget Appendix*, the Public Budget Database, and the *Combined Statement of Receipts, Outlays, and Balances* in our study because they contain government-wide information on collections of fees, fines, and penalties. We excluded the Treasury's *Daily Treasury Statement*, *Monthly Treasury Statement, Financial Report*, and USAspending.gov from this review because we determined that the information presented did not differentiate between types of collections in a way that would allow us to separately

386SP (Washington, D.C.: May 29, 2008); *Federal User Fees: Fee Design Options and Implications for Managing Revenue Instability*, GAO-13-820 (Washington, D.C.: Sept. 30, 2013).

identify fees, fines, and penalties. For example, Treasury's *Financial Report* reports government-wide information in categories that are broader than fees, fines, and penalties. Specifically, it reports "earned revenue," which includes collections of interest payments for federal loan programs. Such collections are not fees. The *Financial Report* also reports fines and penalties combined with interest and other revenues. We also reviewed and excluded CBO products because the data reported are not designed to differentiate between types of collections.

We assessed *Analytical Perspectives*, the *Budget Appendix*, the Public Budget Database, and the *Combined Statement* of Receipts, *Outlays, and Balances* using the criteria we developed for clear and accessible presentation, accurate, and complete. We also assessed the *Budget Appendix,* the Public Budget Database, and the *Combined Statement of Receipts, Outlays, and Balances* using the criteria for useful for the purpose of congressional oversight.[53] Further, we assessed relevant portions of OMB and Treasury instructions using *Standards for Internal Control in the Federal Government*.[54]

We also used OMB and Treasury data to identify and report government-wide totals for fees, fines, and penalties to the extent that they were reported. To assess the reliability of OMB's MAX database data related to the collections of fees, fines, and penalties, we reviewed related documentation, interviewed knowledgeable agency officials, and conducted electronic data testing. To assess Treasury's Bureau of the Fiscal Service data related to the collections of fees, fines, and penalties, we reviewed related documentation and interviewed knowledgeable agency officials. In both cases, we found the data to be reliable for our purposes. We did not examine whether agencies accurately report collections as fees, fines, and penalties to OMB and Treasury.

In addition, we identified and reviewed other sources of data on fees, fines, and penalties that are specific to federal agencies, including annual

---

[53] We did not include *Analytical Perspectives* in our analysis for useful for congressional oversight because the data are presented in aggregate government-wide totals.

[54] Specifically, Principle 13 – Use Quality Information. For more information, see GAO, *Standards for Internal Control in the Federal Government*, GAO-14-704G (Washington, D.C.: September 2014).

financial reports and agency websites. We did not apply the criteria we developed for available and useful for the purpose of congressional oversight to these sources because they contain data for an individual agency rather than government-wide data.

To determine the benefits and challenges to government-wide reporting of fees, fines, and penalties, we interviewed staff of congressional committees on appropriations, budget, and oversight, OMB staff and Treasury officials, staff of CBO, and external organizations, including the Committee for a Responsible Federal Budget, the Data Coalition, the Data Foundation, the Project on Government Oversight, the Peter G. Peterson Foundation, and the Sunlight Foundation, on the potential benefits and challenges of government-wide reporting of fees, fines, and penalties. In addition, we reviewed our prior work on the DATA Act, federal program inventories, and federal fees, to identify and assess issues to consider in government-wide reporting.

We conducted this performance audit from November 2017 to March 2019 in accordance with generally accepted government auditing standards. Those standards require that we plan and perform the audit to obtain sufficient, appropriate evidence to provide a reasonable basis for our findings and conclusions based on our audit objectives. We believe that the evidence obtained provides a reasonable basis for our findings and conclusions based on our audit objectives.

In: Government Reports ...
Editor: Evie Boan

ISBN: 978-1-53615-928-8

Chapter 5

GRANTS MANAGEMENT: AGENCY ACTION REQUIRED TO ENSURE GRANTEES IDENTIFY FEDERAL CONTRIBUTION AMOUNTS*

United States Government Accountability Office

ABBREVIATIONS

ACF	Administration for Children and Families
AHRQ	Agency for Healthcare Research and Quality
ILAB	Bureau of International Labor Affairs
BLS	Bureau of Labor Statistics
CDC	Centers for Disease Control and Prevention
CMS	Centers for Medicare and Medicaid
CEO	Chief Evaluation Office

* This is an edited, reformatted and augmented version of United States Government Accountability Office; Report to Congressional Requesters, Publication No. GAO-19-282, dated March 2019.

COGR	Council on Governmental Relations
USDA	U.S. Department of Agriculture
DOD	Department of Defense
Education	Department of Education
HHS	Department of Health and Human Services
DOL	Department of Labor
ETA	Employment and Training Administration
FDA	Food and Drug Administration
HRSA	Health Resources and Services Administration
IHS	Indian Health Service
MSHA	Mine Safety and Health Administration
NGMA	National Grants Management Association
NIH	National Institutes of Health
OASH	Office of the Assistant Secretary for Health
ODEP	Office of Disability Employment Policy
OGM	Office of Grants Management
ONC	Office of the National Coordinator for Health Information Technology
OSHA	Occupational Safety and Health Administration
SAMHSA	Substance Abuse and Mental Health Services Administration
VETS	Veterans Employment and Training Service
WB	Women's Bureau

WHY GAO DID THIS STUDY

Since 1989, an appropriations provision, colloquially known as the "Stevens Amendment," has reflected Congress's longstanding effort to ensure transparency and accountability in federal grant spending. GAO was asked to review agency guidance and grantee compliance related to the Stevens Amendment.

This chapter (1) describes the guidance DOL, HHS, and Education provide to grantees regarding the Stevens Amendment; (2) examines the extent to which DOL, HHS, and Education are managing grantees' compliance with the Stevens Amendment; and (3) describes what is known about how grantees calculate the dollar amounts and percentages of their federal and nongovernmental funding disclosures. GAO asked for agency guidance documents, reviewed monitoring reports, interviewed officials on agencies' Stevens Amendment oversight efforts, and asked agencies how grantees calculate funding amounts.

WHAT GAO RECOMMENDS

GAO recommends that DOL subagencies (other than ETA), HHS operating divisions, and Education design and implement processes to manage grantees' compliance with the Stevens Amendment. In responding to the report, DOL, one DOL subagency, and HHS agreed with GAO's recommendation. Education disagreed with GAO's recommendation, citing limited monitoring resources and other reasons. GAO believes the recommendation should be fully implemented, as discussed in the report.

WHAT GAO FOUND

The Stevens Amendment is an appropriations provision that requires grantees of the Departments of Labor (DOL), Health and Human Services (HHS), and Education (Education) to disclose for a grant program the percent of the costs financed with federal funds, the federal dollar amount, and the percentage and dollar amount financed by nongovernmental funds.

The provision requires that recipients of grants funded by DOL, HHS, and Education make certain funding disclosures when issuing statements, press releases, bid solicitations, and other documents describing their grant project or program. DOL, HHS, and Education generally provide written guidance to grantees with the exact text of the Stevens Amendment or a paraphrased equivalent. In addition, a number of operating divisions within HHS referenced the HHS Grants Policy Statement, which includes language equivalent to the Stevens Amendment, as a way to instruct grantees. One HHS operating division, the Health Resources and Services Administration, provided grantees with additional guidance in the form of a web page that contained examples of funding disclosure statements and frequently asked questions intended to clarify the Stevens Amendment's requirements. One DOL subagency, the Employment and Training Administration (ETA), whose active grants represented more than 95 percent of DOL's total grant dollars, had processes for managing grantees' compliance that were able to identify instances of grantee noncompliance with Stevens Amendment requirements. ETA's operating plan for grant oversight targets 26 percent of its active grants for risk-based monitoring each fiscal year, representing approximately 2,100 grants in fiscal year 2019. The other DOL subagencies either stated that they did not monitor grantees for compliance with Stevens Amendment requirements or did not have processes in place for managing grantee compliance with the requirements of the Stevens Amendment. Most HHS operating divisions said they did not review grantees for Stevens Amendment compliance. Education also did not monitor for grantee compliance with the Stevens Amendment's requirements. Regulations governing federal agencies' management of grants require federal agencies to manage and administer the federal award in a manner that ensures that programs are implemented in full accordance with U.S. statutory and public policy requirements. Without processes for managing compliance, some DOL subagencies, HHS operating divisions, and Education are unable to ensure that grant programs are being implemented by grantees in full accordance with the statutory requirements of the Stevens Amendment.

Most of the subagencies and operating divisions monitoring compliance did not gather information from grantees about how the grantees calculate the dollar amounts and percentages in their Stevens Amendment funding disclosures. For example, DOL's ETA officials said that they do not know how the dollar amounts reported by grantees were calculated, and have not inquired about the level of detail factored into indirect costs involving the grantee organization's structure and the percentage of funds spent on salaries. Similarly, officials from HHS's National Institutes of Health operating division noted that calculations can be difficult given that a research program can have multiple funding streams that feed into a grant project and grantees' research portfolios are now more complex than they have been in the past.

March 14, 2019

The Honorable Ron Johnson
Chairman
Committee on Homeland Security and Governmental Affairs
United States Senate

The Honorable James Lankford
Chairman
Subcommittee on Regulatory Affairs and Federal Management
Committee on Homeland Security and Governmental Affairs
United States Senate

The Honorable Rand Paul, MD
Chairman
Subcommittee on Federal Spending Oversight and Emergency Management
Committee on Homeland Security and Governmental Affairs
United States Senate

The Honorable Joni Ernst
United States Senate

Federal agency grants management includes ensuring grantee compliance with numerous rules and requirements. Grantees can receive guidance on these requirements in the standard terms and conditions contained in the award notices from federal agencies providing the grants. The President's Management Agenda, released in 2018, established "results-oriented accountability for grants" as a cross-agency priority goal to "maximize the value of grant funding by applying a risk-based, data-driven framework that balances compliance requirements with demonstrating successful results for the American taxpayer."[1]

Requirements for some federal grantees receiving federal funds to disclose the percentage of the total costs of the program or project which will be financed with federal money, the dollar amount of federal funds for the project or program, and the percentage and dollar amount of the total costs of the project or program that will be financed by nongovernmental sources have existed in some form since 1989. The 2018 appropriations law establishing these disclosures requires that recipients of grants funded by the Departments of Labor (DOL), Health and Human Services (HHS), and Education (Education) disclose the total costs of programs or projects paid for with federal funds "[w]hen issuing statements, press releases, requests for proposals, bid solicitations and other documents describing projects or programs."[2] These requirements reflect longstanding efforts to ensure transparency and accountability in federal grant spending.

---

[1] President's Management Council and the Executive Office of the President, *President's Management Agenda: Modernizing the Government for the 21st Century* (Mar. 20, 2018).

[2] For example, the 2018 iteration of the provision is in the Consolidated Appropriations Act of 2018, and applies to DOL, HHS, and Education. Consolidated Appropriations Act, 2018, Pub. L. No. 115-141, div. H, title V, Sec. 505, 132 Stat. 348 (Mar. 23, 2018). Previous iterations have also applied to the Departments of Defense and Agriculture and related agencies, and the agencies of and related to DOL, HHS, and Education. Hereafter, we refer to this provision as the "Stevens Amendment."

The provision has been included in various appropriations acts throughout the last 30 years and is still colloquially referred to as the "Stevens Amendment" as it was first introduced by then-senator Ted Stevens as an amendment to appropriations bills, and was included in the final appropriations for those agencies.[3]

You asked us to review aspects of agency guidance and grantee compliance related to the Stevens Amendment. This chapter (1) describes what types of guidance, if any, DOL, HHS, and Education are providing to grantees about the requirements of the Stevens Amendment; (2) examines the extent to which DOL, HHS, and Education are managing grantees' compliance with the Stevens Amendment; and 3) describes what is known about how grantees calculate the funding percentages and dollar amounts required by the Stevens Amendment, including whether indirect costs are factored into these calculations.

To address these objectives, we researched the legislative history of these requirements to understand their evolution since the original passage in 1989. We spoke to representatives from the National Grants Management Association and the Council on Governmental Relations to obtain their insights into grantees' interpretation and implementation of the Stevens Amendment, which helped inform our discussion topics for later interviews with agency officials. In addition, we reviewed a study published in April 2017 that reviewed 100 National Institutes of Health (NIH) grant projects' press releases for Stevens Amendment compliance.[4]

---

[3] See, e.g., Departments of Labor, Health, and Human Services, and Education, and Related Agencies Appropriations Act, 1989, Pub. L. No. 100-436, Sec. 516, 102 Stat. 1680, 1715 (Sept. 20, 1988), and Department of Defense Appropriations Act, 1989, Pub. L. No. 100-463, Sec. 8136 102 Stat. 2270, 2270-46, (Oct. 1, 1988), Rural Development, Agriculture, and Related Agencies Appropriations Act, 1989, Pub. L. No. 100-460, Sec. 644, 102 Stat. 2229, 2265 (Oct. 1, 1988). There are multiple examples throughout the 30 year history of the Stevens Amendment. This footnote refers to the earliest versions.

[4] "Ivy League Flunkers: Schools Fail on Federal Funding Disclosure," Restore Accountability and White Coat Waste Project, April 2017. This study found that none of the 100 press releases were in compliance with all of the requirements of the Stevens Amendment, and three of the 100 complied with one of the Stevens Amendment requirements (for the dollar amount of the project financed by federal funds).

For the first objective, we asked DOL, all of DOL's grant-making subagencies, HHS, all of HHS's grant-making operating divisions, and Education for copies of relevant guidance documents showing the agencies' instructions to grantees to help them comply with the Stevens Amendment's disclosure requirements.[5]

For the second objective, we asked some of DOL's grant-making subagencies, all 11 of HHS's grant-making operating divisions, and Education to provide us with responses to questions on guidance, monitoring, and enforcement. We also conducted follow-up interviews with officials from DOL's Employment and Training Administration (ETA), HHS operating divisions that initially stated they conducted monitoring, and Education to clarify their written responses and determine whether the agencies had any supporting documentation. We also asked all three agencies what their grants management efforts, including any monitoring, showed with regard to the extent of grantee compliance with the requirements of the Stevens Amendment.

---

[5] HHS has 11 operating divisions that administer a wide variety of health and human services as well as conduct research. These operating divisions are: the Agency for Healthcare Research and Quality, Office of the National Coordinator for Health Information Technology, the Office of the Assistant Secretary for Health, the Substance Abuse and Mental Health Services Administration, the Food and Drug Administration, Centers for Medicare and Medicaid Services, Administration for Children and Families, Health Resources and Services Administration, National Institutes of Health, Centers for Disease Control and Prevention, and the Indian Health Service. HHS noted that the Consolidated Appropriations Act of 2018, appropriated funds for HHS in Division H of the Act, which includes the Stevens Amendment provision, and separately appropriated funds for the Indian Health Service (IHS) in Division G, under the Department of the Interior appropriation which included a subsection for related agencies under HHS. Division G does not contain the Stevens Amendment provision. Despite the appropriation under Interior, for organizational purposes, IHS is an agency within HHS, which is responsible for providing federal health services to American Indians and Alaska Natives. HHS officials stated that IHS was not subject to Division H of the Consolidated Appropriations Act of 2018. The same is true for the appropriations for 2019. For Interior's appropriation which includes IHS, see, Consolidated Appropriations Act, 2019, Pub. L. No. 116-6, div. E, tit. III, 133 Stat. 13, (Feb. 15, 2019), and for the Stevens Amendment provision applicable to Labor, HHS, and Education see, Department of Defense and Labor, Health and Human Services, and Education Appropriations Act, 2019, and Continuing Appropriations Act, 2019, Pub. L. No. 115-245, div. B, tit. V, Sec. 505, 132 Stat. 2981 (Sept. 28, 2018).

We asked each of the subagencies and operating divisions that said or indicated that they conducted monitoring for compliance with the Stevens Amendment for six examples of grantee documents showing compliance or noncompliance with the amendment. For any instances of noncompliance, we asked whether the agency determined appropriate corrective actions and whether the grantees implemented those corrective actions. We also asked the agencies that provided examples whether they tracked the number of instances of compliance or noncompliance.

For the third objective we requested any available information regarding how grantees calculated Stevens Amendment percentages and dollar amounts and whether they factored indirect costs into their calculations. We asked whether the subagencies and operating divisions that stated they conducted monitoring of the Stevens Amendment were aware of the methods grantees used to calculate percentages and dollar amounts of federal funding, and whether grantees factored indirect costs into their calculation of federal spending used in their Stevens Amendment disclosures.

We conducted this performance audit from January 2018 to March 2019 in accordance with generally accepted government auditing standards. Those standards require that we plan and perform the audit to obtain sufficient, appropriate evidence to provide a reasonable basis for our findings and conclusions based on our audit objectives. We believe the evidence obtained provides a reasonable basis for our findings and conclusions based on our audit objectives.

BACKGROUND

Originally the Stevens Amendment was part of appropriations acts for the Departments of Defense (DOD) and Agriculture (USDA), as well as DOL, HHS, and Education.

The provision was dropped from the DOD appropriations act in 1990 and from the USDA appropriations act in 1993.[6] For the version of this requirement that applied to DOL, HHS, and Education, the Stevens Amendment has appeared in all but one of the full appropriations acts passed in Congress since 1993.[7] In proposing the amendment in 1988, Senator Ted Stevens described the role of states, local governments, and the federal government in forging a partnership to share in the costs of many projects and said that the federal contribution should be identified as a matter of taxpayer concern. Further, Senator Stevens said that taxpayers "ought to be informed how much money comes from Federal sources in any program, project, or grant activity."[8] More recently, the Consolidated Appropriations Act of 2018 and the appropriations for these agencies in 2019 renewed this requirement for DOL, HHS, and Education (see sidebar).[9]

The combined amount of grant funding that went to state and local governments from these three departments in federal fiscal year 2017 amounted to approximately $504 billion, or almost 75 percent of the $675 billion total distributed by all federal grant-making agencies to state and local governments that year.

---

[6] Although the provision was dropped from USDA's annual appropriations acts, a different two-part formulation of the Stevens Amendment was subsequently included in USDA's general permanent statutory authority at 7 U.S.C. § 2209d.

[7] While we have previously reported on grantee monitoring practices of DOL, HHS, and Education, we have not done so with regard to the Stevens Amendment. Our prior work on grants monitoring includes: GAO-17-266, *Discretionary Grants: Education Needs to Improve Its Oversight of Grants Monitoring*, (Washington, D.C.: Apr. 18, 2017); GAO-14-832, *International Labor Grants: DOL's Use of Financial and Performance Monitoring Tools Needs to be Strengthened* (Washington, D.C.: Sept. 24, 2014); GAO-14-800, *Health Resources and Services Administration: Action Taken to Train and Oversee Grantee Monitoring Staff, but Certain Guidance Could Be Improved* (Washington, D.C.: Sept. 23, 2014). See also GAO's Key Issues page on Federal Grants to State and Local Governments.

[8] Specifically, Senator Stevens stated that his amendment proposed "that any announcement or publication of these programs specifically and fully identify the Federal contribution. I believe that this approach respects the roles of all participants in such projects, while insuring that the beneficiaries of these activities can perceive the cooperative role of all levels of government." 134 Cong. Rec. S20831-32 (1988) (Statement of Sen. Stevens).

[9] Consolidated Appropriations Act of 2018, Pub. L. No. 115-141, 132 Stat. 348, div. H, Title V, § 505, and Department of Defense and Labor, Health and Human Services, and Education Appropriations Act, 2019, and Continuing Appropriations Act, 2019, Pub. L. No. 115-245, div. B, tit. V, § 505, 132 Stat. 2981 (Sept. 28, 2018).

Stevens Amendment

When issuing statements, press releases, requests for proposals, bid solicitations and other documents describing projects or programs funded in whole or in part with Federal money, all grantees receiving Federal funds included in this Act, including but not limited to State and local governments and recipients of Federal research grants, shall clearly state

1. the percentage of the total costs of the program or project which will be financed with Federal money;
2. the dollar amount of Federal funds for the project or program; and
3. percentage and dollar amount of the total costs of the project or program that will be financed by non-governmental sources.

Consolidated Appropriations Act of 2018, Pub. L. No. 115- 141, 132 Stat. 348, div. H, Title V, Sec. 505 (Mar. 23, 2018).

HHS had the largest amount of grant outlays to state and local governments with about $455 billion (67.4 percent of the total), Education distributed about $42 billion (6.2 percent), while Labor distributed about $7 billion (1.1 percent).[10]

DOL, HHS, and Education Generally Provide Grantees with the Exact Text of the Stevens Amendment or a Paraphrased Equivalent

Generally, agencies or their subdivisions provided grantees with the exact text of the Stevens Amendment, paraphrased its language, or in some cases referred grantees to other guidance containing the Stevens Amendment.

---

[10] Because these figures were calculated using the table of outlays and budget authority in Chapter 14 of the 2019 Analytical Perspectives, "Aid to State and Local Government," they only represent grant outlays to state and local governments and do not include grants to other entities such as universities and nonprofit institutions. Consequently, the dollar figures cited likely understate the total grant amounts distributed by these departments.

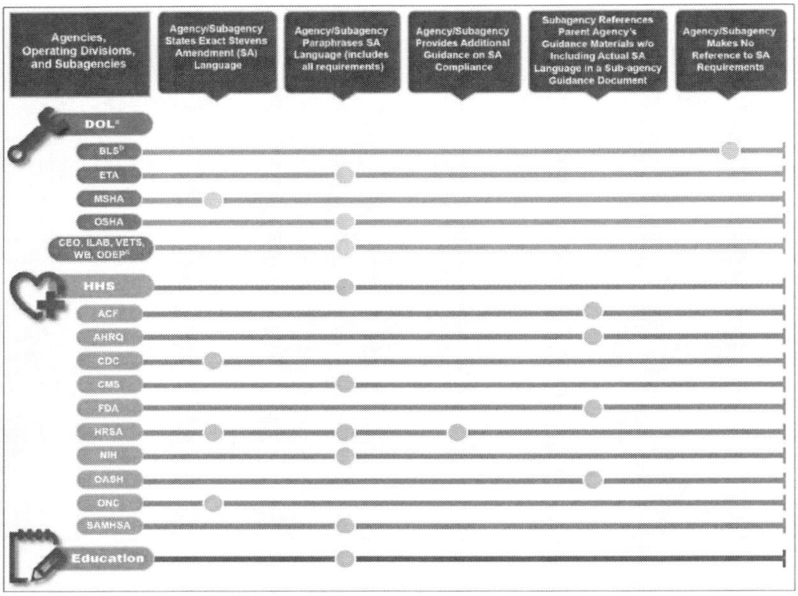

Source: GAO analysis of DOL, HHS, and Education guidance documents and responses to questions about guidance. | GAO-19-282.

Note: The Department of Labor (DOL) subagencies listed are the Employment and Training Administration (ETA), the Occupational Safety and Health Administration (OSHA), the Mine Safety and Health Administration (MSHA), the Bureau of Labor Statistics (BLS), the Chief Evaluation Office (CEO), the Bureau of International Labor Affairs (ILAB), Veterans' Employment and Training Service (VETS), the Women's Bureau (WB), and the Office of Disability Employment Policy (ODEP). The Department of Health and Human Services (HHS) operating divisions listed are the Agency for Healthcare Research and Quality (AHRQ), the Office of the National Coordinator for Health Information Technology (ONC), the Office of the Assistant Secretary for Health (OASH), the Substance Abuse and Mental Health Services Administration (SAMHSA), the Food and Drug Administration (FDA), Centers for Medicare and Medicaid Services (CMS), Administration for Children and Families (ACF), Health Resources and Services Administration (HRSA), National Institutes of Health (NIH), and the Centers for Disease Control and Prevention (CDC).

[a]DOL does not publish grantee guidance at the departmental level, and DOL's subagencies have their own guidance, as shown in this figure.

[b]According to BLS officials, documents produced by their grantees do not fall within the scope of the Stevens Amendment; therefore they do not include a reference to the Stevens Amendment in their guidance.

[c]ETA disseminates its standard terms and conditions template to grantees on behalf of these five DOL grant-making subagencies.

Figure 1. Written Stevens Amendment Guidance Provided By DOL, HHS, and Education to Grantees, 2018.

Figure 1 summarizes what we found at each of the three agencies we reviewed with regard to the Stevens Amendment guidance they provide to grantees.

DOL Instructed Grantees to Follow Stevens Amendment Requirements by Providing a Template for Language in Subagencies' Grant Terms and Conditions

According to ETA officials, grants from DOL's ETA comprised more than 95 percent of DOL's $22.1 billion in active grant awards as of October 1, 2018.[11] ETA's Office of Grants Management (OGM) developed standard terms and conditions that serve as a template for written agreements for grant awards. The terms and conditions template includes language largely similar to the Stevens Amendment, with one instance of paraphrasing, which is permissible under the relevant regulations.[12] ETA's paraphrased language states that the Stevens Amendment requirements apply to "all non-federal entities receiving federal funds," whereas the actual Stevens Amendment wording is that the requirements apply to "all grantees receiving federal funds in this Act, including but not limited to state and local governments and recipients of federal research grants."[13] The Stevens Amendment has been in the agency's terms and conditions library for grant awards since fiscal year 2014. ETA officials said they added the Stevens Amendment requirements to the terms and conditions because they wanted to ensure that grantees knew about the Stevens Amendment's existence.

ETA also disseminates its standard terms and conditions template to grantees on behalf of five other DOL grant-making subagencies, including

---

[11] ETA officials said that their active grant awards include fiscal year 2018 grants as well as multi-year grant funds.

[12] 2 C.F.R. § 200.300(a).

[13] DOL/ETA *Standard Federal Award Terms & Conditions – FY2018*, at 23 (2018).

the Veterans Employment and Training Service, the Chief Evaluation Office, the Bureau of International Labor Affairs, the Women's Bureau, and the Office of Disability Employment Policy. According to ETA officials, OGM administers the front-end application processing for grants awarded by these subagencies, while the subagencies are responsible for any post-award grantee oversight. OGM also administers the final grant closeout for these subagencies. According to DOL officials, together with ETA, these subagencies awarded more than 99.8 percent of DOL's active grant funds as of October 2018.

According to DOL officials, three other DOL grant-making subagencies, the Mine Safety and Health Administration (MSHA), the Occupational Safety and Health Administration (OSHA), and the Bureau of Labor Statistics (BLS), administer their sub-agencies' grant award processes themselves. Officials said that two of these agencies, MSHA and OSHA, disseminate their own separate grant award terms and conditions, and have their own separate guidance for grantees regarding compliance with the Stevens Amendment. For example, OSHA paraphrased the Stevens Amendment language in its terms and conditions. OSHA officials told us that instead of stating the amendment's requirements in three parts, OSHA broke them out into four requirements that reflect the full content of the Stevens Amendment's original language. MSHA also had its own terms and conditions that contain the exact language of the Stevens Amendment's requirements, according to officials. The third agency, BLS, told us that its grantees only produce narrowly focused press releases and that these documents do not fall within the Stevens Amendment description of documents "describing projects or programs funded in whole or in part with Federal money." BLS officials said that since none of the other qualifying public statements mentioned in the Stevens Amendment are part of BLS grantee operations, BLS cooperative agreements do not produce public statements that qualify for Stevens Amendment compliance.

Most HHS Grant Guidance Restated, Paraphrased, or Referenced the Stevens Amendment

At the department level, HHS publishes a Grants Policy Statement that contains language equivalent to the Stevens Amendment, but it does not quote the amendment verbatim.[14] Consistent with the Stevens Amendment, the Grants Policy Statement provision directs grantees to disclose information on the percentage and dollar amount of federal contributions to grantees' programs or projects in addition to the same information for nongovernmental sources, but collapses the three Stevens Amendment requirements into two requirements with slight wording changes. Officials told us that HHS expects its operating divisions to follow the Grants Policy Statement together with the relevant HHS regulations, but does not instruct operating divisions on what to include in their grant award terms and conditions.[15]

A number of HHS operating divisions provide grantees with grant award terms and conditions that contain the exact language of the Stevens Amendment. Examples include:

- Centers for Disease Control and Prevention (CDC) - Provides grantees with general terms and conditions for both research and non-research grants and cooperative agreements that include a requirement for an "Acknowledgement of Federal Support" that is an exact re-statement of the Stevens Amendment.

---

[14] HHS Grants Policy Statement, U.S. Department of Health and Human Services, Office of the Assistant Secretary for Resources and Technology, Office of Grants, Jan. 1, 2007. The HHS Grants Policy Statement states in part, "Acknowledgment of Federal Funding: As required by HHS appropriations acts, all HHS recipients must acknowledge Federal funding when issuing statements, press releases, requests for proposals, bid invitations, and other documents describing projects or programs funded in whole or in part with Federal funds. Recipients are required to state (1) the percentage and dollar amounts of the total program or project costs financed with Federal funds and (2) the percentage and dollar amount of the total costs financed by nongovernmental sources."

[15] The regulations which are specific to HHS are found at, 45 C.F.R. Pt. 75.

- Health Resources and Services Administration (HRSA) - Provides grantees with the Standard Form 424 Application Guide (grants application guide), which includes a section that quotes the exact language of the Stevens Amendment.
- Office of the National Coordinator for Health Information Technology (ONC) - Added a section in 2018 to the terms and conditions section for every Funding Opportunity Announcement that specifically references the Stevens Amendment verbatim.[16]

One operating division, the Centers for Medicare and Medicaid Services (CMS) provides grantees with a section of its terms and conditions titled "Public Reporting" that shows the language of the Stevens Amendment, but with the addition of tribal governments to the list of applicable grant recipients. Another operating division, the National Institutes of Health (NIH), publishes its own grants policy statement separate from the one published by HHS. The NIH grants policy statement contains the standard terms and conditions for all NIH grant awards. It uses the same Stevens Amendment guidance language HHS uses, with the same paraphrasing of the language that collapses the three Stevens Amendment requirements into two requirements.

Four relevant HHS operating divisions told us that they relied solely on a reference to the HHS Grants Policy Statement to instruct grantees with regard to the Stevens Amendment requirements. This reference made no specific mention of the Stevens Amendment and did not include either the exact or paraphrased Stevens Amendment language in the agencies' grant agreement terms and conditions or funding opportunity announcement.[17]

---

[16] Before ONC added a section in its terms and conditions in 2018 that specifically referenced and restated the Stevens Amendment, it incorporated the Stevens Amendment by reference to the HHS Grants Policy Statement in its Notice of Funding Opportunity Announcements.

[17] These HHS operating divisions include the Administration for Children and Families, Agency for Healthcare Research and Quality, the Food and Drug Administration, and the Office of the Assistant Secretary for Health.

HHS's HRSA Provided Additional Guidance to Help Grantees Comply with the Stevens Amendment

HRSA's "Acknowledgement of Federal Funding" provision in its grants application guide contains the exact language of the Stevens Amendment and its requirements. Further, HRSA's application guide provides grantees with what HRSA officials stated was a sample acknowledgement and disclaimer paragraph written in "plain language" that the operating division developed to assist HRSA grantees in complying with the Stevens Amendment. HRSA officials said that they consulted with HHS's Office of General Counsel to simplify the language, while ensuring that it met the requirements of the Stevens Amendment. HRSA's sample acknowledgement and disclaimer paragraph reads, "This [project/publication/program/website] [is/was] supported by the Health Resources and Services Administration (HRSA) of the U.S. Department of Health and Human Services (HHS) as part of an award totaling $XX with xx percentage financed with nongovernmental sources. The contents are those of the author(s) and do not necessarily represent the official views of, nor an endorsement, by HRSA, HHS or the U.S. Government."

Later in the section, HRSA further defines the Stevens Amendment's "other documents describing projects or programs" as including, among other things, HRSA-supported documents such as manuals, toolkits, resource guides, case studies, and issues briefs.

In addition to HRSA's efforts to interpret the Stevens Amendment, HRSA posted a web page in October 2018 that provided grantees with additional written guidance and a list of "frequently asked questions" about communicating and acknowledging federal funding.[18] The HRSA web page provided examples of HRSA disclosure statements to show grantees how disclosure language should be drafted to comply with the Stevens Amendment. The web page also featured frequently asked questions, one of which clarified that the disclosure should reflect the overall amount of

---

[18] For HRSA's webpage on Communicating and Acknowledging Federal Funding see, https://www.hrsa.gov/grants/manage/acknowledge-hrsa-funding, accessed October 24, 2018.

the grant rather than the cost of developing the publication where the acknowledgement appears. The other frequently asked question directed grantees to consult with HRSA officials if they intend to use language that differs from the examples provided to ensure that their alternative wording complies with the Stevens Amendment requirements.

HRSA officials also instructed their grantees on compliance with grant award terms and conditions, including the Stevens Amendment, through informal discussions during workshops and conference calls. HRSA officials provided examples of Stevens Amendment discussions such as a May 2018 Healthy Grants Workshop presentation to grantees, as well as a July 2018 question and answer period during an HRSA conference call with grantees. The grantee conference call featured several HRSA presenters, including one representing the Division of Grants Policy. Officials said that during these technical assistance calls, HRSA wanted to ensure that grantees were made aware of legislative mandates, but the calls were not tailored to focus on a specific mandate.

Education's Grant Awards Terms and Conditions Contain Paraphrased Stevens Amendment Language

Education grantees that receive discretionary and formula grants are provided with information on the Stevens Amendment through a Grant Award Notification attachment. The attachment is included with the terms and conditions of the grant award and has the exact language of the Stevens Amendment's requirements, but paraphrases with regard to the types of entities to which the Stevens Amendment applies. Instead of applying the requirements to "all grantees receiving federal funds included in this act including but not limited to state and local governments and recipients of federal research grants" as noted in the Stevens Amendment, Education's phrasing applies the requirements specifically to "U.S. Department of Education grantees." According to Education officials, the grant notification process involves providing guidance to grantees and ensuring that they are made aware of various statutory requirements, including the Stevens Amendment. Education officials told us that another way that their agency communicates information about the Stevens Amendment to grantees is through Education's required post-award conference call, during which the program offices reinforce grant recipients' need to be aware of the requirements.

DOL's ETA Managed Compliance with the Stevens Amendment through Its Grantee Monitoring Processes, Though Most HHS Operating Divisions and Education Did Not

The regulations that govern DOL, HHS, and Education's management of grant awards state that "the Federal awarding agency must manage and administer the federal award in a manner so as to ensure that Federal funding is expended and associated programs are implemented in full accordance with U.S. statutory and public policy requirements."[19] The Stevens Amendment is a statutory requirement that these federal agencies must ensure is implemented by their grantees. Agencies' management of the grant award so as to ensure implementation of the Stevens Amendment can be accomplished by various means, including the monitoring of grantees, through processes such as reviews of grantee reports and correspondence, desk audits, and grantee site visits. In our review of Stevens Amendment grants management practices at DOL, HHS, and Education, we found that DOL's ETA had processes in place that were able to identify instances of grantee noncompliance with the Stevens Amendment and demonstrate that noncompliance was being remedied.[20]

---

[19] 45 C.F.R. § 75.300(a); 2 C.F.R. § 200.300(a)

[20] As of October 2018, according to DOL officials, active grant awards for their agency totaled approximately $22.1 billion. The remaining DOL grant dollars, almost 5 percent, were divided between DOL's eight other subagencies. These grant making subagencies are Bureau of Labor Statistics, Chief Evaluation Office, Bureau of International Labor Affairs, Mine Safety and Health Administration (MSHA), Occupational Safety and Health Administration (OSHA), Office of Disability Employment Policy, Veterans' Employment and Training Service, and Women's Bureau.

ETA's grants management processes took the form of grantee monitoring. Figure 2 below summarizes the Stevens Amendment monitoring practices of DOL, HHS, and Education.

ETA Had Processes for Managing Grantee Compliance with the Stevens Amendment

ETA officials told us that their subagency's active grants represented more than 95 percent of DOL's total active grant dollars, or approximately $21.1 billion. According to ETA officials, their operating plan for grant oversight targets 26 percent of the active ETA grants universe for monitoring each fiscal year, representing approximately 2,100 grants in fiscal year 2019. The regional office staff in each of ETA's six regional offices conduct a risk analysis of the grants within their regions and assign a risk rating to each grant indicating its risk level. The grant's risk level, which includes factors such as the dollar amount of the grant award and whether the grantee is on track to meet the grant's performance goals, determines which grants ETA selects for monitoring and inclusion in its regional monitoring plans for that fiscal year.

Each annual regional monitoring plan consists of a list of grants and schedule of ETA staff monitoring reviews. According to ETA, monitoring reviews are used to measure grantee progress toward achieving project goals, identify areas of grantee compliance, offer opportunities for technical assistance to help resolve compliance issues, and ensure that federal funds are used responsibly. ETA conducts these reviews either through an on-site monitoring visit or an "Enhanced Desk Monitoring Review" that is conducted remotely. ETA officials stated the regional monitoring plans are designed to be flexible management tools, and are updated throughout each fiscal year to ensure that ETA meets its operating plan's goal to monitor 26 percent of its grants annually.

According to ETA's Grantee Handbook, upon completion of the monitoring review, ETA drafts a monitoring report to each of the grantees reviewed. The monitoring report includes, among other things, compliance findings and the required grantee corrective action for any noncompliance with the findings, along with the due date for the corrective action. In response to our request for examples of grantee noncompliance with the Stevens Amendment requirements, ETA officials from each of the agency's six regional offices conducted a manual search of monitoring reports from fiscal years 2016 and 2017.

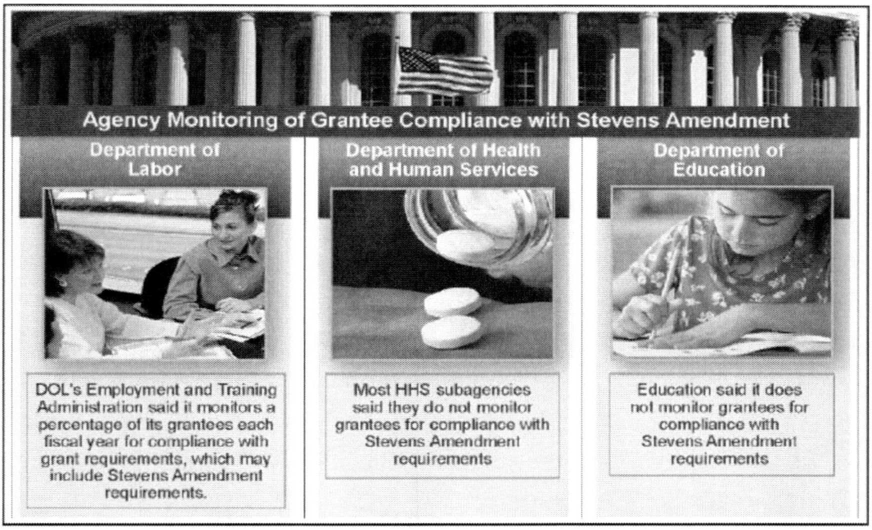

Source: GAO analysis of DOL, HHS, and Education information and responses to questions about monitoring practices, and photos from GAO image library collections Eyewire, Digital Visions, and Creatas. | GAO-19-282.

Figure 2. Stevens Amendment Monitoring Practices at DOL, HHS, and Education.

ETA officials in four of the six ETA regional offices located monitoring reports with a finding stating that grantees' public materials did not include the Stevens Amendment's required language or information to properly identify the project's federal funding dollar amount and the project's percentage of federal and nongovernmental funding. Three of the four monitoring reports provided the grantee with the exact language of the Stevens Amendment and instructed the grantee to ensure that statements, such as brochures, promotional materials, and other public announcements, contain a statement that identifies the project's funding sources in accordance with the three requirements of the Stevens Amendment.

In the fourth monitoring report, while finding that the grantee did not include the required funding source statement in its documents, ETA's comments in the monitoring report did not provide the grantee with the full language of the Stevens Amendment and had omitted the requirement to provide the percentage and dollar amount of costs financed by nongovernmental sources. For each of these examples, ETA officials showed that the grantees subsequently corrected their documents to bring them into compliance with the Stevens Amendment requirements. In the fourth example, the grantee's subsequent inclusion of the required funding source statement in its documents showed that the program was 100 percent funded by federal dollars.

In August 2018, ETA also created a "Core Monitoring Guide" that references the Stevens Amendment requirements as an element to be monitored by ETA officials when speaking with grantees. ETA intended this guide to be used as a tool in the on-site review of a grantee's activities, and it provides officials with a series of checklists as well as the steps to take when conducting monitoring. For Stevens Amendment compliance, the guide includes a "Question for Review and Discussion" that uses the exact language of the Stevens Amendment. However, the Stevens Amendment is only one issue among many addressed in the guide, and ETA officials said they do not have the resources to audit all of the elements included in the guide. ETA officials said that their grant reviewers select from one to four sections of the guide to use when conducting monitoring, depending on the nature of the grant, and that the choice of which items to monitor is based on a risk analysis of the grantee and the grant projects' quarterly financial reports. ETA officials acknowledged that the scope of their monitoring overall is limited to 26 percent of their grant universe for a given fiscal year, therefore the extent of noncompliance among ETA grantees cannot be determined.

Of the eight DOL subagencies we spoke to other than ETA, two, OSHA and BLS, stated that they did not monitor grantees for compliance with Stevens Amendment requirements. These subagencies' officials said they did not monitor for Stevens Amendment compliance because monitoring is not explicitly required under the statute and, in the case of BLS, because it believes that the type of press releases generated by their grantees do not fall within the scope of the Stevens Amendment. Six of the eight DOL subagencies told us that they conducted grantee compliance monitoring. However, based on the information and documents provided by officials from these six subagencies, they have not demonstrated that they have processes to manage grantees' compliance with the Stevens Amendment. For example, the Chief Evaluation Office, the Bureau of International Labor Affairs (ILAB), and the Veterans' Employment and Training Service stated that they do not track the extent of grantee compliance; and the Mine Safety and Health Administration said that it does not maintain records of grantee compliance with the Stevens Amendment. In addition, both ILAB and the Women's Bureau, while stating that they conducted monitoring of grantee compliance with the Stevens Amendment, provided examples of grantee disclosures that did not meet all of its requirements. Further, the Office of Disability and Employment Policy (ODEP) said that all of its grantees were fully compliant with the Stevens Amendment, but produced no examples of grantee disclosures.

The Uniform Administrative Requirements that govern certain federal agencies, including DOL, state with regard to the management of grants that "the Federal awarding agency must manage and administer the Federal award in a manner so as to ensure that Federal funding is expended and associated programs are implemented in full accordance with U.S. statutory and public policy requirements."[21] Other than ETA, DOL's subagencies have not developed the processes needed to manage and administer grantees' compliance with the Stevens Amendment. Without these processes, these DOL subagencies are not able to ensure that grant programs are being implemented by grantees in full accordance with the statutory requirements of the Stevens Amendment.

---

[21] 2 C.F.R. § 200.300(a).

Most HHS Operating Divisions Said They Did Not Review Grantees for Compliance with Stevens Amendment Requirements

At the department level, HHS officials said that they have no knowledge about whether their operating divisions conduct monitoring and enforcement of the Stevens Amendment, and they did not collect information from their operating divisions on grantee compliance with the Stevens Amendment's requirements. According to HHS officials, any efforts to manage grant awards for adherence to Stevens Amendment requirements would be carried out by staff at the agency's 10 relevant operating divisions. HHS officials said that operating divisions have an obligation to monitor their grantees for compliance with all of the agency's standard grant award terms and conditions, which includes the Stevens Amendment.

Of the 10 relevant HHS operating divisions we spoke with in our review, officials from eight of them—the Administration for Children and Families (ACF), the Agency for Healthcare Research and Quality (AHRQ), the Centers for Disease Control and Prevention (CDC), the Food and Drug Administration, the Health Resources and Services Administration (HRSA), the National Institutes of Health (NIH), the Office of the Assistant Secretary for Health (OASH), and the Substance Abuse and Mental Health Services Administration—told us that they did not monitor grantees' compliance with Stevens Amendment requirements. Two of these operating divisions, ACF and AHRQ, further stated that the Stevens Amendment did not require them to monitor for grantee compliance. These operating divisions maintained the position that they are not required to monitor for grantee compliance despite HHS policy regarding operating division monitoring of grants that states "...to fulfill their role in regard to the stewardship of Federal funds, OPDIVs monitor their grants to identify potential problems and areas where technical assistance might be necessary. This active monitoring is accomplished through review of reports and correspondence from the recipient, audit reports, site visits, and other information available to the OPDIV."[22] As mentioned earlier in this chapter, agencies are required to manage grant awards and have a number of possible means available to do so—including grant monitoring. However, grant monitoring is not explicitly required by the Stevens Amendment.

NIH officials stated that they do not specifically monitor for Stevens Amendment compliance and that NIH officials have not received any reports of noncompliance with the Stevens Amendment. They said they would address any non-compliance issues if they were raised. Similar to NIH, HRSA officials told us that they conduct grantee monitoring, but do not specifically review grantee documents for compliance with Stevens Amendment requirements unless there is a cause for concern regarding noncompliance. Similarly, CDC officials said that their grantee monitoring practices do not specifically target Stevens Amendment compliance. CDC officials further explained that while grant program officers may find instances of noncompliance during a grant review, it would be tangential to other issues more central to the focus of the grant review, such as grantee financial performance and goal accomplishment.

Officials from OASH stated that while they do not specifically review grantees' written statements for Stevens Amendment compliance, they provide grantees with guidance regarding how to comply with its requirements. For example, a grantee asked whether a Stevens Amendment acknowledgement statement had to be included on billboards the recipient rented to promote their program's services. OASH determined that the grantee did not need to include the statement on the billboards.

ONC officials told us that all of their grantees were in compliance with the Stevens Amendment. ONC officials stated that while they do not specifically look for Stevens Amendment compliance, it was their belief that ONC monitoring practices would identify instances of noncompliance for their small number of grantees.[23] ONC officials told us their belief is based on interactions with a wide range of grantees' employees during

---

[22] HHS Grants Policy Statement, U.S. Department of Health and Human Services, Office of the Assistant Secretary for Resources and Technology, Office of Grants, Jan. 1, 2007. The term "OPDIV" is an abbreviation used by HHS to refer to its operating divisions.

[23] ONC had 13 active grants as of April 2018.

monitoring visits that seek to ensure that all compliance issues among their grantees are addressed.

The remaining HHS operating division in our review, CMS, told us that its monitoring processes include reviews for Stevens Amendment requirements and that CMS had a process for reviewing grantee documents. According to HHS policy, the results and accomplishments of the activities CMS funds should be made public and CMS requires grantees to make the results and accomplishments of their activities available to the research community and to the public at large. The grantee must submit any materials to CMS in advance of publication, including brochures, recruitment materials, informational materials, advertisements, website copy, website pages, videos, and op-ed articles that report results from or describe information obtained through the grant award. CMS officials told us they reviewed for Stevens Amendment compliance, and provided us with examples of materials they said were from grantees that were in compliance. However, in our analysis of the sample grantee materials from CMS, we found that the grantees were not in compliance with the cost requirements of the Stevens Amendment.

Despite the claims and efforts of some HHS operating divisions with regard to monitoring for Stevens Amendment compliance, none of HHS's operating divisions could demonstrate that they had a process to manage and administer grantees' compliance with the Stevens Amendment requirements. In addition to the previously-mentioned Uniform Administrative Requirements applicable to all grant awards, HHS regulations that govern the agency's grant making state that, "The Federal awarding agency must manage and administer the Federal award in a manner so as to ensure that Federal funding is expended and associated programs are implemented in full accordance with U.S. statutory and public policy requirements."[24] Further, these regulations also state, "The Federal awarding agency must communicate to the non-Federal entity all relevant public policy requirements, including those in general

[24] 45 C.F.R. § 75.300(a).

appropriations provisions, and incorporate them either directly or by reference in the terms and conditions of the Federal award."[25]

Neither HHS, nor its operating divisions, had developed processes to manage and administer grantees' Stevens Amendment compliance. Without having processes to manage and administer their grantees' compliance with the Stevens Amendment, which is included in HHS's appropriations provisions, there is no way for HHS or its operating divisions to ensure that grantees are in full accordance with the statutory requirements of the Stevens Amendment appropriations provision and the agency-communicated conditions of the federal award.[26] Further, without monitoring grants in accordance with their Grants Policy Statement, HHS and its operating divisions are not able to identify potential problems related to grantees' Stevens Amendment compliance.

Education Does Not Monitor for Grantee Compliance with the Stevens Amendment

Education officials stated that its program offices do not explicitly track individual grantees for Stevens Amendment compliance. Education officials told us that their grant review process does not collect Stevens Amendment documentation nor do they gather information regarding the extent of grantee compliance with the appropriations provision. As a consequence, Education cannot determine the extent of their grantees' compliance with the requirements of the Stevens Amendment.[27]

---

[25] 45 C.F.R. § 75.300(a).

[26] For example, Consolidated Appropriations Act, 2018, Pub. L. No. 115-141, div. H, title V, Sec. 505, 132 Stat. 348 (Mar. 23, 2018).

[27] In our prior work we found that Education grant staff did not consistently document key required monitoring activities in the agency's official grant files. GAO-17-266, *Discretionary Grants: Education Needs to Improve Its Oversight of Grants Monitoring*, (Washington, D.C.: Apr. 18, 2017).

Representatives from Education's Office of General Counsel stated that Education has an "obligation to correct" instances of Stevens Amendment noncompliance, but does not have an "obligation to monitor" its grantees to determine whether they are in compliance. Education officials told us that due to limited resources, they use risk assessment results to identify and prioritize which items among their standard terms and conditions they will monitor during the course of a grant review. Officials told us they had not received any complaints related to the Stevens Amendment.

The uniform regulations that govern federal agencies, including Education's management of grants, state that "the Federal awarding agency must manage and administer the federal award in a manner so as to ensure that Federal funding is expended and associated programs are implemented in full accordance with U.S. statutory and public policy requirements."[28] Education has not developed the processes it needs to manage and administer grantees' compliance with the Stevens Amendment which is included in Education's appropriations provisions. Without these processes, Education is not able to ensure that grant programs are being implemented by grantees in full accordance with the statutory requirements of the Stevens Amendment appropriations provision and the agency-communicated conditions of the federal award.

Most Subagencies and Operating Divisions Monitoring Stevens Amendment Compliance Did Not Gather Information about Grantees' Cost Calculations

With two exceptions, the subagencies and operating divisions we reviewed that stated they conducted monitoring had no information on the methods used by grantees to calculate the federal funding dollar amounts or funding percentage figures required by the Stevens Amendment. As an example, DOL's ETA officials told us that they do not know how the

---

[28] 2 C.F.R. § 200.300(a).

dollar amounts reported by grantees were calculated, and they have not inquired about the level of detail factored into indirect costs involving the grantee organization's structure and the percentage of funds spent on salaries. In addition, officials at DOL's ILAB said that it is not always clear how grantees calculate these costs, and the Stevens Amendment does not provide specific guidance on how costs should be determined. Officials also noted that some grantees expressed confusion regarding the requirements and how to calculate the total federal funds, including in cases where there may be collaboration across federally-funded programs. Similarly, officials from HHS's NIH operating division noted that calculations can be difficult given that research programs can have multiple funding streams that feed into a grant project and grantees' research portfolios are now more complex than they have been in the past.

Officials at one DOL subagency, ODEP, said that grantees calculate the total funds received in the grant awarding document and that these funds include negotiated indirect cost rates. The remainder of the DOL subagencies and HHS operating divisions that produced examples of either compliance or noncompliance with the amendment did not have information on how grantees made their disclosure calculations. In addition, officials at one HHS operating division, HRSA, said the HRSA Notice of Award lists the total federal and non-federal amounts for the grant project or program. Grantees can use this information to calculate the percentage of federal funding and nongovernmental funding. However, in the Stevens Amendment compliance examples that HRSA provided to us, this calculation was not necessary because these projects were 100 percent funded by the HRSA grant award. In addition, HRSA officials told us that they are not aware of any other methods that grantees would need to use to arrive at the percentage. With regard to indirect costs, HRSA officials said that these costs are already included in the federal award amount and, therefore, any calculation of funding percentage should already account for the inclusion of both direct and indirect costs.

CONCLUSION

Congress has repeatedly taken action to include the Stevens Amendment requirements with agencies' appropriations. Ensuring grantee compliance with accountability requirements is achieved through investment of federal agency resources that reflect decisions regarding how best to ensure efficient and effective use of grant funds while reinforcing statutory requirements.

DOL's largest grant making subagency, ETA, showed that its grantee review processes were, to some extent, actively monitoring for Stevens Amendment compliance and that when ETA found compliance issues, it was able to provide grantees with the technical assistance needed to correct them. While a couple of HHS operating divisions showed some evidence that they were enhancing their guidance to grantees with regard to the Stevens Amendment, none of the operating divisions could demonstrate that they had a process to manage and administer grantees' compliance with the Stevens Amendment requirements. Education officials stated that while their agency does not have an "obligation to monitor" its grantees to determine whether they are in compliance with the Stevens Amendment, they do have an "obligation to correct" instances of noncompliance if brought to their attention. While none of the agencies in this review can determine the extent of their grantees' compliance with the Stevens Amendment, DOL's ETA has monitored grantee compliance with the provision, and when noncompliance is found, has taken steps to bring their grantees into compliance. However, with no such processes in place, the remaining DOL subagencies, HHS's operating divisions, and Education are not able to manage or administer grantee compliance with the Stevens Amendment appropriation provision so as to ensure that grant funds are being expended in full accordance with these statutory and regulatory requirements.

Recommendations for Executive Action

We are making a total of three recommendations, one to each of the three agencies in our review, to take steps to manage grantees' compliance with the Stevens Amendment. Specifically:

The Secretary of Labor should direct its subagencies, other than ETA, to design and implement a process to manage and administer grantees' compliance with the Stevens Amendment, including determining to what extent to provide guidance to grantees on calculations. (Recommendation 1) The Secretary of Health and Human Services should direct its operating divisions to design and implement processes to manage and administer grantees' compliance with the Stevens Amendment, including determining to what extent to provide guidance to grantees on calculations. (Recommendation 2)

The Secretary of Education should design and implement a process to manage and administer grantees' compliance with the Stevens Amendment, including determining to what extent to provide guidance to grantees on calculations. (Recommendation 3)

Agency Comments and Our Evaluation

We provided a draft of this chapter to DOL, HHS, and Education for review and comment. We received written concurrence from DOL, and written comment letters from DOL's OSHA, HHS, and Education. The comment letters are reprinted in appendixes I, II, and III, respectively and are summarized below.

DOL

DOL stated that it concurs with our recommendation. OSHA provided written comments and stated that it generally agreed with GAO's recommendation. OSHA said it will take steps to establish processes to monitor grantee compliance with Stevens Amendment requirements, to include reviewing what assistance the agency can provide to grantees on how to calculate funding percentages. OSHA further stated that it has begun updating its grant and cooperative agreement instructions to include the Stevens Amendment language verbatim, rather than paraphrasing the language, and is adding guidance to grant monitoring guidelines to assist OSHA's Regional Offices in reviewing compliance with the Stevens Amendment.

DOL subagencies ILAB, BLS, ETA, and ODEP also provided technical comments, which we incorporated into the report where appropriate.

HHS

In its written comments, HHS stated that it concurs with our recommendation and would implement the recommendation to the fullest extent feasible. HHS officials said they would direct all operating divisions to design a process for implementing and monitoring the Stevens Amendment and would update HHS grants policy to reflect this new process.

HHS also provided technical comments, which we incorporated into the report where appropriate.

Education

Education provided written comments stating that it did not concur with our recommendation, but would consider enhancing its existing approach to compliance with the Stevens Amendment. We reiterate our recommendation that Education should design and implement a process to manage and administer grantees' compliance with the Stevens Amendment, including determining to what extent to provide guidance to grantees on calculations.

Education had three concerns regarding the recommendation. First, Education said that our recommendation is not based on any evidence of noncompliance with the Stevens Amendment by Education grantees. As noted in our report, we found that Education lacks information regarding whether its grantees are, or are not, complying with the requirements of the Stevens Amendment. As indicated in this chapter, Education officials told us that they do not collect documentation from grantees to monitor their compliance with the Stevens Amendment, nor do they analyze information regarding the extent of grantee compliance with the Stevens Amendment. As a consequence, Education does not know the extent to which its grantees are or are not complying with the statutory requirements of the Stevens Amendment. Without this knowledge, Education does not have assurance that its grant awards are managed and administered in accordance with federal regulations.

Second, Education referred to its tiered risk-based approach to grantee monitoring that balances compliance requirements with limited monitoring resources in alignment with the President's Management Agenda. According to Education, implementation of the recommendation would require them to devote limited resources to managing and administering grantee compliance with the Stevens Amendment when there is no evidence of grantee noncompliance. We acknowledge that the cross-agency priority goal in the President's Management Agenda refers to maximizing the value of grant funding by applying a risk-based, data-driven framework that balances compliance requirements with demonstrating successful results. However, because Education does not collect information or documentation on this aspect of grantee compliance, it lacks the data needed to make an informed risk-based assessment with regard to monitoring for Stevens Amendment compliance. The recommendation could be implemented within the context of Education's risk-based approach to grantee monitoring as long as Education gathers the grantee compliance information needed to apply their risk-based, data-driven framework.

Third, Education said that it has already taken numerous steps to make its process for awarding and overseeing grant funds transparent to the public. However, these steps do not eliminate the legal requirements that grantees must comply with the Stevens Amendment, and that federal agencies, including Education, must manage and administer the federal award in a manner that is fully in accordance with statutory requirements. Education did state that it would consider enhancing its existing approach to Stevens Amendment compliance with actions that further explain the requirements to grant recipients. While such efforts could enhance grantees' understanding of the Stevens Amendment, they would not give Education the grantee compliance information it needs to apply to a risk-based, data-driven framework or to manage and administer its grant awards in accordance with federal regulations. For all of these reasons we continue to believe that our recommendation to Education is valid and that Education should fully implement it.

We are sending copies of this chapter to the Secretaries of Labor, Health and Human Services, and Education, as well as interested congressional committees and other interested parties.

Michelle Sager
Director, Strategic Issues

APPENDIX I: COMMENTS FROM THE DEPARTMENT OF LABOR'S OCCUPATIONAL SAFETY AND HEALTH ADMINISTRATION

Ms. Michelle Sager
Director, Strategic Issues
U.S. Government Accountability Office 441 G Street,
NW Washington, DC 20548

Dear Ms. Sager:

Thank you for the opportunity to comment on the Government Accountability Office's (GAO) draft report, Grants Management: Agency

Action Required to Ensure Grantees Identify Federal Contribution Amounts. The following comments are submitted on behalf of the Department of Labor's (DOL) Occupational Safety and Health Administration (OSHA) and relate only to those sections of the report that address OSHA directly.

The report notes that most DOL subagencies provide either verbatim or paraphrased Stevens Amendment language to grantees, but do not have processes in place to monitor grantee compliance with those requirements, which is not statutorily required. The report also notes that DOL subagencies do not gather information from grantees about how grantees calculate the dollar amounts and percentages in their Stevens Amendment funding disclosures. GAO recommends that DOL subagencies, other than ETA, should design and implement a process to manage and administer grantees' compliance with the Stevens Amendment, including determining to what extent to provide guidance to grantees on calculations.

OSHA generally agrees with GAO's recommendation and will take steps to establish processes to monitor grantee compliance with Stevens Amendment requirements, to include reviewing what assistance the agency can provide to grantees on how to calculate funding percentages.

OSHA has begun updating grant and cooperative agreement instructions to include the Stevens Amendment language verbatim, rather than paraphrasing the language, and is adding guidance to monitoring guidelines for State Plans, Consultation, and Harwood programs to assist OSHA's Regional Offices in reviewing compliance with the Stevens Amendment. The agency will continue to take additional steps to ensure that all OSHA grant programs are managed in accordance with legal requirements, including those of the Stevens Amendment.

OSHA welcomes this process review, and appreciates the opportunity to respond to GAO's draft report.

Loren Sweat
Acting Assistant Secretary

Appendix II: Comments from the Department of Health and Human Services

DEPARTMENT OF HEALTH & HUMAN SERVICES OFFICE OF THE SECRETARY

Assistant Secretary for Legislation
Washington, DC 20201

FEB 14 2019

Michelle A. Sager
Director, Strategic Issues
U.S. Government Accountability Office
441 G Street NW
Washington, DC 20548

Dear Ms. Sager:

Attached are comments on the U.S. Government Accountability Office's (GAO) report entitled, "*Grants Management: Agency Action Required to Ensure Grantees Identify Federal Contribution Amounts*" (GAO-19-282).

The Department appreciates the opportunity to review this report prior to publication.

Sincerely,

Matthew D. Bassett
Assistant Secretary for Legislation

GENERAL COMMENTS FROM THE DEPARTMENT OF HEALTH & HUMAN SERVICES ON THE GOVERNMENT ACCOUNTABILITY OFFICE'S DRAFT REPORT ENTITLED - GRANTS MANAGEMENT: AGENCY ACTION REQUIRED TO ENSURE GRANTEES IDENTIFY FEDERAL CONTRIBUTION AMOUNTS (GAO-19-282)

The U.S. Department of Health & Human Services (HHS) appreciates the opportunity from the Government Accountability Office (GAO) to review and comment on this draft report.

Recommendation 2
The Secretary of HHS should direct its operating divisions to design and implement processes to manage and administer grantees' compliance with the Stevens Amendment, including determining to what extent to provide guidance to grantees on calculations.

HHS Response
HHS concurs with the above recommendation and will implement it to the fullest extent feasible. In the short term, the Assistant Secretary for Financial Resources' Office of Grants and Acquisition Policy and Accountability, Division of Grants (OGAPA/DG), will utilize a Policy Action Transmittal to direct all operating divisions to design processes for implementing and monitoring the Stevens Amendment, and will update HHS grants policy to reflect the contents of the same Action Transmittal. This proposed action will be communicated to all HHS Chief Grants Management Officers at the next Executive Committee for Grants Policy Administration meeting.

APPENDIX III: COMMENTS FROM THE DEPARTMENT OF EDUCATION

UNITED STATES DEPARTMENT OF EDUCATION

OFFICE OF GRANTS ADMINISTRATION

February 13, 2019

Ms. Michelle A. Sager
Director, Strategic Issues
Government Accountability Office
Washington, DC 20548

Dear Ms. Sager:

Thank you for the opportunity to review the Government Accountability Office (GAO) draft report titled, *Grants Management: Agency Action Required to Ensure Grantees Identify Federal Contribution Amounts* (GAO-19-282). This draft report identifies one recommendation regarding GAO's findings about the monitoring of grants by the U.S. Department of Education (ED), particularly the extent to which ED: (1) provides guidance to grantees regarding the Stevens Amendment; and (2) manages grantees' compliance with the Stevens Amendment.

ED provides guidance to its grantees regarding the Stevens Amendment at the time of issuing a grant award through the Grant Award Notification (GAN) attachments for discretionary and formula grants. GAN Attachment 11, "Specific Conditions for Disclosing Federal Funding in Public Announcements," specifically provides guidance on the Stevens Amendment. Additionally, ED program offices address the amendment as part of their post-award conference call to grantees. ED's monitoring of its grantees does not center on compliance with grant assurances and certifications, such as the Stevens Amendment, unless there is a reason for such review. Instead, ED employs a risk-based monitoring approach to ensure grantees have the capacity to manage grant funds consistent with Federal requirements.

RECOMMENDATION FOR EXECUTIVE ACTION

The following provides our specific response to the recommendation.

Recommendation 3: The Secretary of Education should design and implement a process to manage and administer grantees' compliance with the Stevens Amendment, including determining to what extent to provide guidance to grantees on calculations.

Response: We do not concur with the recommendation but would consider enhancing our existing approach to compliance with the Stevens Amendment. Specifically, we have three concerns with this recommendation. First, the recommendation is made in the absence of any evidence of non-compliance with the Stevens Amendment by ED grantees. Second, it unnecessarily calls into question ED's risk-based approach to monitoring, which allows it to concentrate its limited resources on those issues that are most critical to successful and effective implementation of ED grants. Third, ED's decision reflects its commitment to transparency on how ED grant funds are used in ways beyond the limited scope of this recommendation.

First, the only information referenced in the draft report concerning non-compliance by grantees with the Stevens Amendment is a study titled, *Ivy League Flunkers: Schools Fail on Federal Funding Disclosure*, conducted by Restore Accountability and White Coat Waste Project.[2] (See page 2, footnote 4, of the draft report.)
As the draft report indicates, none of the 100 press releases issued by various Ivy League institutions that concerned studies funded by the National Institutes of Health and the National Science Foundation complied with the Stevens Amendment. This study and the draft report do not identify any instance where a violation of the Stevens Amendment involved an ED grantee. In light of these circumstances, it does not seem appropriate to recommend that ED alter its approach to implementation of the Stevens Amendment.

Second, a significant part of ED's approach to implementing the Stevens Amendment, which the draft report notes, involves providing grantees with notice of the requirement through an attachment to their GANs and discussing the requirement during post-award conference calls. (See page 11 of the draft report.) As we explained during the exit conference, ED uses a tiered risk-based approach to monitoring that aligns with the President's Management Agenda, released in 2018 and quoted on page 1 of the draft report. Specifically, on page 1, the draft report notes that the President's Management Agenda "established 'results-oriented accountability for grants' as a cross-agency priority goal to 'maximize the value of grant funding by applying a risk-based, data-driven framework that balances compliance requirements with demonstrating successful results for the American taxpayer.'" ED's tiered risk-based approach to monitoring is in line with this directive.

In identifying grantees and issues to monitor, we at ED focus our limited resources on those issues and situations where there is a higher risk of non-compliance with requirements that will have a significant impact on fiscal accountability and programmatic outcomes. For that reason, issues such as the effectiveness of grantee internal controls, possible waste, fraud, and abuse, and compliance with key programmatic requirements (such as serving eligible beneficiaries and providing them with key services) take precedence over other issues in allocating ED's monitoring resources. The time and effort expended in monitoring one requirement is necessarily time and effort not spent on monitoring another requirement. For that reason, recommending that ED devote limited resources to managing and administering grantee compliance with the Stevens Amendment, when there is no evidence that our current approach of informing grantees of the requirement is not working, is contrary to both our tiered risk-based approach and the results-oriented compliance of the President's Management Agenda.

Third, ED appreciates the importance of transparency and the role the Stevens Amendment plays in making more transparent the way in which Federal grant funds are used. ED has taken numerous proactive steps to make its process for awarding and overseeing State-administered and discretionary grant funds, as well as the recipients of those funds, transparent to the public. External stakeholders can obtain information on all recipients of ED grants and subgrants through www.spendingusa.gov. For discretionary grant programs, ED also typically identifies the recipients of grants under those programs each year and provides information on the grant application. We also post on our website Elementary and Secondary Education Act (ESEA) State

[2] https://www.restoreaccountability.com/sites/restoreacc/uploads/images/Ivy_League_Flunkers_WCW-RA.pdf

plan submissions[3] and Individuals with Disabilities Education Act (IDEA) Part B and C grant award letters and determination letters responding to annual performance reports.[4]

Thus, while we do not concur with the specific recommendation to "manage and administer grantees' compliance with the Stevens Amendment," we would consider enhancing our existing approach to Stevens Amendment compliance. We could give this requirement additional emphasis in post-award conferences and include a page on ed.gov that explains the requirement and provides information on commonly asked questions (such as calculating the percentage of Federal funding in a project) and a point of contact for questions. This approach would foster enhanced understanding and grantee compliance with this requirement without diverting limited ED monitoring resources from more critical compliance activities.

Thank you for the opportunity to respond to the draft report. We are available to discuss these comments with you and encourage GAO to consider the information provided in this response when preparing its final report. As indicated, we will use the information in this report to enhance our existing approach to Stevens Amendment compliance.

Sincerely,

Jim Stader, P.E.
Director
Office of Grants Administration
Office of Finance and Operations

[3] https://www2.ed.gov/admins/lead/account/stateplan17/statesubmission.html
[4] https://www2.ed.gov/fund/data/award/idea/ptballyears.html, https://www2.ed.gov/fund/data/award/idea/ptcallyears.html, and https://www2.ed.gov/programs/oseppsg/performance.html.

In: Government Reports …
Editor: Evie Boan

ISBN: 978-1-53615-928-8

Chapter 6

U.S. POSTAL SERVICE: ADDRESSING POLICY GAPS COULD IMPROVE PILOT DESIGN AND EVALUATION FOR POSTAL INNOVATIONS*

United States Government Accountability Office

ABBREVIATIONS

MTAC	Mailers' Technical Advisory Committee
PRC	Postal Regulatory Commission
USPS	U.S. Postal Service.

* This is an edited, reformatted and augmented version of United States Government Accountability Office, Report to the Ranking Member, Permanent Subcommittee on Investigations, Committee on Homeland Security and Governmental Affairs, U.S. Senate, Accessible Version, Publication No. GAO-19-293, dated March 2019.

WHY GAO DID THIS STUDY

USPS faces a challenging business environment that has led to reduced demand for its traditional services and significant financial losses. USPS aims to address this challenge by offering innovative products and services. The success of these efforts will depend, in part, on how effectively USPS tests each innovation's performance on a small scale to determine whether, how, and when to launch an innovation more broadly—a practice known as "piloting."

GAO was asked to review USPS's efforts to develop postal innovations. This chapter (1) describes key innovations that USPS recently piloted and (2) examines the extent to which USPS's policies reflect leading practices for pilot design and evaluation. GAO analyzed information on USPS pilots from fiscal years 2013 through 2017; compared USPS policies for piloting innovations to leading practices for pilot design and evaluation in prior GAO work and relevant standards for internal control; and selected four key innovations based on various characteristics (e.g., innovation type) to serve as illustrative examples of USPS's piloting efforts.

WHAT GAO RECOMMENDS

GAO recommends that USPS (1) develop policies that fully reflect leading practices for pilot design and evaluation and (2) develop tools or training to ensure consistent documentation of lessons learned from pilots. USPS neither agreed nor disagreed with the recommendations but described actions it plans to take related to each.

WHAT GAO FOUND

From fiscal years 2013 through 2017, the U.S. Postal Service (USPS) piloted 24 key innovations intended primarily to generate revenue or improve customers' experience. The following four selected innovations illustrate these efforts:

- Same-Day Delivery: USPS delivered goods consumers bought online or in stores. The pilot sought to test the product's feasibility and revenue potential.
- Grocery Delivery: USPS delivered groceries to consumers in metropolitan areas. The pilot sought to test the product's feasibility and revenue potential.
- Informed Delivery: USPS emailed customers an advance image of the mail they would receive. The pilot sought to test the service's potential benefits, such as generating new revenue from advertisers that may use the service.
- Keyless Parcel Lockers: USPS is testing lockers where customers can independently pick up packages at post offices. The pilot seeks to test the service's operation and potential benefits for USPS and customers.

Source: United States Postal Service and GAO. | GAO-19-293.

(From Left to Right) Metro Post (same-day delivery), Grocery Delivery Tote Bag, Informed Delivery Email Notification, and Keyless Parcel Locker Unit.

USPS's policies for piloting innovations do not fully reflect the five leading practices for pilot design and evaluation identified in GAO's prior work. The policies fully reflect two of the leading practices because they require articulating a methodology for evaluating pilot performance and documenting lessons learned. The policies do not fully reflect the other three practices because they do not require: (1) linking pilot objectives to identified performance measures; (2) documenting conclusions based on pilot results; or (3) communicating with key external stakeholders, as appropriate. These policy gaps limit the extent to which USPS can ensure that it is making good resource allocation decisions based on pilot experiences. For example, GAO found that USPS did not document its conclusions based on the results of its pilots of same-day delivery, grocery delivery, and Informed Delivery. Documenting conclusions can be especially important when USPS continues to offer the product or service after the pilot has concluded, even though the pilot did not achieve all of its objectives, as was the case with these three innovations. Further, while USPS's policies require documenting lessons learned from its pilots, USPS did not do so for some pilots GAO reviewed. Senior USPS officials said that USPS did not consistently follow this policy because it had not developed tools or training that could help ensure such consistency. As a result, USPS risks losing information that could be relevant to future innovation efforts.

March 14, 2019

The Honorable Thomas R. Carper
Ranking Member
Permanent Subcommittee on Investigations
Committee on Homeland Security and Governmental Affairs
United States Senate

Dear Mr. Carper:

The U.S. Postal Service (USPS) faces a challenging business environment that has reduced demand for traditional postal services and led to significant financial losses. Revenue from USPS's most profitable postal-service category—First-Class Mail—has declined over the last decade, from $38.2 billion in fiscal year 2008 to $25 billion in fiscal year 2018. According to USPS, offering innovative products and services is critical to adapting to evolving business and customer needs and improving its financial condition. The success of any particular innovation will depend, in part, on how effectively USPS tests the innovative product's or service's performance on a small scale to determine whether, how, and when to launch the innovation more broadly—a practice known as "piloting." Effectively piloting innovations can help ensure that USPS invests its limited resources on innovations that are most likely to improve its long-term viability.

You asked us to review USPS's efforts to develop innovative products and services. This chapter (1) describes key innovations USPS has recently piloted and (2) examines the extent to which USPS's policies for piloting key innovations reflect leading practices for pilot design and evaluation.[1]

To identify key innovations that USPS has recently piloted, we first requested information from USPS on all such innovations piloted between fiscal years 2013 and 2017.[2] In response, USPS identified 24 key piloted innovations. We compared the list provided by USPS against information in USPS, USPS Office of Inspector General, and Postal Regulatory Commission (PRC)—an independent agency with regulatory oversight over USPS—documents to help corroborate the completeness and accuracy of USPS's response. We conducted an in-depth review of 4 of the 24 innovations to provide illustrative examples of USPS's piloting efforts. We selected the 4 innovations—Metro Post (i.e., same-day delivery), Customized Delivery (i.e., grocery delivery), Informed Delivery, and keyless parcel lockers—to represent a range of the innovations' primary

---

[1] For the purpose of this chapter, we focused on "key innovations," which USPS defines as new products and services that may have a significant effect on cost, the end consumer, the shipper, or the mailer.

[2] We selected fiscal year 2013 because it corresponds with the fiscal year that USPS issued its Five-Year Business Plan to return USPS to financial and operational viability, including actions to confront revenue declines through innovation. We selected fiscal year 2017 because it was the most recent fiscal year for which USPS had available information on piloted innovations at the time of our review.

characteristics, such as innovation type (e.g., new product or new service); primary innovation goal (e.g., generating revenue or improving customer service); and investment level.[3]

To evaluate the extent to which USPS's policies for piloting key innovations reflect leading practices for pilot design and evaluation, we compared policies identified by USPS officials as applicable to its efforts to pilot innovative products and services[4] against five leading practices we identified in our prior work, as well as standards for internal control related to documenting key information:[5] The five practices we identified include:

---

[3] A postal "product" is statutorily defined as a postal service with a distinct cost or market characteristic for which a rate or rates are, or may reasonably be, applied, and a "postal service" refers to the delivery of letters, printed matter, or mailable packages, including acceptance, collection, sorting, and transportation, or other ancillary function. See 39 U.S.C. §§ 102(5), (6). In addition, the Postal Service was statutorily authorized, subject to Postal Regulatory Commission approval, to provide "nonpostal services" offered as of January 1, 2006. In general, the term "nonpostal service" is defined by statute to mean any service that is not a "postal service." See 39 U.S.C. § 404(e)(1). We did not independently evaluate whether USPS's categorization of each innovation aligned with these definitions. For the purpose of this chapter, we collectively refer to USPS's three types of key innovations—new service, new product, or enhancement to an existing product or postal/nonpostal service—as "innovative products and services." We are not reporting specific investment, cost, revenue, or volume data for piloted innovations because USPS considers this information to be proprietary.

[4] USPS, Handbook F-66, *General Investment Policies and Procedures* (Sept. 2018) and Handbook F-66D, *Investment Policies and Procedures — Business Initiatives, Alliances, Real Estate Development, and Major Operating Expense Investments* (February 2006).

[5] Our prior work identifies leading practices for designing and evaluating pilot programs. In our prior work, we have applied these practices to multiple federal agencies and programs. For the purpose of this chapter, we made some modifications to these leading practices. For example, we modified the leading practice related to evaluating pilot performance to make explicit that the leading practice includes documenting lessons learned. For the prior work that we reviewed to identify these five leading practices, see GAO, *Tax Administration: IRS Needs to Strengthen Its Approach for Evaluating the SRFMI Data-Sharing Pilot Program*, GAO-09-45 (Washington, D.C.: Nov. 7, 2008); *DATA Act: Section 5 Pilot Design Issues Need to Be Addressed to Meet Goal of Reducing Recipient Reporting Burden*, GAO-16-438 (Washington, D.C.: Apr. 19, 2016); *Performance Partnerships: Agencies Need to Better Identify Resource Contributions to Sustain Disconnected Youth Pilot Programs and Data to Assess Pilot Results*, GAO-17-208 (Washington, D.C.: Apr. 18, 2017); and *Identity Theft: Improved Collaboration Could Increase Success of IRS Initiatives to Prevent Refund Fraud*, GAO-18-20 (Washington, D.C., Nov. 28, 2017). For standards for internal control that we reviewed, see GAO, *Standards for Internal Control in the Federal Government*, GAO-14-704G (Washington, D.C.: Sept. 10, 2014), Principle 3, Paragraph 9, and Committee of Sponsoring Organizations of the Treadway Commission, *Internal Control-Integrated Framework* (2013), Chapter 4, Additional Considerations, Documentation.

- establish appropriate and measurable objectives linked with identified performance measures;
- articulate a methodology for evaluating pilot performance;
- evaluate pilot performance and identify and document lessons learned;
- draw and document conclusions about scalability (i.e., determining whether, how, and when to launch the innovation more broadly) based on pilot results; and
- ensure appropriate two-way communication at all stages of the pilot with key internal and external stakeholders in order to understand and address their views.

We discussed these leading practices with senior USPS officials, and they agreed that the practices were reasonable and relevant to USPS's efforts to pilot innovative products and services.

We examined how USPS followed its policies and applied these leading practices for the four selected key innovations by reviewing the pilot proposals and revenue and other performance data.[6] Our findings related to these four selected key innovations are not generalizable to all innovations piloted by USPS but provide illustrative examples of how USPS has followed its policies and applied the leading practices that we identified.

For both objectives, we also interviewed USPS officials and representatives from four postal associations knowledgeable about USPS's efforts to develop innovative products and services, as well as two mailers directly affected by USPS's Informed Delivery innovation.[7]

---

[6] As we discuss later in this chapter, USPS had not concluded the pilot for one of the four key innovations we selected for review. Consequently, for this innovation, we did not compare USPS's application of two leading practices: evaluate pilot performance and identify and document lessons learned and draw and document conclusions about scalability based on pilot results.

[7] We did not interview mailers for other innovations that we selected either because representatives of mailers that worked directly with USPS during the pilots of these innovations were no longer available or because individual mailers were not directly affected by the innovation.

We conducted this performance audit from December 2017 to March 2019 in accordance with generally accepted government auditing standards. Those standards require that we plan and perform the audit to obtain sufficient, appropriate evidence to provide a reasonable basis for our findings and conclusions based on our audit objectives. We believe that the evidence obtained provides a reasonable basis for our findings and conclusions based on our audit objectives.

BACKGROUND

USPS's Financial Position and Strategic Goals

USPS's mission is to provide universal postal service while operating as a self-financing entity, but USPS's current financial position is not sustainable. To achieve its mission, USPS must cover its expenses through revenues generated from the sale of its products and services. However, USPS's total operating expenses have exceeded total operating revenue each year since fiscal year 2007, including a $2.6 billion loss from operations in fiscal year 2017 alone (see Figure 1). Moreover, we have reported that USPS's overall financial condition is deteriorating.[8] For example, in August 2018 we reported that USPS had about $149 billion in unfunded liabilities and debt at the end of fiscal year 2017.[9] As a result, USPS's financial condition remains on our list of high-risk areas needing attention by Congress and the executive branch.[10]

According to USPS financial documents, its ability to sell innovative products and services will be a key factor in improving its financial

---

[8] For example, see GAO, *U.S. Postal Service: Key Considerations for Restoring Fiscal Sustainability*, GAO-17-404T (Washington, D.C.: Feb. 7, 2017) and *U.S. Postal Service: Action Needed to Address Unfunded Benefit Liabilities*, GAO-14-398T (Washington, D.C.: Mar. 13, 2014).

[9] GAO, *Postal Retiree Health Benefits: Unsustainable Finances Need to Be Addressed*, GAO-18-602 (Washington, D.C.: Aug. 31, 2018).

[10] GAO, *High-Risk Series: Progress on Many High-Risk Areas, While Substantial Efforts Needed on Others*, GAO-17-317 (Washington, D.C.: Feb. 15, 2017), p.130. We added USPS's financial condition to our list of high-risk areas in July 2009.

condition. Thus, USPS established a strategic goal to "innovate faster to deliver value" to its customers, by making investments in innovations that respond to rapidly evolving customer needs.[11] A key element of this effort is to accelerate testing of innovative products and services to better serve these needs, according to USPS.

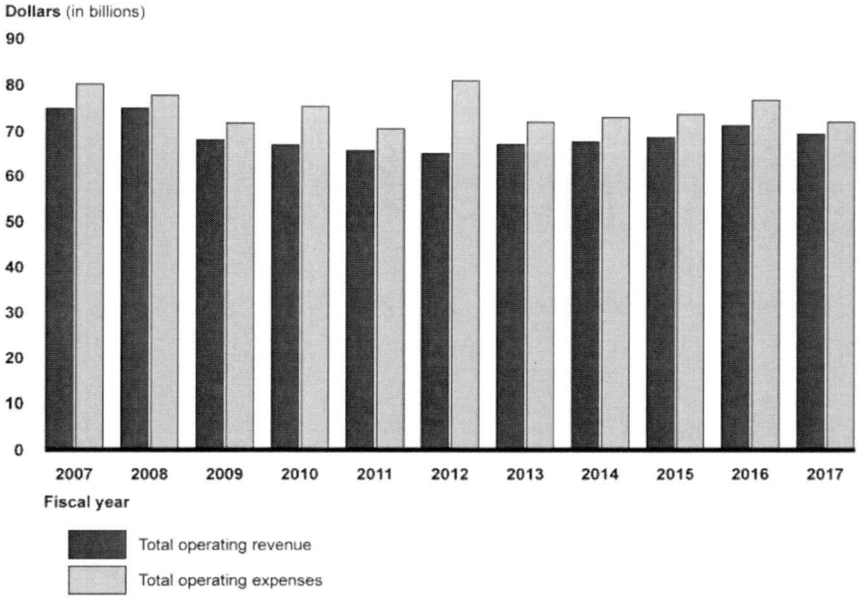

Source: USPS, Forms 10-K. | GAO-19-293.

Figure 1. U.S. Postal Service (USPS) Total Operating Revenue and Total Operating Expenses, Fiscal Years 2007 through 2017.

While USPS is allowed to develop certain new postal products and services, there are statutory restrictions that currently limit the range of innovations USPS can offer. For example, under current statute, USPS is not permitted to ship alcoholic beverages.[12] Similarly, although USPS is explicitly authorized to provide services to federal executive agencies (e.g., passport services), such authorization does not include services to state,

[11] USPS, *Future Ready: U.S. Postal Service Five-Year Strategic Plan Fiscal Years 2017 to 2021* (Sept. 30, 2016).

[12] 18 U.S.C. § 1716(f).

local, and tribal governments. Legislation has been introduced in previous sessions of Congress that would permit USPS to deliver alcoholic beverages and allow USPS to provide property and services to state, local, and tribal governments under certain conditions.[13] According to USPS officials, USPS supports these legislative proposals, which could enhance its ability to offer innovative products and services.

USPS Postal Innovation Pilot Policies and Responsibilities

According to USPS officials, two USPS handbooks include policies applicable to piloting key innovations. Specifically, the first handbook includes requirements, procedures, and responsibilities for all types of investment programs and projects undertaken by USPS, regardless of size, cost, or complexity.[14] This handbook, for example, requires the identification and documentation of lessons learned for all investments and projects. The second handbook includes requirements and procedures specifically for major operating expense investments.[15] This handbook, among other things, establishes requirements and procedures meant to ensure that new and enhanced products and services consistently meet customer needs, generate new revenue, and strengthen USPS as a business. This handbook further states that USPS has a responsibility to subject new initiatives to rigorous financial analysis, testing, and measurement, to determine whether these initiatives will make a positive financial

---

[13] For provision of property and services to state, local, and tribal governments, see e.g., S. 1486, § 302, 113th Cong (2013); S. 2629, § 203, 115th Cong (2018); H.R. 756, § 204, 115th Cong (2017); and H.R. 6076, § 204, 115th Cong (2018). In addition, for shipment of alcoholic beverages, see e.g., S. 1486, § 303, 113th Cong (2013) and S. 2629, § 204, 115th Cong (2018).

[14] USPS, *Handbook F-66, General Investment Policies and Procedures* (Washington, D.C.: September 2018).

[15] USPS, *Handbook F-66D, Investment Policies and Procedures — Business Initiatives, Alliances, Real Estate Development, and Major Operating Expense Investments* (Washington, D.C.: February 2006). A major operating expense investment is an investment associated with a new initiative, project, or program and may include ongoing operating expenses associated with the initiative, as well as capital expenditures that may fall under $5 million.

contribution to the organization and ensure that USPS's leadership has appropriate information for effective decision-making.

USPS's Office of Product Innovation generally has lead responsibility for piloting innovations.[16] According to USPS's policies, a project manager is responsible for establishing and coordinating a cross-functional team to design and evaluate the pilot. This team typically includes officials from a variety of USPS departments, such as finance, general counsel, information technology, marketing, and operations. The project manager, with support from the cross-functional team, is responsible for preparing a proposal for the pilot that includes key information, such as the pilot's objectives and performance measures, and overseeing pilot implementation and communication with key stakeholders.

In some cases, PRC has a role in overseeing postal innovation pilots.[17] For example, USPS must notify PRC before it pilots any postal product innovation for which it will impose a price (i.e., a pilot that generates revenue for USPS) and must subsequently report quarterly revenue, volume, and cost data.[18] PRC also ensures that certain safeguards are maintained during the pilot, such as limitations on the pilot's duration and revenue. However, according to PRC officials, the commission has limited involvement in other areas of USPS's efforts to develop innovations.

---

[16] According to USPS officials, other USPS offices have lead responsibility for piloting some innovations. For example, the Office of the Chief Information Officer may have lead responsibility for piloting information technology-based innovations.

[17] The PRC is composed of five commissioners and exercises regulatory oversight over USPS. It was created by the Postal Reorganization Act of 1970, with expanded responsibilities under the Postal Accountability and Enhancement Act of 2006. We did not assess actions taken by PRC to consider and approve innovation pilots, including grocery delivery and same-day delivery.

[18] See 39 U.S.C. § 3641, 39 C.F.R. Part 3035. In September 2014, PRC issued a final rule for conducting "market tests" of "experimental products" that it regulates See Market Tests of Experimental Products, 79 *Fed. Reg.* 54552 (Sept. 11, 2014). We refer to these tests as "pilots" and products as "postal product innovations" for purposes of our report. In January 2019, PRC issued an order amending these rules to revise the method for calculating applicable revenue limitations, among other things. See PRC Order Amending Rules Relating to Market Tests, Order No. 4973 (Jan. 8, 2019).

USPS Piloted Key Innovations Are Intended Primarily to Generate Revenue or Improve Customers' Experience

USPS piloted 24 key innovations from fiscal years 2013 through 2017.[19] For example, USPS piloted an Identity Verification Service that allows users to verify their identity either remotely (i.e., online) or in person at a postal facility. Similarly, USPS piloted an innovation to allow mailers to print shipping labels, track packages, and schedule package pick-ups by accessing USPS data. The primary goal of the majority of these key innovations (16 of 24) was to generate revenue, while the primary goal for the remaining innovations was generally to improve customers' experience using USPS products or services (see Figure 2). Appendix I includes a complete list of key innovations USPS piloted from fiscal years 2013 through 2017.

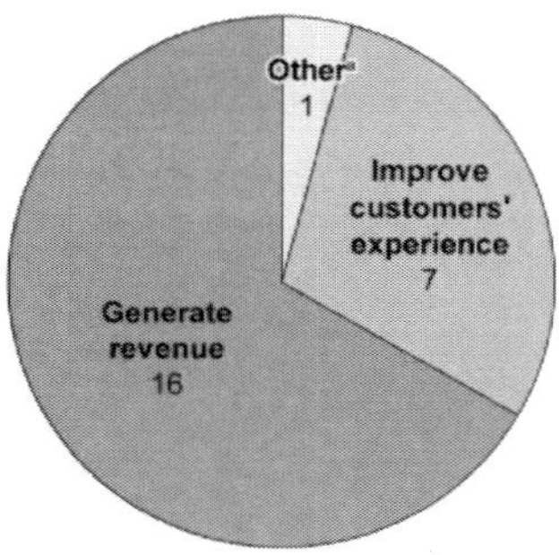

Source: GAO analysis of USPS information. | GAO-19-293.

[a]USPS stated that the primary goal of one innovation was to improve internal infrastructure.

Figure 2. Key Piloted U.S. Postal Service (USPS) Innovations by Primary Goal, Fiscal Years 2013 through 2017.

---

[19] USPS officials noted that USPS implemented a variety of other key innovations during this time frame, but did not pilot them because the investments carried relatively low risk or implementation cost. For example, USPS introduced High Density Plus, a product enhancement for mailers delivering more than 300 pieces on a single mail route. Similarly, USPS offered annual-mailing promotions (i.e., postal rate discounts offered over a limited period to qualifying mailings) intended to create awareness of innovative uses of mail.

The following discussion provides additional information about the 4 key innovations we selected as illustrative examples of USPS's efforts to pilot innovative products and services.

- *Same-Day Delivery:* From December 2012 to December 2015, USPS piloted same-day delivery for consumer e-commerce purchases (see Figure 3). According to the pilot proposal, this innovation was intended to generate revenue for USPS by allowing it to leverage its existing delivery infrastructure to capture part of the growing e-commerce market. To determine the potential scalability of same-day delivery, USPS first tested its operational feasibility and potential demand in several major metropolitan areas, including San Francisco, New York, and Phoenix. During the pilot, USPS delivered photos, chocolates, water, electronics, and other goods from 38 participating mailers to consumers in these areas. At the pilot's conclusion, USPS decided to continue offering same-day delivery to interested participating mailers under Priority Mail contracts.[20]
- *Grocery Delivery:* From November 2014 to October 2017, USPS piloted a grocery delivery product in nine selected metropolitan areas.[21] According to USPS, the innovation was intended to generate additional revenue by taking advantage of the growing market for grocery delivery. To test the innovation's operational feasibility, USPS required the pilot's sole participating mailer to bring totes containing groceries and other prepackaged goods ordered by customers directly to post offices (see Figure 4). USPS was then responsible for sorting the totes and delivering them to customers. According to its proposal for this pilot, USPS expected grocery delivery to provide a substantial revenue generation opportunity. At the pilot's conclusion, like same-day delivery,

---

[20] According to USPS, as of October 2018, it has signed nine Priority Mail contracts with eight mailers that participated in the pilot. Priority Mail provides flat-rate 1- to 3-day expected delivery for domestic parcels.

[21] Metropolitan areas included San Francisco, Los Angeles, San Diego, New York, Sacramento, Stamford, Philadelphia, Boston, and the Washington/Baltimore capital region.

USPS decided to continue offering grocery delivery with the participating mailer under a Parcel Select contract.[22]

Source: United States Postal Service (USPS.com, October 4, 2018). | GAO-19-293.

Figure 3. Snapshot of U.S. Postal Service Website for Same-Day Delivery Product Innovation.

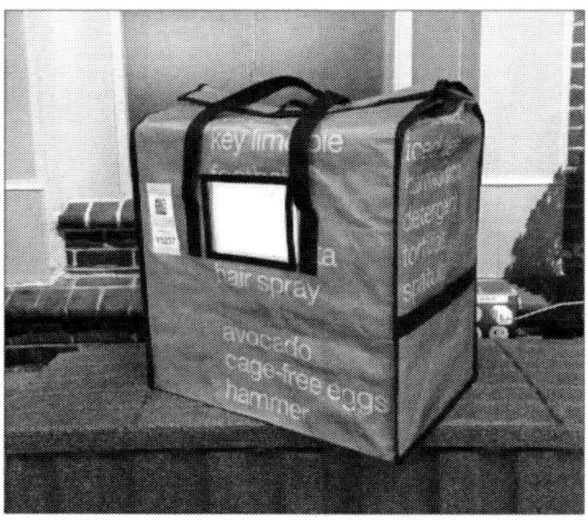

Source: GAO. | GAO-19-293.

Figure 4. Illustration of a Tote Used for U.S. Postal Service Grocery Delivery Product Innovation.

---

[22] Specifically, USPS signed a Parcel Select contract with the participating mailer in October 2017 that was reviewed and approved by the PRC. According to USPS, Parcel Select is a ground delivery product for bulk package shipments.

Sources: United States Postal Service and GAO. | GAO-19-293.

Figure 5. Snapshot of U.S. Postal Service Informed Delivery Notification.

- *Informed Delivery:* From spring 2014 through July 2016, USPS piloted a notification service called Informed Delivery in Northern Virginia and New York.[23] According to USPS, this innovation is intended to bridge the gap between the physical and digital worlds by, for example, emailing customers with a scanned image of the exterior address side of letter-sized mail they should receive later that day (see Figure 5). Informed Delivery can also allow mailers to conduct marketing campaigns by integrating other elements—such as hyperlinks to mailers' websites—into the email and other notifications that customers receive. In its proposal to pilot Informed Delivery, USPS stated the pilot was intended to help USPS understand the service's business opportunity and increase the certainty of its potential benefits, which included retaining mail

[23] According to USPS officials, the Informed Delivery pilot did not start during any one month, but rather was rolled out over a few months during the spring of 2014.

volume and generating new revenue from large advertisers. In addition, the pilot aimed to generate "statistically valid data" on how subscribers respond to marketing campaigns that mailers conduct. According to USPS, more than 70,000 customers were actively using the service at the pilot's conclusion. In July 2016, USPS decided to end the pilot and launch the service nationally. According to USPS, about 13 million customers were subscribed to the service as of October 2018. USPS aims to have 40 million customers subscribed to the service by 2020.

- *Keyless Parcel Lockers:* Since October 2013, USPS has piloted keyless parcel lockers that allow customers to independently pick up packages in 98 selected post offices. According to USPS, among other things, this innovation is intended to reduce the number of missed package deliveries to customers' post office boxes and thereby reduce USPS's delivery costs (see Figure 6).[24] The purpose of the pilot is to assess the performance and use of the lockers and to assess their performance. In October 2013, USPS began pre-testing the technical performance of 10 prototype keyless parcel locker units at post offices in New York City and Northern Virginia.[25] Following this pre-test, in February 2015, USPS approved the installation of 50 made-to-order locker units in selected post offices across the country. Finally, in May 2016 USPS expanded the pilot to include an additional 50 units, including 2 units that a senior USPS official told us were not yet installed. As of November 2018, the pilot is still ongoing.

[24] According to USPS, missed deliveries to post office boxes occur when a package is unable to fit into a post office box and a parcel locker is unavailable, or when package does not fit into an available locker.

[25] According to USPS's proposal for the pilot, a keyless locker unit typically contains 12 individual lockers and is capable of electronically recording inventory and locker use.

Source: GAO. | GAO-19-293.

Figure 6. Photo of U.S. Postal Service Keyless Parcel Locker Unit.

USPS'S POLICIES FOR PILOTING KEY INNOVATIONS REFLECT SOME BUT NOT ALL LEADING PRACTICES FOR PILOT DESIGN AND EVALUATION

USPS's policies applicable to piloting key innovations fully reflect two of the five leading practices for pilot design and evaluation that we identified in prior GAO work and relevant standards for internal control (see Table 1).[26] These policies do not, however, fully reflect the other three leading practices due to policy gaps. Further, we found that USPS had not consistently followed its policies to document lessons learned at the conclusion of each pilot, as discussed below.

---

[26] As discussed earlier, we identified leading practices from prior GAO reports on pilot design and evaluation, including GAO-09-45 and GAO-16-438, as well as from our review of standards for internal controls related to documentation in GAO-14-704G and the Committee of Sponsoring Organizations of the Treadway Commission's *Internal Control-Integrated Framework* (2013). USPS officials identified Handbook F-66 and USPS Handbook F-66D as policies applicable to its piloting of key innovations.

Table 1. Extent to Which the U.S. Postal Service's (USPS) Policies for Pilot Design and Evaluation Reflect Leading Practices

Leading practices for pilot design and evaluation	Assessment of USPS's policies
Establish appropriate and measurable objectives linked with identified performance measures	Do not fully reflect
Articulate a methodology for evaluating pilot performance	Fully reflect
Evaluate pilot performance and identify and document lessons learned	Fully reflect
Draw and document conclusions about scalability (i.e., determining whether, how, and when to launch the innovation more broadly) based on pilot results	Do not fully reflect
Ensure appropriate two-way communication at all stages of the pilot with key internal and external stakeholders in order to understand and address their views	Do not fully reflect

Source: GAO. | GAO-19-293.

Senior USPS officials acknowledged that gaps exist in its policies for pilot design and evaluation because they were not developed by USPS to fully reflect all leading practices. These policy gaps limit the extent to which USPS can ensure that it is making good resource allocation decisions based on pilot experiences. Below we further discuss the extent to which USPS's policies reflect the five leading pilot practices we identified as well as how USPS applied these leading practices among the four piloted innovations that we reviewed.

Establish Appropriate and Measurable Objectives Linked with Identified Performance Measures

We found USPS's policies do not fully reflect this leading practice. While USPS policies require that project managers establish pilot objectives and performance measures, they do not require that each objective be linked with identified performance measures. As a result, some pilots may have objectives without an associated performance measure.

For example, although USPS established both objectives and performance measures for each of the four innovations we selected for review, it did not consistently link each established objective to performance measures. USPS's proposal to pilot same-day delivery, for example, had objectives of generating new revenue and improving customers' experience. However, while the proposal included performance measures associated with generating new revenue—i.e., package volume, gross revenue, and net revenue—it did not identify and link any performance measures with its objective of improving customer experience. Similarly, USPS's proposal to pilot keyless parcel lockers included improving customers' experience as one of its objectives. However, while the proposal included a variety of performance measures—reduction in the number of missed deliveries to post office boxes, locker rate utilization, and on-time locker installation—it did not identify and link any performance measures with its improving customers' experience objective. Absent such measures, USPS may not know whether customers have experienced an improvement using keyless parcel lockers compared to using manual, keyed parcel lockers. Linking all objectives to performance measures could help ensure that USPS has the performance information to assess the extent to which a pilot has achieved all of its objectives.

USPS officials told us that it can be difficult to measure performance for some objectives related to customer experience. While measuring customers' experience can be challenging, it is important to understand the extent to which a pilot has achieved all of its objectives. Further, USPS has demonstrated that it can measure improvement in customers' experience. For example, during its Informed Delivery pilot, USPS conducted a consumer survey with approximately 5,500 Informed Delivery subscribers to collect data on consumer adoption and satisfaction. In the survey, USPS found that over 80 percent were satisfied or very satisfied with the service. According to USPS officials, this data helped USPS to measure the pilot's success in meeting its objective of improving customers' experience.

Articulate a Methodology for Evaluating Pilot Performance

We found that USPS's policies fully reflect this leading practice because the policies require officials to develop and communicate a methodology for evaluating pilot performance. Articulating such a methodology helps managers to identify the types and sources of performance information necessary to evaluate the pilot.[27] USPS's policies require project managers to work with the pilot's cross-functional team to develop and reach consensus on the methodology. These policies also require the project manager and cross-functional team to identify data needs, data sources, and how the data will be evaluated.

For the four innovations we reviewed, we found that USPS articulated a methodology for evaluating the pilot's performance. For example, for the Informed Delivery pilot, USPS identified its customer registration system as the method for tracking progress toward performance measures related to the number of Informed Delivery subscribers. Similarly, in its proposal to pilot keyless parcel lockers, USPS identified its central parcel locker monitoring system as a method of tracking progress toward performance measures related to utilization of keyless parcel lockers.

Evaluate Pilot Performance and Identify and Document Lessons Learned

We found that USPS's policies fully reflect this leading practice, but USPS did not consistently follow its policy that requires documenting lessons learned. Specifically, the policies require project managers to evaluate performance and document lessons learned at the conclusion of each pilot. Doing so can enable USPS to identify information needed to make conclusions about the pilot's scalability and ensures that such information will be accessible to inform future related efforts. However,

---

[27] GAO-16-438.

among the key innovations we selected for review USPS had not consistently documented lessons learned (see Table 2).

Table 2. Extent to Which the U.S. Postal Service (USPS) Documented Lessons Learned for Key Piloted Innovations Selected by GAO

Key piloted innovations	Documented lessons learned at pilot's conclusion
Metro Post (i.e., same-day delivery)	Not documented
Customized Delivery (i.e., grocery delivery)	Not documented
Informed Delivery	Documented
Keyless parcel lockers	As of November 2018, USPS had not concluded its pilot for keyless parcel lockers.

Source: GAO. | GAO-19-293.

[a]As of November 2018, USPS had not concluded its pilot for keyless parcel lockers.

USPS officials told us that they discussed lessons learned during ongoing monitoring of pilot performance for these innovations, but had only documented lessons learned for its Informed Delivery pilot. Specifically, USPS identified lessons learned in its July 2016 proposal to launch its Informed Delivery service nationally. In this proposal, we found that USPS identified some lessons learned about the pilot related to user satisfaction and adoption rates. USPS officials told us that this information helped to inform USPS's decision to launch the service nationally. However, USPS officials acknowledged that USPS did not document lessons learned for the other two concluded pilots that we selected for review (same-day delivery and grocery delivery).

Senior USPS officials told us that USPS had not consistently documented lessons learned at the conclusion of pilots across the 24 key innovations because it had not developed tools, such as a template, or training that could help ensure such consistency. Without consistently documenting lessons learned for all of its pilots, USPS risks losing information garnered during pilot implementation that could be relevant to future innovation efforts. Doing so can be particularly important because, according to a senior USPS official, officials responsible for pilot projects sometimes retire or leave USPS for employment elsewhere, creating a gap in knowledge of pilot experiences. Standards for internal control underscore the importance of maintaining documentation in order to retain organizational knowledge and mitigate the risk of having knowledge limited to a few personnel.[28]

Draw and Document Conclusions about Scalability Based on Pilot Results

USPS's policies do not fully reflect this leading practice. These policies require that project managers draw conclusions based on the results and lessons learned from the pilot. According to USPS officials, conclusions may include determining scalability—i.e., whether, how, and when to integrate pilot activities into overall efforts. However, USPS's policies do not specifically require that officials document these conclusions. Documenting conclusions about scalability based on pilot results helps to ensure retention of organizational knowledge related to the pilot that may inform future decisions.

Among the three innovations that we selected for review for which the pilots had concluded (i.e., same-day delivery, grocery delivery, and Informed Delivery), USPS officials told us that senior leadership discussed the results and lessons of the pilots and made determinations regarding whether, how, and when to launch them more broadly, but that they did not document these decisions or the rationale for them.[29] By not documenting conclusions, USPS risks losing information that could affect the success of future related efforts and that could inform future USPS leadership of the rationale for maintaining investments in activities upon which pilots were based.

---

[28] GAO-14-704G and Committee of Sponsoring Organizations of the Treadway Commission, *Internal Control-Integrated Framework* (2013).

[29] In August 2017, USPS proposed purchasing over 1,400 additional keyless parcel locker units. However, according to a senior USPS official, USPS did not approve the purchase because the pilot had not demonstrated that the benefits of providing keyless parcel lockers to consumers outweighed installation, maintenance, and other costs.

Documenting conclusions for innovation pilots can be especially important in cases in which USPS decides to continue or expand pilot activities even when the pilots do not meet all of their intended objectives. For example, USPS's same-day delivery and grocery delivery pilots had revenue objectives, along with associated performance measures; however, neither pilot achieved these objectives. For the same-day delivery pilot, costs exceeded revenue in 12 of the 13 fiscal year quarters in which the pilot was conducted, according to data USPS reported to PRC. Likewise, USPS data indicate it did not reach its annual revenue target for its grocery delivery pilot. Similarly, USPS's pilot of Informed Delivery was intended to generate "statistically valid data" on how consumers respond to mailer marketing campaigns. However, according to a senior USPS official, the pilot did not generate the data as intended, because no such campaigns were conducted during the pilot.

As discussed earlier in this chapter, USPS did not discontinue any of these three selected innovations when their pilots concluded. Although USPS may have had good reasons to continue with, or more broadly launch, these innovations despite the pilots not meeting all of their objectives, the lack of documentation regarding its reasoning and decisions limits information relevant to whether USPS is making judicious use of limited resources.

Ensure Appropriate Two-Way Communication at All Stages of the Pilot with Key Internal and External Stakeholders in Order to Understand and Address Their Views

USPS's policies do not fully reflect this leading practice.

USPS's policies require the involvement of key internal stakeholders in pilots. Specifically, USPS's policies require the involvement of cross-functional teams—which include legal, finance, and other departments—and varying levels of review during the design and implementation of pilot proposals. However, USPS's policies do not address communication with key external stakeholders. According to USPS officials, some pilot projects may be confidential or have limited or no direct effect on external stakeholders and, thus, communication with external stakeholders may not be appropriate. While external stakeholder communication may not be appropriate with some pilots, such communication, as appropriate, can help to ensure that issues critical to the success of a pilot activity are identified and addressed.

Among the innovations that we selected for review, USPS officials explained various steps taken to involve internal stakeholders in the design and evaluation of the pilots, such as the involvement of cross functional teams to develop pilot proposals. Further, while USPS's policies do not address external stakeholder communication, we found that USPS employed strategies for some of the innovations we selected for review to communicate with some external stakeholders—i.e., industry associations and mailers. For example, a representative of a postal association told us that USPS shared information and sought input about its Informed Delivery pilot during a quarterly meeting with industry groups. Similarly, a mailer we interviewed told us that USPS had shared information and sought input on the Informed Delivery pilot through direct outreach with the mailer.

However, USPS did not consistently employ strategies to communicate with some key external stakeholders among the innovations that we selected for review. Specifically, USPS did not design or implement strategies to obtain feedback from consumers on its pilots for same-day delivery, grocery delivery, or keyless parcel lockers, despite the fact that each of these innovations directly affected consumers. In contrast, as previously discussed, for its Informed Delivery pilot, USPS planned and conducted a survey to obtain consumer feedback, the results of which helped USPS project managers support the proposal to expand the service nationally. Absent communication with all key stakeholders, USPS risks not having a complete understanding of perspectives that could inform the viability of its innovations.

Conclusion

In recent years, USPS has sought to compete in a challenging business environment by piloting innovations intended primarily to generate revenue and enhance customers' experience. The policies that USPS uses for piloting key innovations fully reflect some leading practices for pilot design and evaluation, such as articulating a methodology for evaluating pilot performance. However, addressing gaps between USPS's policies and leading practices related to linking objectives and performance measures, documenting conclusions, and communicating with key external stakeholders would enable USPS leadership to better assess the outcomes of its pilots, understand the rationale for conclusions about scalability based on pilot results, and gauge customers' reactions to innovative products and services. Moreover, developing tools or training to ensure that USPS consistently implements its policy of documenting lessons learned from pilots would provide USPS with key information to inform future related efforts.

Recommendations for Executive Action

We are making the following two recommendations to USPS:

The Postmaster General should direct the Vice President of Product Innovation to develop policies that fully reflect leading practices for pilot design and evaluation in areas such as linking objectives and performance measures; documenting conclusions about scalability based on pilot results; and communicating with key external stakeholders, as appropriate. (Recommendation 1).

The Postmaster General should direct the Vice President of Product Innovation to develop tools, such as a template, or training to help ensure USPS consistently documents lessons learned at the conclusion of pilots, as required by USPS policies. (Recommendation 2).

AGENCY COMMENTS AND OUR EVALUATION

We provided a draft of this product to USPS and PRC for comment. USPS provided a written response, which is reproduced in appendix II of this chapter. In its response, USPS did not state whether it agreed with our recommendations, but described actions that it plans to take related to each. These actions, if fully implemented, would meet the intent of our recommendations. For example, USPS stated that it would develop policies specifically for pilot design, and would reflect leading practices for pilot design and evaluation based upon best practice research. USPS also noted that it would develop training to ensure consistent documentation of lessons learned from its pilots. USPS added that this planned training would cover best practices for pilot tests.

Regarding our first recommendation USPS said that pilots are only one step in a larger process for developing innovations. We agree with this and noted in our report that piloting is one key element of USPS's efforts to innovate. Nonetheless, given USPS's financial position, effectively piloting innovations is a critical step to ensure that USPS invests its limited resources on innovations that are most likely to improve its longterm viability. USPS also stated that flexibility is important in innovation pilots, particularly as it pertains to linking pilot objectives with performance measures. We continue to believe that linking objectives with performance measures is key to effectively evaluating pilots. In so doing, however, there is flexibility to adjust pilot objectives and performance measures as new information is gleaned during the pilot. Finally, with regard to communication with external stakeholders during pilots, USPS said that it communicates consistently with external stakeholders regarding pilots at Mailers' Technical Advisory Committee meetings (MTAC).[30]

In our report, we noted that USPS employed strategies to communicate with some external stakeholders—i.e., industry associations and mailers. We continue to believe, however, in the importance of communication with all key external stakeholders, which may include stakeholders, such as consumers, that do not participate in MTAC meetings.

USPS and PRC also provided technical comments, which we incorporated as appropriate.

We are sending copies of this chapter to the appropriate congressional committee, the Postmaster General, Chairman of PRC, and other interested parties.

Sincerely yours,

Lori Rectanus Director
Physical Infrastructure Issues

APPENDIX I: LIST OF U.S. POSTAL SERVICE KEY PILOTED INNOVATIONS, FISCAL YEARS 2013-2017

The U.S. Postal Service (USPS) piloted 24 key innovations from fiscal years 2013 through 2017 (see Table 3).[31]

---

[30] The Mailers' Technical Advisory Committee is a venue for USPS to share technical information with mailers and to receive their advice and recommendations on matters concerning mail-related products and services. The committee holds meetings on a quarterly basis.

[31] USPS defines "key innovations" as those that have a significant effect on cost, the end consumer, the shipper, or the mailer. The 2006 Postal Accountability and Enhancement Act defines (a) postal "product" as a postal service with a distinct cost or market characteristic for which a rate or rates are, or may reasonably be, applied, and (b) "postal service" refers to the delivery of letters, printed matter, or mailable packages, including acceptance, collection, sorting, and transportation, or other ancillary function. USPS defines an "enhancement" as any improvement to the quality or value of a postal product or service.

Table 3. U.S. Postal Service (USPS) Key Piloted Innovations, Fiscal Years 2013 through 2017

Innovation name	Description	Innovation Primary goal
Metro Post (i.e., same-day delivery)	Package delivery product that delivers packages from participating retailers to customers in selected areas on the same day.	Generate revenue
Customized Delivery (i.e., grocery delivery)	Package delivery product that delivers groceries and other prepackaged goods from a participating retailer to customers in selected areas.	Generate revenue
Standard Post / Retail Ground	Package delivery product that reduces customer costs by providing "zone pricing" (i.e., lower prices for boxes shipped shorter distances) for less-than-urgent deliveries and oversized packages.	Generate revenue
Parcel Return Service pick-up locations	Offering that reduces the number of USPS locations shippers must visit to pick-up returned packages.	Generate revenue
Priority Mail regional rate	Alternative shipping product that reduces customer costs by providing "zone pricing" (i.e., lower prices for boxes shipped shorter distances) for some Priority Mail shipments.	Generate revenue
Informed Delivery Platform	Service that provides consumers with a digital preview of their household mail arriving soon. Mailers can integrate digital campaign elements to engage the consumer.	Generate revenue
MyUSPS	Portal that allows customers to see all packages destined to their address, create return labels, and request mail holds or redelivery. This feature in now a part of the Informed Delivery platform so customers can see all mail and packages in one place.	Improve customers' experience
Expected Delivery	A service that provides customers with: a delivery timeframe (currently 2 hours) on the day of delivery; and predictions for the expected delivery date and delivery timeframe at least the day before the actual delivery day.	Improve customers' experience
Mobile Check Payment	A service that allows commercial customers to make deposits using a mobile device, thereby avoiding the need to visit a retail location, enhancing the customer experience, and expediting the clearance of funds.	Improve customers' experience

Innovation name	Description	Innovation Primary goal
Keyless parcel lockers	Lockers installed in some USPS post offices that serve as a "last mile" delivery point for packages that cannot be delivered directly into P.O. Boxes.	Improve customers' experience
Identity Verification Service	A service that would allow users to verify their digital identity either remotely (i.e., online) or in person.	Generate revenue
Electronic Postmark	A service that assures the integrity, authenticity, and accuracy of electronic data content.	Generate revenue
Priority Mail redesign	Enhanced Priority Mail product by providing expected delivery, free insurance up to $50, and new packaging.	Generate revenue
Parcel Select rural pricing	Enhanced Parcel Select product by developing two-tiered (i.e., rural and non-rural) pricing to meeting shipper needs.	Generate revenue
Parcel Select next day delivery	Enhanced Parcel Select product by allowing shippers to drop packages at USPS processing plants with lower sorting requirements.	Generate revenue
Parcel Select Return Service	Enhanced Parcel Select product by expanding the number of USPS locations that accept package returns from shippers.	Generate revenue
Click-N-Ship Business Pro	Developed software that allows mailers to pay postage electronically and provides enhanced reporting features for some shipments.	Generate revenue
Merchant Return scan base payment	Streamlined package returns process by using electronic scan data to calculate payment in lieu of manually weighing and rating each package.	Generate revenue
Developed online tools for shippers	Developed software that allows mailers to, for example, print shipping labels, track packages, schedule package pick-ups by accessing USPS data.	Improve Internal Infrastructure
Next Generation Mailbox	Developed larger mailbox receptacle capable of accommodating more package deliveries and locations with multiple delivery points.	Improve customers' experience
Informed Visibility / GEO delivery	Developed software that provides mailers with near real-time end-to-end tracking information for some mailpieces and mail aggregates (e.g., containers).	Improve customers' experience
USPS returns automated	Developed capability to charge for returns based on captured attributes, such as capturing package weight from mail processing equipment, accurately assessing postage, and easily collecting postage due.	Generate revenue

Table 3. (Continued)

Innovation name	Description	Innovation Primary goal
Near real time package delivery notification	Developed capability of on-street devices used by carriers to transmit mail scan information at the time of the scanning.	Improve customers' experience
E-Commerce Program	A service to enable printing and payment of shipping labels from customers' home or office.	Generate revenue

Source: GAO analysis of USPS information. | GAO-19-293. Note: USPS did not discontinue any key piloted innovations from fiscal years 2013 through 2017.

APPENDIX II: COMMENTS FROM THE U.S. POSTAL SERVICE

Gary C. Reblin
Vice President
Product Innovation

UNITED STATES
POSTAL SERVICE

February 15, 2019

Ms. Lori Rectanus
Director, Physical Infrastructure Issues
United States Government Accountability Office
Washington, DC 20548-0001

Dear Ms. Rectanus:

This responds to the draft report, U.S. Postal Service: Addressing Policy Gaps Could Improve Pilot Design and Evaluation for Postal Innovations (GAO-19-293).

Thank you for providing the United States Postal Service (USPS) with the opportunity to review and comment on the draft report titled *U.S. Postal Service: Addressing Policy Gaps Could Improve Pilot Design and Evaluation for Postal Innovations* (GAO-19-293). Our comments on the draft report and our responses to the GAO's Recommendations for Executive Action are set forth below.

Product Innovation has established comprehensive product development processes where pilots are only one step in those processes. These processes are documented in the F-66D section 4.6, "Overview of Development Process" and the Product Innovation new product development process that was provided to the GAO on January 4, 2018. In many cases, a pilot is part of the Ideation stage of product development. This stage is part of the creative process of generating, developing, and communicating new ideas, where an initiative and the pilot being conducted are not fully defined and are exploratory, which require deeper and broader research to finalize. Therefore, pilots may have general metrics/objectives because they are part of ideation and fact finding. Much of this report refers to generic best practices tailored to traditional product pilots with set metrics and precedents, and not as applicable to disruptive and exploratory product and service innovation with no precedent in the organization. Therefore, the GAO stated best practice of *"Linking pilot objectives to identified performance measures"* is not always applicable to our innovation pilots. Sometimes a pilot is created for one opportunity and the data may unveil or prove a new or different opportunity. This is the nature of innovation and why pilots for innovation need to be flexible.

In addition, the USPS communicates consistently with external stakeholders regarding pilots through the Mail Technical Advisory Committee (MTAC): MTAC and MTAC user groups. MTAC members consist of key external stakeholders. MTAC is a way for the USPS to share technical information with the industry, and to receive their advice and recommendations on matters concerning mail-related products and services, in order to enhance customer value and expand the use of these products and services for the mutual benefit of industry stakeholders and the Postal Service.

GAO Recommendations:

1. *The Postmaster General should direct the VP of Product Innovation to develop policies that fully reflect leading practices for pilot design and evaluation in areas such as linking objectives and performance measures, documenting conclusions about scalability based on pilot results; and communicating with key external stakeholders as appropriate.*

   USPS Response:

   The USPS will develop policies specifically for pilot design and continue to use MTAC to communicate with key external stakeholders. The USPS will reflect leading practices for pilot design and evaluation based on thought leader and best practice research.

   The USPS believes that "best practices" for innovation should predominantly follow "Agile Development." Agile development recognizes the need to pilot (test) a preliminary, exploratory concept and iterate to learn and be adaptable on the final concept. For innovation, the pilot itself is done to help better define the performance metrics that are feasible and to clarify the goals that should be set for the program. We agree that pilot tests for traditional pilots with incremental changes with clear precedents and metrics should follow the recommendations in this report. However, for the majority of our pilots for new concepts, with variables and unknowns, we need to follow a more "agile" approach, which recognizes the pilot itself will help frame and flush out the concept to help define expectations. We agree with GAO that we should document lessons learned and ensure that all learnings are required to be clearly documented in the process.

2. *The Postmaster General should direct the VP of Product Innovation to develop tools such as templates or training to help ensure USPS consistently documents lessons learned at the conclusion of pilots as required by USPS policies.*

   USPS Response:

   The USPS will develop training to ensure consistent documentation of lessons learned from pilots. The USPS is in the process of developing the training for the Chief Customer and Marketing Officer (CCMO organization), led by the Product Innovation organization to ensure all departments under the CCMO who develop or enhance products have completed the training by September 30, 2019. Training planned will provide best practices for pilot tests that include checklists, leading practices for pilot design and evaluation, templates to ensure consistency, post analysis process that includes documenting lessons learned, and a central repository to store all pilot test information to ensure easy archiving and retrieval. In addition, the Finance and the Business Analysis team is updating and refreshing F-66D with completion November 2019.

Again the USPS appreciates the opportunity to respond to the GAO draft report and Recommendations for Executive Action.

Sincerely,

Gary C. Reblin

Appendix III: Accessible Data

Data Tables

Accessible Data for Figure 1: U.S. Postal Service (USPS) Total Operating Revenue and Total Operating Expenses, Fiscal Years 2007 through 2017

Fiscal year	Total operating revenue (billions)	Total operating expenses (billions)
2007	74.778	80.105
2008	74.932	77.738
2009	68.09	71.83
2010	67.052	75.426
2011	65.711	70.634
2012	65.079	80.964
2013	67.195	72.128
2014	67.764	73.178
2015	68.79	73.826
2016	71.429	76.899
2017	69.593	72.21

Accessible Data for Figure 2: Key Piloted U.S. Postal Service (USPS) Innovations by Primary Goal, Fiscal Years 2013 through 2017

Other	Improve customers' experience	Generate revenue
1	7	16

INDEX

#

A

B

C

D

E

F

G

H

I

J

L

M

N

O

P

R

S